INSIGHTS

*General Editor*: Clive Bloom, Lecturer in En⌣
Polytechnic

*Editorial Board*: Clive Bloom, Brian Docherty, Gary Day, Lesley
Bloom, Hazel Day

**Insights** brings to academics, students and general readers the
very best contemporary criticism on neglected literary and cultural
areas. It consists of anthologies, each containing original
contributions by advanced scholars and experts. Each contribution
concentrates on a study of a particular work, author or genre in
its artistic, historical and cultural context.

*Published titles*

Clive Bloom (*editor*)
JACOBEAN POETRY AND PROSE: Rhetoric, Representation and
the Popular Imagination
TWENTIETH-CENTURY SUSPENSE: The Thriller Comes of Age

Clive Bloom, Brian Docherty, Jane Gibb and Keith Shand (*editors*)
NINETEENTH-CENTURY SUSPENSE: From Poe to Conan Doyle

Gary Day and Clive Bloom (*editors*)
PERSPECTIVES ON PORNOGRAPHY: Sexuality in Film and
Literature

Brian Docherty (*editor*)
AMERICAN CRIME FICTION: Studies in the Genre
AMERICAN HORROR FICTION: From Brockden Brown to
Stephen King

Rhys Garnett and R. J. Ellis (*editors*)
SCIENCE FICTION ROOTS AND BRANCHES: Contemporary
Critical Approaches

Robert Giddings, Keith Selby and Chris Wensley
SCREENING THE NOVEL: The Theory and Practice of Literary
Dramatisation

*list continued on next page*

*continued from previous page*

Mark Lilly (*editor*)
LESBIAN AND GAY WRITING: An Anthology of Critical Essays

Christopher Mulvey and John Simons (*editors*)
NEW YORK: City as Text

Jeffrey Walsh (*editors*)
VIETNAM IMAGES: War and Representation

**Series Standing Order**

If you would like to receive future titles in this series as they are published, you can make use of our standing order facility. To place a standing order please contact your bookseller or, in case of difficulty, write to us at the address below with your name and address and the name of the series. Please state with which title you wish to begin your standing order. (If you live outside the United Kingdom we may not have the rights for your area, in which case we will forward your order to the publisher concerned.)

Customer Services Department, Macmillan Distribution Ltd
Houndmills, Basingstoke, Hampshire, RG21 2XS, England.

# New York

## City as Text

*Edited by*

### CHRISTOPHER MULVEY

*Principal Lecturer in English*
*King Alfred's College, Winchester*

*and*

### JOHN SIMONS

*Co-ordinator, American Studies*
*King Alfred's College, Winchester*

MACMILLAN

First published 1990

Published by
THE MACMILLAN PRESS LTD
Houndmills, Basingstoke, Hampshire RG21 2XS
and London
Companies and representatives
throughout the world

Typeset by Wessex Typesetters
(Division of The Eastern Press Ltd)
Frome, Somerset

Printed in Hong Kong

British Library Cataloguing in Publication Data
New York: City as text.
1. New York (City). Arts
I. Mulvey, Christopher    II. Simons, John
700'.9747'1
ISBN 0–333–47502–X (hc)
ISBN 0–333–47503–8 (pbk)

# Contents

# List of Maps

# Acknowledgements

This volume consists largely of papers which were first presented at the annual conference of the British Association for American Studies held at King Alfred's College, Winchester, in April 1986. Thanks are due to the organising committee of that conference, especially John Bentley, Elinor Davenhill, David Firth and Geoffrey Ridden, and to the students who remained on campus to help. Thanks are also due to King Alfred's College, which provided John Simons with study leave in order to complete the editing of the typescript. The editors acknowledge the permission given by Harper & Row, Publications, Inc. to Derek Pollard to quote from the edition of John Sloan's diary edited by Bruce St John with an introduction by Helen Farr Sloan, published in New York in 1965.

C. M.
J. S.

# Notes on the Contributors

**Roma Barnes** has been a WEA lecturer and a lecturer in American Studies at Hull University. She is currently lecturing in British and American Social History at Bristol Polytechnic. She is writing *Impatient for Justice: Black Americans Post-1945* for the BAAS/Longman series.

**Graham Clarke** is a lecturer in English and American literature at the University of Kent where he teaches on the American Studies programme. He has published material on a number of writers and is the editor of *The American City: Literary and Cultural Perspectives*. He is currently writing a book on Alfred Stieglitz and New York City.

**John F. Davis** is a lecturer in American Geography at Birkbeck College, University of London. He has published extensively in the field of American geography with a specialism in the railways.

**James L. de Jongh** is an Associate Professor at the City College of New York, where he has taught in the Department of English since 1972. He is currently working on a book for the Cambridge University Press on the Harlem Renaissance.

**Eric Homberger**, Reader in American Literature at the University of East Anglia, was born and raised in Atlantic City, New Jersey. He has edited a volume in the Critical Heritage Series on Ezra Pound and was co-editor of *The Second World War in Fiction* and *The Troubled Face of Biography*. He is the author of *The Art of the Real: Poetry in England and America since 1939*, *American Writers and Radical Politics, 1900–1939: Equivocal Commitments* and *John Le Carré*.

**Allen J. Koppenhaver** is Professor of English and American Studies at Wittenberg University, Springfield, Ohio. He has taught on a Fulbright Lectureship at Exeter University. He has written and produced numerous plays and opera libretti.

**Christopher Mulvey** is a Principal Lecturer in English and American Studies at King Alfred's College, Winchester, and taught at the

City College of New York for ten years. He has published extensively in the field of Anglo-American travel literature, including *Anglo-American Landscapes* (Cambridge, 1983), and is presently engaged in writing a further book for Cambridge to be called *Transatlantic Manners*. He is shortly to move to Regent's College, London, to take up the position of Academic Dean.

**John Osborne**, Lecturer in American Studies at the University of Hull, is the editor of the arts magazine *Bête Noire* and the author of *The Poetry of Philip Pacey* and of more than fifty essays and reviews. He is presently co-authoring a study of post-1945 British and American poetry.

**Arthur E. Paris** is a Professor in the Department of Sociology at the University of Syracuse, New York. He has published extensively in the sociology of the American city and has lectured widely in Europe. Before moving to Syracuse, he taught at the University of Rutgers, New Jersey.

**Derek Pollard** has been Head of American Studies at the Liverpool Institute of Higher Education since 1967 and has regularly contributed papers, reviews and workshops to both the British Association for American Studies and the British Association for Canadian Studies. He has been involved in promoting art and architecture within integrated study programmes to explore cultural development.

**John Simons** is a Senior Lecturer in English and American Studies at King Alfred's College, Winchester. He is co-editor of an edition of Henry Porter's *The Two Angry Women of Abington* and co-editor of *The Poems of Lawrence Minot*. He has published numerous articles on medieval, Renaissance, nineteenth-century and modern American literature.

*Map 1*

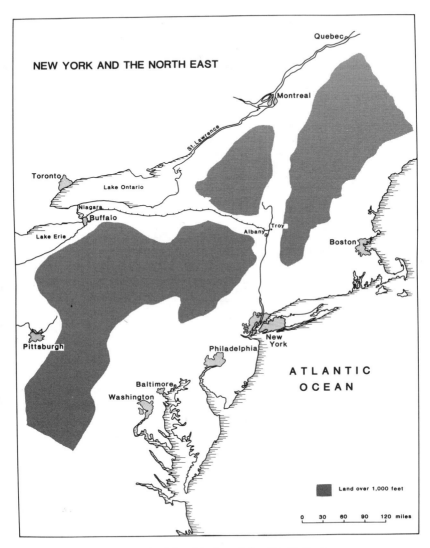

*Map 1    New York and the North East*

# 1

# Citytext: A Theoretical Introduction

CHRISTOPHER MULVEY and JOHN SIMONS

New York City has long faced both towards America and towards Europe. This provides it with an ambiguous status, so that New York can represent both a spiritual antithesis to the middle America that would repudiate it and an American epitome to the rest of the world that would embrace or repudiate it. In the nineteenth century, New York served as a port of entry to millions of immigrants; in the twentieth century, New York serves as a point of entry to many areas of American cultural, social, political, intellectual and sexual life. The issues of both American culture and American studies can be problematised by study of the city precisely because it remains the fact that in terms of American Studies, the wealth of material and diversity of sources make New York simultaneously a problem and a solution. The deafening rush of new subject-matter demands integration into the culture study while it points to its limitation.

Readings of America, geographical, historical or cultural, that do not lead to New York are partial readings. But readings of the cartographic, topographic, demographic and photographic text of New York, readings of the filmic, televisual and videolic text of New York (like any readings of the lyric, epic, dramatic and narrative text of New York City which operate by isolating the phenomenon called 'New York City' by a combination of geographical, historical and cultural specifications) engage in an exercise which raises as many problems as it provides solutions. We need to problematise issues somewhat better than that. To treat New York City as unique is to fall victim to a methodological error which is fatally attractive both to the American and the Americanist: the exceptionalist fallacy. The exceptionalist presumes that American phenomena are exclusively American. The exceptionalist discusses America or something American with insufficient reference to or

1

consciousness of other continents or worlds. More perversely, the exceptionalist of a middling order of raised consciousness sets out to explain the unique quality of the object American, expending ingenious and extraordinary energy to do so. The exceptionalist approaches the general in such a way that it appears particular; the exceptionalist makes the worldwide appear to be local.

When Emerson talked in 'Nature' about 'American Nature', he isolated, in a way characteristic of nineteenth-century nationalist thinking, a phenomenon of peculiar importance. Emerson talked to, or of, an entity around which might crystallise a whole series of notions which would give security to the ethnocentric, phallocratic and privileged reader who was the projected recipient of the text. It is unprofitable to engage in the late twentieth century in discussion of Emerson's 'American Nature' except as a construct of his world-view, except in so far as it would tell us what kind of mind and culture it was that required so exceptional a phenomenon by which to know its world. Emerson was not talking about anything with which we must engage in its own terms. There was and is no noumenon which was or is 'American Nature', any more, for that matter, than there was or is 'Nature'.

If there is something exceptional to be studied in American Studies, it might be that Americans have, potentially from the seventeenth century, implicitly from the eighteenth century, and explicitly from the nineteenth century, believed themselves to be an exceptional people and believed profoundly in the myth of American exceptionalism. The nineteenth-century American historian did not believe that the determinations of European history, still less those of Asian history, were operative on the North American continent. Lessons learned in Europe did not apply; dangers implicit for European peoples and European constitutions were not implicit for the American people and the American constitution; patterns of tyranny and oppression, of exploitation and excess, which marked European development, were neither the lot nor the destiny of the United States. So frequent, strong and varied are the claims of American culture and history and geography to the exceptional status of the United States of America in terms of its culture, history and geography, that it is difficult to engage in the subject without engaging in it in exceptional terms.

But America has been dreaming about itself for far too long and it is time to wake up from the American Dream to the common light of day. There is no more actuality to the 'American Dream' than there is to 'American Nature'. We must cease to treat America in American terms; the subject must not set the agenda. This means that we must not only cease to treat American history as a story of a chosen people or to think of the 'American way' as having some exceptional measure of commonplace human decency; it must also mean that we cease to regard America as being unusually materialistic, hedonistic, oppressive, imperialist. America, and with it New York, must be treated as no better and no worse than the country and the city next door. It should be the object of American Studies to make its subject seem ordinary, commonplace, pedestrian.

We need to undermine mythos by systematic scepticism and we need to forgo the pleasures of finding redemptive hope or apocalyptic despair in the American scene and within New York City. The citytext needs to be read in terms of larger intertextual phenomena which would pursue the particular text to localities in Amer-European (at least) macro-textualisations, in the constructs of mythological fictions and the resistant patterns of ideological obfuscations. The boundaries of the subject exist only within the boundaries of its environment, and while the subject may begin to shape that environment through political, aesthetic and technical interventions, the gross materially of the physical world, however transformed, stays one step ahead of the human beings who inhabit it. Environmental change is structural and therefore the transformations of one generation become the limitations of the next. The abolition of Nature as a meaningful physical entity has been accomplished, yet the need for a category of Being which takes Nature's place, or rather fulfils its role as an inviolate and absolute materiality which eludes human transformation may be said to remain with us as an indispensable order of discourse. In this sense Nature might always be said to appear *sous rature* just as the land itself, 'first Nature', exists under the bar of the street, the skyscraper and the factory.

The point then is to understand the subject which itself feels barred by the monstrous transformations of its own precursors. History may be defined as a progressive force tending always to the further promotion of the environment as a specialised capsule for the human being. Unfortunately, this view remains a possibility only while we see history as a narrative of the past and write it by projecting ourselves back into it. From this vantage-point all human endeavour will appear to tend towards the amelioration of the conditions of life. However, let us, theoretically, propose that we should write a history of the future and project the point at which we stand away from ourselves and into the centuries which have not yet been. From here we see history as a narrative of limitation, and a persistent closing off of human potential as each successive generation struggles to make over to itself the estates of its predecessors who, inevitably, died intestate. Walter Benjamin, a connoisseur of the urban in his writings on Paris, Moscow, Marseilles, Naples and Berlin, pointed out in the ninth of his *Theses on the Philosophy of History* that the angel of history looks into the past from which a storm is blowing:

> This storm irresistibly propels him into the future to which his back is turned, while the pile of debris before him grows skyward. This storm is what we call progress.[1]

As a roll-call of famous acts and deeds, the history of the future is, of course, not possible. Considered, however, as a theoretical position in historiography – that all history might be a history of the future if only we adjust our perspective correctly, swing our necks against the storm as it were – it is perfectly feasible and, indeed, if history is to perform its most important task, to reveal the making and the processes of the subject, it is mandatory.

In *All That is Solid Melts into Air*, Marshall Berman has drawn on Marx, among others, in attempting to analyse the experience of the modern as it manifests itself in the cities of the late nineteenth and twentieth centuries. In his commentaries he has specifically concentrated on the idea of 'modernism' both as an aesthetic and as a mode of being and elaborated its incursions into the everyday lives of city-dwellers:

> When students at Columbia University rebelled in 1968, some of their conservative professors described their action as 'modernism in the streets'. Presumably those streets would have been calm and orderly – in the middle of Manhattan yet! – if only modern culture could somehow have kept them off, and confined to university classrooms and libraries and Museums of Modern Art.[2]

In so far as New York is concerned, Berman reserves his most poignant critique for the modernistic destruction of the Jewish communities of the Bronx by the expressway cut through it under the tutelage of Robert Moses. Nowhere in his essentially romantic work is the sense of the modernist city as a lost opportunity more fully realised than in the constant autobiographical references in this section. Berman points out that many of New York's most characteristic monuments were designed with the specific purpose of projecting value, of symbolising the modernity of the new urban space and, of course, Allen Trachtenberg's analysis of the Brooklyn Bridge more than bears out this point. However, there is a duality in the message which the chain of urban developments generates and the value that it bears:

> The cumulative impact of all this is that the New Yorker finds himself in the midst of a Baudelairean forest of symbols. The presence and profusion of these symbols make New York a rich and strange place to live in. But they also make it a dangerous place, because its symbols are endlessly fighting each other for sun and light, working to kill each other off, melting each other along with themselves the air.[3]

Berman goes on to allude explicitly to *Love's Labour's Lost* and to *Macbeth*, but in this quotation we do find allusions to Shakespeare's 'American' play, *The Tempest*. It is worth pausing to reflect on these as through them a central aspect of Berman's excellent analysis of modernity may be perceived, though it is one that inexorably draws him from hard socioeconomic critique and into a traditionally humanistic paradigm in which the political determinations of capitalism in the urban centre are transformed into expressive moods analogous to the genres of aesthetic production.

Plainly, Berman has, all along, seen the connection between Marx's 'All that is solid melts into air' and Prospero's:

> These our actors
> As I foretold you, were all spirits, and
> Are melted into air, into thin air;
> And, like the baseless fabric of this vision,
> The cloud-capp'd towers, the gorgeous palaces,
> The solid temples, the great globe itself,
> Yea, all which it inherit shall dissolve,
> And, like this insubstantial pageant faded,
> Leave not a rack behind.
> (*Tempest* iv.i.148–56)

For Berman, the forest of the city dissolving itself takes on, as the Shakespearean language shines through his argument, the dress of a vision and then, a stage. How well the glorious edifices enumerated by Prospero adumbrate the major architectural features of New York. The denizens of the top floor of the World Trade Center phoning down to find out the weather at ground level might well feel their situation very accurately described in Prospero's words. However, it is not only the city that dissolves through this meeting of Shakespeare and New York, but also Berman's own sense of the solidity of the urban space. Try as he might he is unable to maintain such a grip on the city as to be able to believe in it as a reality which will be docile to the tools of political analysis, and thus New York slides off into the realm of the aesthetic: the 'real world' which Berman feels so keenly about becomes swiftly covered by its own propensity to generate symbols. Myth is, essentially, depoliticised ideology and here Berman allows his usually rigorous analysis through ideology to slip into the realm of analysis through myth.

This is not necessarily, of course, a conscious process. What is being demonstrated here is the difficulty of operating as a commentator who is disentangled from the symbolic web which is the subject of comment. The point is developed through Berman's sense of the city as a 'rich and strange place'. The phrase 'rich and strange' derives from a song in *The Tempest* which is sung by Prospero's servant Ariel in an attempt to delude the shipwrecked Ferdinand:

> Full fathom five thy father lies;
> Of his bones are coral made;
> Those are pearls that were his eyes;
> Nothing of him that doth fade
> But does suffer a sea-change
> Into something rich and strange.
> (*Tempest* i.ii.396–401)

The dialectical vision of Ariel's song fits well with Berman's own sense of the flux of urban modernism, but the import of this allusion in his work is deeper than this. As we saw above, New

York collapses into a stage ruled by Prospero, by name and nature an obvious cipher for the capitalists who made the city possible and, equally, are responsible for its constant and savage, or saving, reformations. It is they who orchestrate the symbolic dance of the New York skyline and they who arbitrate the grammar of its architectural language. The political fragility of their regime is blended with huge powers and thus, like Prospero, they are able to dissolve the system which they have built at any moment of crisis or Caliban's plot. Here the shipwrecked prince learns the pretended fate of his father, which is not so much death as mutation, from the magician's captive.

In the context of the quotation in Berman's book, immediately preceding his lament for the Bronx and the devastating public works which 'had come into my life just before my Bar Mitzvah, and helped bring my childhood to an end', the allusion, and its Shakespearean context take on a rich Oedipal complexion.[4] Indeed Berman will, within two pages, himself allude to Oedipus in his citation of Ginsberg's *Howl* with its 'sphinx of cement and aluminum'.[5] What we see here is another implication of the subject in the fabric of the city and the apparent impossibility of a disengagement which operates through a series of consciously defensive discourses.

The riddle of New York posed by the sphinx-like Robert Moses becomes the fate of the community and the individual whose fate – both childhood and the Bronx Jews are coterminous for Berman – is itself bound into the space which gave the community its original definition. Just as the origin of the individual is the father, so the origin of the community is the environment, and, like the father, the environment may be a forbidding authority. In mourning for a lost communal father Berman turns upon the environment as positioning itself just where the father might himself stand: towering above the vengeful, fearful infant and laying down an arbitrary law. The richness and strangeness that Berman finds in New York thus becomes a metaphor of reconciliation with the ghost of the murdered father through its rediscovery in the fabric of the city. Architecture, Capitalism, Father, Community: all four crowd together in Berman's richly overdetermined language and pull him into discourses which are much more truly defensive than those of Marxism and modernism. Though his claim is, at least partially, that modernism can be recuperated and seen as other than a force of monolithic alienation, this is not something which can be maintained on the ground of political science or sociology but something undermined by the unconscious which reasserts an understanding of the world as the symbolic form of its own ineffable desire.

We can see, then, how even such an intelligent and astute commentator as Berman can be seduced away from his own intentions, like Ferdinand by Ariel, the lost orphan by the creature of capitalist production, and retreat into aesthetic and psychological realms which leave the political battle unfought and serve to show just how deeply the subject is penetrated by the protocols of its own object. This rather lengthy analysis of a short passage from Berman's book is designed to show how the act of analysis is, in a sense, inalienable. There is no ground on which we can stand to move the object of argument away from our own implication in and with it. The problem comes when the object is an environment such as New York City, which is itself a symbol of alienation.

Compared with most European countries (Germany, Italy, France, the Republic of Ireland, Finland, the whole of the Eastern bloc, etc.) the USA is a very old state. One of its triumphs is to have retained its sense of itself as an experiment in governmental form and democratic ideology. Thus, modernism quickly found a home, not least in New York, which formed its port of entry through, for example, the Armory Show. Whether it is truly the case that New York is essentially a modernist city is, however, another matter. Modernism is a development of European traditions of high art and depends perilously on an understanding of romantic and post-romantic aesthetics for its effects.

Was there ever a romantic New York in which the modernist reaction could bear fruit? The drawing-rooms of Henry James? The puffing Dutchmen of Washington Irving? We are, of course, speaking not of architecture here but of symbol. There was a romanticised New York, of course, and that romanticisation met its nemesis in the sheds of Ellis Island but perhaps New York and modernism truly grew together: the one a new city, the other an aesthetic, thoroughly uprooted and thoroughly modified by transatlantic transportation. In the USA a cultural movement was grafted on to a fertile yet ingrown stock and flourished not, we shall suggest, as modernism, but as a specifically American transitional phase between modernism and post-modernism which, like Woolworth's Gothic, soon obtained its own traditions and its own claim to be the 'natural' style of the city. One might ask why Eliot and Pound went to Europe where their cultural predilections enabled them to become unambiguously modernist, and where their belief that their home country was, in some sense, culturally undeveloped could be constantly reinforced.

What Pound and Eliot were escaping, however, was not a cultural waste land (paradoxically Eliot was to find that in Europe) but a lack of the firm lines and cultural borders which would have enabled them to establish themselves as a literary elite. In other words, Walt Disney's nightmare that one day Mickey Mouse cartoons would be an object of academic study and aesthetic admiration was already coming true in the blurring of the distinction between high art and popular culture, and was to come to its finest development in the government-sponsored art of the Depression, the WPA murals and the *Index of American Design* as well as the burgeoning monumentality of New York City. It is clear that a volume such as this concerns itself with this spirit of, to use the word in its peculiarly American sense, democracy.

The contributions all point towards the popular arts (rock music); the high arts, painting, literature, rhetoric, practised with a deliberate consciousness of their relationship to the popular; or photography, which is perhaps, together with cinematography, the one truly twentieth-century art form, the classic manifestation of the work of art in the age of mechanical reproduction and the art form which has perhaps the most commonly available medium. Alongside these essays are pieces which orient themselves to the topography and political life of the city; these serve not so much to provide a context for the essays on cultural manifestations as to underpin the point hinted at in the treatment of Berman above: that the aesthetic may not be contextualised but rather forms part of field in which the various discourses of the urban environment are mutually determinate and distinct neither from each other nor from the perceiving subjects that they serve both to constitute and to interpellate.

As the subject itself comes under pressure and the idea of its unity becomes increasingly illusory so the idea of a totalised aesthetic vision which will serve as a complete explanatory model of the human condition fades away. Modernism was such a model and its supersession by post-modernism should not be considered as a development of the same order as the supersession of romanticism by modernism. Essentially both of these aesthetics inhabited a cultural paradigm produced by mechanised industry

and its social institutions and ideological apparatuses. Post-modernism is the product of a paradigm shift in which the mechanical
has been replaced by the electronic, the unique utterance (or
artefact) by the record, performance by competence. Marshall
McLuhan was, obviously, a prophet of this shift, as were Walter
Benjamin and Theodor Adorno, but the full effects could not have
been apparent to them and are only now becoming so to us. It is,
however, clear that the modern has never really been separate
from the post-modern in the USA, and New York City may act as
the exemplar of that cultural fold.

Thus, the sense of the urban space which is explored in this
volume is multifaceted and multimedial. No claims are made for
the privileging of one articulation above another and no attempt
is made to give a prior claim to authenticity to any one approach.
This is a book about New York which discusses the ways in which
the cultural life of the city is both expressive of the environment
and determined by it. The question which faces anyone who looks
at the intricate web of modern American culture may be posed
thus: 'Do we define our topic by its content or by the method we
propose to use to create a problematic for study?' This is not a
methodologically unified volume but one thing should be clear
from it: while the city itself provides an obvious unity through
content the idea of problematising the urban space and its cultural
boundaries and the theoretical positions that such a process
necessarily entails refuses the easy option of allowing the city to
remain as an ultimately untouched determinant, 'Nature' as it
were.

Instead the city is consistently textualised; it can be read as itself
a product of the culture which it may also be said to produce. We
saw how Berman's attempt to present a version of New York which
could be read as a narrative of lost community collapsed into an
introverted meditation as the unpredictable sublimations of the
intertextual manifested themselves in his allusions to Shakespeare.
Thus textualisation begets text and text begets textualisation.
Everything is not a text but we perceive it as if it were.

Methodologies and theories which are drawn from the broadened
cultural studies model of critical enquiry may prove more appropriate for the study of the city as text than those which derive from a
traditional literary critical base. However, we cannot say that we
have a specific theoretical or methodological 'line' apart from a
commitment to self-awareness and the determination to provide

in each of the essays of *New York: City as Text* a rewarding and rigorous statement about the city. In a pluralistic spirit the essays embrace topics such as the artist and the artist's journal, the photographer and the urban image, the artists and the power of the market, the entrepreneur and the cultural commodity, the activist and the social context, the political speaker and the street, the black migrant and the economic magnet, the ghetto-dweller and the welfare economy, but the different contributors bring their own preferred approach to the citytext. All such approaches are complemented by the consideration of environment and history which enables the perception of culture as a unified, if unevenly textured, entity. Our approach is pluralist and eclectic but we do not allow the relationship of, say, literature and history to be merely one of text and context but rather see it as a single discursive formation which allows multiple points of entry and which is generated by specific academic protocols, and focuses on the diverse culture of New York City.

The historical development of American Studies as a distinct subject has been marked by a preparedness to extend the canon, but it might be argued that the theoretical bases of such extension and their implications have not found a firm place in the general domain of the subject. The subject of English, on the other hand, has revolutionised the theoretical aspects of literary study but has not succeeded markedly in revising its canon. We are working here towards the blending of the new canon with a sophisticated base in cultural theory. We thus feel able to construct a New York City which will not immediately fall prey to reacculturation by the determinations of specifically English perspectives by introducing content which deflects the imposition of values inscribed on the received canon of literature and history. In summary, the theoretical core of our multifaceted approach is a vision of New York City as a complex entity which holds together in tension the highly diverse cultural interests which are reflected in this book's contents.

NOTES

1. Walter Benjamin, *Theses on the Philosophy of History*, in *Illuminations*, ed. H. Arendt (London: Fontana, 1977) pp. 259–60.
2. Marshall Berman, *All That is Solid Melts into Air* (London: Verso, 1985) p. 31.
3. Ibid., p. 289.
4. Ibid., p. 291.
5. Ibid., p. 291.

# 2

# The City as Ideal Text:
## Manhattan and the Photography of Alfred Stieglitz, 1890–1940

## GRAHAM CLARKE

The period 1890–1940 was an auspicious time for New York City. It not only consolidated its position as *the* metropolis of continental America, it emerged as the primary centre of an American avant-garde intent on establishing a metropolitan milieu to rival those of Europe: Zurich, Berlin, London and, above all, Paris. Growing from a population of some 1.4 million in 1890 to some 7.4 million in 1940 New York seemed the apogee of energy and activity: a whirl of constant construction in which, literally, a new America was seen to be in the making.

And nowhere was this more obvious than in the way the *look* of the city changed during that period. Manhattan Island, with twenty-two square miles, offered an image of a city seemingly made for the twentieth century and a 'tradition of the new'. In 1892, for example, *King's Handbook of New York City*, a leading gazetteer of the city, published a series of eight photographs which, collectively, offer a panorama of Manhattan Island.[1] The obvious point is how low the buildings are: how nineteenth century the look of the city is. It is a city of brownstones and warehouses, of dense East Side tenements and tightly berthed sailing ships. Apart from Brooklyn Bridge and the 'El' it is a city which shows little of the *visual* icons so basic to our sense of Manhattan today.

And yet over the next fifty years that skyline is to emerge as *the* quintessential image of the modern metropolis: what Le Corbusier sensed as part of Manhattan's essentially 'sublime' aspect. Even by the early 1900s the skyscraper had established itself as the central icon of the city. With the construction between 1900 and the 1930s of such buildings as the Woolworth Building, the Chrysler and Singer Buildings, and the Empire State Building, so the city emerged as a visual symbol of a unique urban ethos and energy:

wholly appropriate to a new America in the making.

Artists and writers alike celebrated this novel image: portraying a city of energy, radiance and potential.[2] As distinct from the naturalism of Dreiser and Stephen Crane, and the 'realism' of artists such as John Sloan and Edward Glackens, the city was viewed as an image of the future, particularly by the group of figures associated with Alfred Stieglitz. The Stieglitz Group, most obviously linked to Stieglitz's gallery '291' (at 291–3 Fifth Avenue) or published by Stieglitz in *Camera Work* and the *291* magazine, made of Manhattan an ideal locale on which to base its image of American promise and potential. John Marin, Abraham Walkowitz and Georgia O'Keeffe, for example, forged an art which celebrated the city as essentially a transcendent condition.[3] Like Nick Carraway in *The Great Gatsby* (1925) their vision of Manhattan is always the city seen for the first time,[4] whether in Marin's watercolours, where Manhattan appears repeatedly as a complex of inspired (almost magical) energies; a dynamic geometry in which buildings are dissolved as part of a single but continuous flux, or in O'Keeffe's skyscraper paintings, where the buildings are offered as urban icons with an overwhelming and mysterious presence bordering on the spiritual. And yet the vision of these artists is essentially rhetorical; for they seek a myth of the city which robs it of its history. The condition they visualise is never social: it is aesthetic. Their art, so to speak, seeks an ideal condition at the expense of the human. The specificity of the moment is always referred to an assumed (higher) abstract meaning of which it is a part.

I want to suggest that, like the artists he championed, Alfred Stieglitz also saw Manhattan as an ideal image and that in his photographs of New York he constructs a view of the city informed precisely by an abstract rather than human context. From his return to New York in the 1890s[5] to his last photographs in the 1930s Stieglitz sees the city in relation to a sacred typology: seeking in Manhattan a 'synergy' of the kind Hart Crane invoked in his own paeon to the urban myth, *The Bridge* (1930): a symbolic iconography to fulfil Walt Whitman's transcendent image of 'Manhattan'. Whether it is the photographs of the Lower East Side, or those taken in the 1910s around the Madison Square and '291' area, or those taken from his studio, 'An American Place', on Madison Avenue (at 53rd Street), or from the Shelton (on Lexington Avenue) in the 1930s, the camera seeks a consistent ideal image: an urban equivalent appropriate to America's true significance (for Stieglitz):

the white light of a celestial city sanctified by God and Manifest
Destiny. What he found, ultimately, was its direct opposite: a
brutal and material condition in which the image spoke to an
increasing commercialism which Stieglitz detested.

It is characteristic then, that in *America and Alfred Stieglitz* (1934)
he is seen as a 'vital figure', a 'missionary', a 'revolutionary',[6]
whose camera becomes an 'eye' to an assumed ultimate condition.
As Paul Rosenfeld insisted in *Port of New York* (1924),[7] Stieglitz's
photographs are essentially revelations in which the city is 'full of
quotidian stuff charged with vital power'. Similarly, they are
'expressive of unseen forces at work in things', part of 'the spirit
of ideal aspiration and spiritual growth'.[8] As H. J. Seligman
commented, 'Stieglitz saw the world as a series of pure forms'.[9] It
is no coincidence that one of his favourite texts was Kandinsky's
*The Spiritual in Art* (1912) nor that in Picabia's 1915 'portrait' Stieglitz
has been jokingly transformed into a camera; a mechanism in
search of its subject suggested by the word 'IDEAL' suggestively
placed in front of the lens.[10] Stieglitz stalks the city as an ideal
image but one which is increasingly ambivalent to its construction
in the photographs. As Stieglitz characteristically announced,
'photography brings what is not visible to the surface'.[11]

And part of that revelation found its source for Stieglitz in a
supreme natural order: a transcendent other based essentially in
the responses of Emerson and Thoreau as much as in nineteenth-
century American landscape painting. Indeed if Stieglitz made
New York his absolute urban habitat, he equally had an alternative
rural habitat to which, especially in the 1910s, he (and later Georgia
O'Keeffe, his second wife) would retreat: the family property on
Lake George in Upper New York State. Lake George had been
familiar to Stieglitz since his childhood and summers there continued to be a necessary respite from the city: a point of rest
and refreshment from the 'hothouse' of Manhattan. Indeed he
consistently divided his year between the two: staying at Lake
George often as late until November; returning to New York for
the winter and spring (the two seasons of his most famous
Manhattan images).

Lake George and Manhattan, in other words, became the two
poles of his symbolic register. As habitats they were not so much
opposed as complementary, for Lake George not only 'lifted'
Stieglitz spiritually, it underpinned his sense of the city and
formed the basis of his urban iconography. If, 'in reality all [his]

photographs are equivalents',[12] so Lake George existed as an equivalent to Manhattan. The energy he sought to photograph there had its source in his other ideal base. Lake George establishes, in other words, the ideal image of so much that we are offered in the photographs of Manhattan. It does not only remain as a symbolic presence; it frames the terms by which the city is seen. As his letters consistently stress, it is an area of purity and stillness, of original and fundamental natural images and processes of the kind he photographs in his equivalents (clouds, trees, grasses).

But significantly Lake George was also an important area for painters and artists associated with luminism. Martin Heade, for example, painted a view of it (*Lake George*) in 1862, as did John Frederick Kensett (*Lake George*) in 1869, and Seneca Ray Stoddard photographed it in the 1880s and 1890s. All images appropriate to the transcendent base of luminism as a *visual* attempt to picture a 'spiritual' America.[13]

Indeed, characteristic of much luminist work are precisely those qualities so associated with Stieglitz's own photography: an objective accuracy, a concern with light, atmosphere and form, and a 'direct' treatment of the subject rather than viewing it through literary and pictorial convention. In short, luminism seeks a transcendent visual equivalent of the world at which Emerson and Thoreau looked. Luminist images offer us a caught moment of spiritual repose, evinced through a spatial sense of light, silence and 'purity'. This is one reason why, as Barbara Novak suggests, 'water has a special significance in American landscape painting'.[14]

This is essentially the way in which Stieglitz approaches his experience of Lake George. He does not seek composed 'scenes' so much as frozen moments which imply a purity and abstraction of form. The photographs fix an imagery of assumed energy: a natural world pervaded by transcendent meaning. They are equivalents of the eye's 'scale' in the way it reads the world as a spiritual emblem. Like Emerson, Stieglitz saw his American world as a 'poem' in his 'eyes'.

The formal elements of *Dancing Trees* (1921), *Music* (1922), *Chicken House, Lake George* (1923) and *Chestnut Trees, Lake George* (1927) for example, appear again and again in the photographs of New York.[15] As 'shapes' and caught moments of a 'natural' world they seek to image what Rosenfeld called 'a profound revelation of life' in which an 'infinite light' becomes the 'substance' of Stieglitz's art.

This 'spiritual' America, then, is the essence of Stieglitz's view
of the city. The 'natural' imagery of his Lake George experience is
basic to the way he images Manhattan. The city is viewed through
an iconography of the transcendent: stillness, light, atmosphere,
sky and water, all qualities redolent of a 'natural' rather than urban
world.

Indeed one of the most basic of aspects associated with Stieglitz's
New York photographs is water. As Lewis Mumford noted,
'Weather and sky came into his pictures, again and again'.[16]
Stieglitz admitted that he 'always loved snow, mist, fog, rain [and]
deserted streets'.[17] An aspect, perhaps, most obvious in the
photographs from the 1890s and early 1900s. In these the essential
element is, literally, water in all its forms: as ice, snow, storm,
rain, mist and vapour. It becomes *the* supreme element just as the
'colour' white has a similar symbolic presence. As snow or as
stone, it becomes part of a *fluid* iconography in which the solid
gives way to the transmutable: an aspect basic to the lyric intensity
of so much of Stieglitz's New York images.

Water and whiteness (as snow) as part of a visual vocabulary in
which Stieglitz's 'ideal' is held; mediums of a natural environment
which signify a 'spiritual' condition. As such, the rhetoric of an
ideal 'America' encounters the solidity of the actual: of an urban
environment made substantial by its extension in time and space.
Consider, for example, Stieglitz's response to the Flat-Iron
Building:

> 'I stood', he said, 'spellbound as I saw that building in that storm
> . . . I had watched the structure in the course of its erection, but
> somehow it had never occurred to me to photograph it in the
> stages of its evolution. But that particular snowy day, with the
> streets of Madison Square all covered with snow, fresh snow, I
> suddenly saw the flat-iron building as I had never seen it before.
> It looked, from where I stood, as if it were moving toward me
> like the bow of a master ocean-steamer, a picture of the new
> America which was still in the making'.[18]

The language is of obvious significance here. Stieglitz suggests that
he is seeing the building for the first time and that its effect is to
make him stand 'spellbound'. In turn, what had caused this change
was the fall of, in his word, 'fresh snow'. Again the building is
related to an 'ocean-steamer': it has been turned into a boat and

thus, by implication, of a 'picture of the new America which was still in the making'. And 'still' is wholly apposite, both as part of a wider (assumed) energy to which it is a clue, but also as a static image of the dynamic Stieglitz seeks – *stilled* amidst flux – a fixed moment out of time. In other words the photographic image makes still those ideal energies of which the camera is a spectator. A series of social and historical referents have been stilled (controlled) by the lens in search of an ideal: a picture of the new America, 'still in the making'.

What then does his photographic image of the Flat-Iron offer? First, it records an image of the Fuller Building (the 'Flat-Iron') at the triangular junction of 5th Avenue and Broadway which, when it was completed in 1902 with twenty-one storeys, was the highest building in the city. Second, however, the image is of the building giving way to 'fresh snow', as if the city has been transformed, 'dehistoricised', as it were, into an image of whiteness and, by implication, of purity. As such we view the Flat-Iron through the images and tones of Lake George. The tree, for example, is almost a silhouette and, in its triangular-like structure, both recalls the 'Flat-Iron' shape but also offers that shape as a *natural* form. In turn, the trees in the middle distance are both delicate and fragile as they merge with the building behind. In other words, the image as a whole establishes a pattern of horizontals and verticals which reduce the photograph to a series of spatial arrangements.

The effect is to rob the building of depth and extension: of *substance*. The Flat-Iron is held within a 'geometry' of trees and as we look at this image of a 'new America' so its presence is reduced to a *flat area* just as, in tone, it merges with the whites and silver-greys which surround it. It has been transposed into a setting of implied energies: integers of the Stieglitz scene / seen. An aspect made obvious, perhaps, by the way in which the figures at the bottom of the photograph are 'lost'.

Anyone who has seen the actual building will realise just how much Stieglitz's image flattens and reduces it. The building has about it a detail, texture and substance which are wholly lost in the Stieglitz photograph. As Paul Goldberger notes, 'The facade is a richly detailed tapestry of rusticated limestone' while 'the French Renaissance detail is ornate.'[19] In Stieglitz's image there is none of this detail or solidity. Windows become patches of tone: they are not part of an interior into which we look. The building, in Stieglitz's image, could never 'house' human activity.

This response is elicited once again by a 1900 photograph: *Spring Showers, New York*,[20] where the vertical significance is again stressed. The tree exists as a 'found object', as it were, but photographed in relation to an urban surrounding almost wholly dissolved by water and mist. One's eye might move to the traffic (cabs) in the top half, but the effect is to suggest a series of surfaces and reflections which shine. The tree remains the focus just as the figure (again a formal 'patch') has almost dissolved into the water atmosphere. Indeed the image looks forward to Stieglitz's photograph of the Flat-Iron, for *Spring Showers* is based, like *The Flat Iron*, in Madison Square and gives us, behind the tree, the very junction at 5th Avenue and Broadway on which, two years later, the building is erected. At the time of the photograph (as contemporary photographs and, significantly, Theodore Dreiser in *The Color of a Great City* make clear) the site is occupied by a conglomeration of shabby buildings which, like the Flat-Iron, have about them a remarkable and ornate detail wholly lost (or 'dissolved') by Stieglitz. The spot in 1900 is full of advertising and notices: a profusion of signs and texts announcing the very commercial city in which Stieglitz seeks his ideal base. In *Spring Showers* the city, in this sense, has all but disappeared.

The effect is similar in *Winter, Fifth Avenue* (1893) and *The Terminal* (1892) – caught moments in which, despite an ambivalent urban scene, the inference is upon natural energies. The city as a human and working environment is displaced in favour of snow, light, steam and *stilled* energies: a geometry of line and fluid substance which dissolves, once again, the very structures (economic, social, personal) in which the scene is 'lived'.

Indeed Stieglitz's way with his urban world is especially evident in another early image, *The Street* (1892), which again shows the city in winter covered with snow and bathed in a mist. In addition, the tree and horse imply other energies which supplant the figures. Indeed the figures are barely present. They walk away from us just as the scene is fixed in a moment of *dissolution*: a flatness which evinces an ethereal quality typical of these views. The substantial and the solid is dissolved in the way we are distanced from any activity *on* 'the Street'. Any human trace, so to speak, has been erased by the snow and the whiteness in which it is held. What Mark Kuspit has called an aspect of the way the *city* is 'ameliorated',[21] or, as I have suggested, 'dissolved' in favour of an assumed ideal condition.

The way in which a specific sense of 'the Street' has been constructed for us here is made obvious if we relate the photograph to the original area in which it was taken. What we have, and what we so easily miss, is that this is an image of 5th Avenue, close to where Stieglitz was to establish '291'. And yet it gives little sense of what was happening in the area in the 1890s, for it was no longer the domain of wealthy houses, but, like Madison Square along the way, it was becoming more and more a *commercial* area, and newspapers of the time commented upon the rapid change in the use of buildings. We might, for example, note the fact that the building in the background of Stieglitz's image is not an ornate private residence: it is the original Waldorf Astoria Hotel – a building which had replaced one of the grandest residences of a more traditional 5th Avenue.

As a street, then, the image remains ambivalent and certainly has little to do with one's sense of a street as part of an immediate urban reality. Indeed, Stieglitz's viewpoint is made clearer in relation to another major New York photographer of the period, Lewis Hine, who, unlike Stieglitz, was essentially committed to the life and work he found in the deeply textured streets of Manhattan.

The *Literary Digest* made such a distinction in a 1920 review of Hine's work, calling him a 'sociological photographer'.[22] As such Hine is in the tradition of Jacob Riis – photographing what Paul Kellogg called 'piled-up actualities'.[23] The difference I want to establish, however, is the way in which Hine makes the human figure central, whereas Stieglitz virtually expunges and erases it from the space of the photograph. In other words, Hine offers an image of the city quite different from that of Stieglitz. If Hine looks at labour, he does so in order to establish the *context* of that labour, and the life to which it belongs. The fundamental elements of Hine's images are, as it were, social and historical; Stieglitz's are aesthetic and mythic.

Just as Stieglitz 'flattens' public space (and avoids private space) so Hine mines it – allowing his figures to establish their mark in an integral but complex series of relationships within the immediate context of the city. Thus Hine's subjects in the 1900s are the immigrants entering Ellis Island (opened 1892) and the tenements of the Lower East Side. In his images of these groups his photographs catch the detail of street-level activity and celebrate the evidence and trace of the human rather than, as with Stieglitz, the aesthetic contemplation of the city as spectacle.

The difference, for example, between Stieglitz's *The Street* and Hine's *Children on the Street, Lower East Side, New York City*[24] becomes obvious. In Hine there is no single focal point, but equally there are no tonal or formal patterns which dominate the photographic space. The eye is drawn to the richness and density of detail and texture just as it is allowed to range in depth rather than merely move over the surface of the image. As the lettering in the photograph suggests, we are invited, literally, to 'read' the environment. It is, as it were, before us – open to our gaze and, significantly, at street level. It does not spread away from us, it spreads around us even though it remains separate and distanced from our intrusion. The figures here are photographed in time: they are not given over to orders of space.

And this is similar to other of Hine's images in the period, for example, *Beggar, New York City* (1900), *Italian Immigrant* (1907) and *East Side, New York* (1910). Equally Hine intrudes into private spaces and domestic interiors (areas wholly alien to Stieglitz) partial orders and orderings which contain the measure of the lives being lived: in *Finishing Clothing* (1906) and *New York Sweatshop* (1908), just as much as in his images of immigrant groups on Ellis Island, *Jews at Ellis Island* (1904) and *Slovak Group* (1906), for example.

In all these the human figure is central. The photographs offer images of the private and strange and record, so to speak, environments being read by the participants. Even though often 'posed' they create a distance which both draws us into the histories imaged and their difference and separation from us. Their presence remains complex and compelling. All are attempts, finally, to create a knowable space amidst the public extension of the city: at once amorphous, ambiguous and unfeeling – as in, for example, *Man Asleep in Doorway* (1910). As Hine moves through the plurality of the Lower East Side so his camera records a rich but ambivalent human potential. The figure is central to the effect – and the figure, it is detail, is evidence of a culture and history that we seek to know. It gives to their images a caught individuality.

In contrast consider how Stieglitz responds to the Lower East Side in his *The Five Points* (1892), an area the New York *WPA Guide* called 'historically infamous' (and so described by Charles Dickens in his *American Notes*).[25] In the area pictured and written about by Jacob Riis in *How the Other Half Lives* (1891) it was also, in the 1890s, close to where Stieglitz worked on Leonard Street.

As so often in a Stieglitz image we are 'physically' distanced
from the scene, just as virtually all the figures have their backs to
us. They turn away from the camera. The 'human', as it were, has
been deflected to the 'sign' for Fineburg's store which is given no
specific social dimension. Rather, the scene has been offered (like
*The Steerage*) as a series of shapes and tonal areas – flattened and,
by implication, ameliorated.[26] The street-level here distances us
from the image; it does not engage with, nor does it appear to
seek, the 'life' of the area. It is a photograph of space, not time; of
light and shade, not bricks and mortar.

The relationship to the 'subject' is made more obvious if we
think of how Paul Strand photographed street figures in New York
during the 1900s: finding images of people whom 'life had battered
into some sort of extraordinary interest'. Those of 1915–16, for
example, focus upon the figure – wholly committed to the experience of the street, catching images at once separate and fiercely
compelling: once again, human contexts rather than abstract
energies. Rarely, in Stieglitz, do we confront figures in this sense –
of, on or from the street. Rarely do we have a sense of their
presence, of their trace as individual histories. Rather, the fascination is that of the city as spectacle. The human, ultimately, is
always subordinate to a photographic image and its potential as
an 'ideal text'. Even with the semi-abstract *Wall Street* (1915) Strand
achieves a marvellously caught web of different relationships in
which the human is held, literally, within a larger historical and
cultural context.

If we recall what Stieglitz said of his experience in the area the
relationship is clear: 'From 1893 to 1895', he said, 'I often walked
the streets of New York downtown, near the East River, taking
my hand camera with me. I wandered around the Tombs, the old
post office, Five Points. I loathed the dirty streets, yet I was
fascinated.'[27] And as Stieglitz is 'fascinated' so he is always
distanced. He 'loathes' the 'dirty streets' as if dirt implies the mark
and trace of the human. Stieglitz seeks a pure image: an ideal
rhetoric in which the stain of the human, and of history, has been
expunged. Water is, once again, part of a symbolic cleansing,
restoring the environment to its condition as ideal text, not as
human space.

In one sense, then, the concern with light, with whiteness and
water, is one aspect of the way the camera in Stieglitz 'restores'
the environment – 'bathes', as it were, the city in search of an

assumed ideal energy which 'holds' those energies that the camera might 'catch'. 'The Hand of Man' has simultaneously created the city but disparaged and polluted the radiant American light and land of which Stieglitz is in search. Thus, as Alan Trachtenberg suggests, where in Hine the 'place of the picture is a solid space in which individuality is defined'[28] we might say that the place of the picture in Stieglitz is an inferred ideal space in which an idea is given its found but constructed equivalent, but an equivalent at the cost of the 'human' and the social. The city at its most obvious working level – the pavement and the street – is all but invisible.

Certainly this increasingly underlies Stieglitz's photographs of the city in the later 1900s and perhaps suggests why the images from the 1930s are so ambivalent. The photographs of 1910 and 1911, for example, although centred on Lower Manhattan, now move away from the street and the density of the Lower East Side to the waterfront and the East River, and record the changing skyline as part of an assumed 'dynamic' energy.

In these photographs the city is given over to water and sky as the dominant categories – not 'composed', but, once again, stilled moments of larger unities – light, for example, and large-scale abstract movement. Thus *City of Ambition* (1910) (so ambiguous in its sense of 'power') offers an image of Lower Manhattan once again on the verge of 'dissolution'. Water, sky and smoke predominate over any sense of the city in a human or social context. Equally *The Aquitania* (1910) looks to the Port of New York – and again stresses movement and change. Its use of white makes form rather than subject significant. This is not the city of immigrants, but of energies. In *The City Across the River* (1910) once again water and steam stress the sense of distance and dissolution. The city is reduced to a silhouette just as in *Lower Manhattan* (1910) it is space, sky and light which dominate: the city held, as it were, amidst a geometry of 'natural' energies.

Indeed this is fundamental to the way in which Stieglitz photographs the increasingly massive visual changes the city undergoes between 1900 and the 1930s. Unlike Lewis Hine or Berenice Abbott, for example, Stieglitz characteristically seeks the most *insubstantial* aspects of the new construction. He looks up (to the sky) and photographs buildings being built (or, let us say, momentarily stilled: there are never any figures in these studies). Manhattan emerges as a series of skeletal patterns in which the dominant medium is not brick or steel but light amidst space. Once again

Manhattan in these photographs is a city divorced from the street. Stieglitz is at his furthest point from Hine and Riis. Their habitats are the street and alley: dense and enclosed urban spaces; dark areas of dirt and constriction. Stieglitz, in contrast, seeks out the *avenues* of Manhattan: wide public thoroughfares where the eye is freed to the sky above.[29] As the city grows upward so he constructs a mythic spectacle, less and less dependent upon its historical site.

In *Old and New New York* (1910), for example, although we are given an image of the city in the making its viewpoint is wholly characteristic, I think, of the early photographs. Even though we are at street level the 'eye' is given over to an upward gaze towards the central Stieglitz presence – the sky: an encompassing medium as source of light. In other words, we move from the solidarity, depth and texture of a nineteenth-century brownstone New York to its 'new' equivalent: not a building so much as a geometry – a grid of direction in which 'space' is 'sky'.

Indeed this concern with the 'new' and the increasing sense of 'distance' is underlined by Stieglitz's own position within Manhattan. In the 1900s, at '291' he is between 30th and 31st Streets on 5th Avenue – at street level or photographing from the upper floor of his studio. From there he moves up-town. The Intimate Gallery was at 59th Street and Park Avenue and, perhaps ironically in retrospect, An American Place at 53rd Street on Madison Avenue – on the seventeenth floor. By 1924 he and Georgia O'Keeffe are living on 49th Street and Lexington Avenue – on the thirtieth floor of the then Shelton Hotel (opened in 1924 and thirty-four storeys high).

Stieglitz not only moves further away from the human and local environment of the 1890s – moving 'deeper' into a corporate Manhattan – he moves higher and higher above street level. Not only does he leave the street behind, he views the city from on high, behind the 'glass' of his apartment or gallery window. Contact, as it were (so crucial a term in the 1920s), is now from *above* the city: he views it as a large-scale form not made up of intimate and disturbing details.

This is in part suggested by *Two Towers* (1913), a photograph which shows a newer Manhattan but does so, once again, by means of those basic Stieglitz elements: snow, whiteness and trees – all 'natural' images which frame the city and establish their terms on which we receive the two towers – once again on Madison Square (opposite the Flat-Iron): the old Madison Square Garden

'Giralda' Tower and, behind, the Metropolitan Life Insurance Building, fifty storeys high. Completed in 1909 it was, for a brief period, the tallest building in New York. Significantly it is 'dissolved'. What Ben Lubeschz called 'a great white sentinel' is offered to us as a presence, a referent of other energies.[30] It has no function, certainly not as insurance headquarters. It stands as a 'mysterious' and, by implication, spiritual symbol.

This, however, is the city Stieglitz constructs: seeing, as it were, not insurance headquarters, but 'white sentinels' redolent of, once again, his ideal energy as characteristic of an 'America' in the making. As he moves into this new environment he does so in terms of energies rather than economies. The Woolworth Building (1913) – that 'Cathedral of Commerce', the American Radiator Building (1924) and, in the 1930s (some of which he photographs from the Shelton), a series of buildings basic to the iconography of mid-town Manhattan: (1923) the Empire State Building (1931) the Rockefeller Center, (1930–40) the Chrysler Building, (1931) the (fifty-one-storey) General Electric Building, and, just by the Shelton (again in 1931), the Waldorf Astoria: all icons of a new and ever *higher* Manhattan; seemingly images of promise (and wonder) as part of the rhetoric of New York as ideal image.

This is, in part, the New York we see from the seventeenth floor of An American Place. Thus in the photograph entitled *An American Place* (1931) the use of shadow allows the upper half of the photograph to dominate. The resulting diagonal stresses the vertical nature of the scene. Once again, the texture and detail of the lower half gives way to the white skyscrapers in the top half. The eye is invited to move up although the tendency is to move down – into that 'mass' of detail below but, significantly, the street below is blacked out by shadow. It *refutes* our gaze just as, once again, there are no figures.

Consider how different are Hine's photographs of the Empire State Building's construction in the 1930s. In *Construction Workers* (1930), for example, we are once again, placed in an environment which is both determined and *constructed* by the figures. The movement here is of the eye in the photographic space as it traces specific movements and areas of human direction. As Hine said, 'cities do not build themselves'. Similarly in *Construction Workers, New York City* (1930) we see the city 'through' the figure, just as the area of 'dark' suggests weight and substance – an environment in the making by individuals. As Trachtenberg argues, in the photographs of the Empire State Building, 'Hine could follow with his camera a process that culminated in a tangible product: not "power", something abstract, metaphysical, beyond sight, but a *building*, a tower, an unmistakable presence.'[31] As distinct from Hine's, Stieglitz's move into a skyscraper allows him to observe the changing city from a needful distance. The city becomes a panorama (and spectacle) of geometrics and tonal patterns. Once again it exists as mythic spectacle rather than as human environment.

The Shelton thus is Stieglitz's 'final' vantage-point – this urban 'pole' to match his other residence at Lake George. Just as his wife, Georgia O'Keeffe, 'became eager to take rooms in the ultra-modern brick skyscrapers . . . to sleep and paint high above the nerve-jangling cacophony of the city side-walks and shadowed streets, up in the sky, the infinite space', so too Stieglitz, we are told, 'was also interested in the idea of living in a skyscraper'.[32] Significantly then it is from the Shelton that we have Stieglitz's last photographs of the city. They image a city in the making but, collectively, they construct a mid-town Manhattan dominated by a sense of shadow and emptiness: large blocks of tonal contrast in which detail invariably reveals a half-finished skyscraper, devoid of inhabitants. See, for example, *From the Shelton, Westward* (1931) or *From the Shelton, Looking Northwest* (1932).

And yet there is a peculiar, ghost-like, quality about those views. What Harold Clurman saw as an image of Manhattan as an 'intricate gigantic tomb', Lewis Mumford as images of the 'cold exhalations of a depopulated world' and Doris Bry as 'a brooding poetic quality, . . . of great loneliness' increasingly overwhelms the view of Manhattan which is so basic to the mythic city constructed in *Port of New York*.[33] It is as if, unwittingly, the visual rhetoric so basic to Stieglitz's ideal has leaked away to leave only an empty reflection. The myth, so to speak, has been overwhelmed by history.

And perhaps this is suggested by two of the buildings so central to these later photographs, the Waldorf Astoria, just west of the Shelton (which in the photographs appears with those telling diagonal crosses in each of the windows) and the General Electric Building. Stieglitz photographs a hotel and a company building – central integers of a mid-town Manhattan he would rather view as surface, shadow and light: as an image of America endlessly STILL in the making. There is a sense, finally, of mystery which Stieglitz can only capture in the night pictures from the Shelton itself: *From the Shelton, Looking West* (1933) and *Night, New York* (1931). But now, as it were, his play of light is centred on the production of light. The General Electric Building, while it sustains the image in structural and aesthetic terms, also sustains the city in economic and social terms. It is, therefore, perhaps more than a little ironic that one of the final and dramatic images of Stieglitz's New York suggests a corporation which produces the very commodity on which Stieglitz is so dependent – the light he constantly sought to capture – a city of light and, presumably, of lightbulbs. But the light is not a transcendent light; it is instead a light traceable to its productive source: a light, indeed, created, not caught, by 'The Hand of Man'.

NOTES

1. See *King's Handbook of New York City*, ed. Moses King (Boston, Mass.: Moses King, 1892).
2. See Peter Conrad's *The Art of the City* (Oxford and New York: Oxford University Press, 1983).
3. The most useful study of this group in relation to Stieglitz remains William Innes Homer, *Alfred Stieglitz and the American Avant-Garde* (Boston, Mass.: New York Graphic Society, 1977).
4. In Chapter IV Carraway tells us that 'The city from the Queensboro Bridge is always the city seen for the first time, in its first wild promise of all the mystery and beauty in the world.'
5. For detailed information on Stieglitz's life and development see the excellent biography by Sue Davidson Lowe, *Stieglitz: A Memoir / Biography* (New York: Farrar, Straus & Giroux, 1983).
6. *America and Alfred Stieglitz: A Collective Portrait*, ed. Waldo Frank, Lewis Mumford *et al.* (1934: re-issued New York: Aperture, 1979). The whole volume is of importance.
7. See the chapter on Stieglitz in Paul Rosenfeld, *Port of New York* (Urbana and London: University of Illinois Press, 1966, with an introduction by Sherman Paul) pp. 237–79.
8. Paul Rosenfeld, 'The Photography of Alfred Stieglitz', *Nation*, 23 March 1932, vol. 134, no. 3481.
9. H. J. Seligman, *Alfred Stieglitz Talking: Notes on Some of His Conversations, 1925–1931* (New Haven, Conn.: Yale University Press, 1966) p. 2.
10. Published in *291*, nos 5–6, July–August, 1915. See the illustration in Homer, *Stieglitz and the American Avant-Garde*, p. 191.
11. See Stieglitz's essay 'Pictorial Photography', reprinted in *Classic Essays on Photography*, ed. Alan Trachtenberg (New Haven, Conn.: Leete's Island Books, 1980) pp. 116–123.
12. Alfred Stieglitz, in *Twice a Year* (Fall–Winter 1938) p. 99.

13. See *American Light: The Luminist Movement, 1850–1875*, ed. John Wilmerding (Washington DC: National Gallery of Art, 1980).

14. Barbara Novak, *Nature and Culture: American Landscape Painting 1825–1875* (New York: Oxford University Press, 1980) p. 40, but see pp. 39–41.

15. Virtually all of the photographs mentioned in this article can be found in: *America and Alfred Stieglitz*, ed. Frank *et al.*; Doris Bry, *Alfred Stieglitz: Photographer* (Boston, Mass.: Museum of Fine Arts, 1965); and Dorothy Norman, *Alfred Stieglitz: An American Seer* (New York: Aperture, 1973).

16. See Mumford's essay 'The Metropolitan Milieu', in *America and Alfred Stieglitz*, ed. Frank *et al.*, pp. 27–37.

17. Norman, *Alfred Stieglitz: An American Seer*, p. 36.

18. Alfred Stieglitz, 'Six Happenings', *Twice a Year*, nos 13–15 (Fall–Winter 1946–7) pp. 188–9.

19. Paul Goldberger, *The City Observed: New York* (New York: Vintage Books, 1979) p. 97.

20. The photograph is given this title in *Camera Work: A Pictorial Guide*, ed. Marianne Fulton Margolies (New York: Dover Books, 1978).

21. See Henry M. Sayre, *The Visual Text of William Carlos Williams* (Urbana and Chicago: University of Illinois Press, 1983) p. 67.

22. 'Treating Labor Artistically', *Literary Digest*, 67 (4 December) pp. 33–4.

23. Paul Kellogg, *America and Lewis Hine: Photographs 1904–1940* (New York: Aperture, 1970) with an essay by Alan Trachtenberg, p. 126.

24. Ibid.

25. *The WPA Guide to New York City*, intr. William H. Whyte (1939; re-issued New York: Pantheon Books, 1982).

26. Stieglitz, on looking at the scene he photographed as *The Steerage* noted that, despite all the figures in the scene he saw only 'a picture of shapes and underlying that the feeling that [he] had about life'. See Alfred Stieglitz, 'Four Happenings', *Twice a Year*, nos 8–9 (Spring–Summer, Fall–Winter 1942) p. 128.

27. Norman, *Alfred Stieglitz: An American Seer*, p. 39.

28. Trachtenberg, in Kellogg, *America and Lewis Hine*, p. 125.

29. For a discussion on the distinctions between such areas see Joseph Rykwert's essay, 'The Street: The Use of its History', in *On Streets*, ed. Stanford Anderson (Cambridge, Mass. and London: Harvard University Press, 1978) pp. 15–26.

30. Ben Lubeschz, *Manhattan: The Magical Island* (New York, 1927).

31. Trachtenberg, in Kellogg, *America and Lewis Hine*, p. 135.

32. Laurie Lisle, *Portrait of an Artist: A Biography of Georgia O'Keeffe* (New York: Seaview Books, 1980) pp. 144–6.

33. See *America and Alfred Stieglitz*, ed. Frank *et al.*, *Alfred Stieglitz: Photographs and Writings* (Washington, D.C.: National Gallery of Art, 1986). Sarah Greenough notes (p. 32) that 'of the sixty-five photographs of New York City from the 1930s in the National Gallery collection, over two-thirds can be grouped into series depicting the construction of buildings'.

# 3

# John Reed, Mabel Dodge and Sexual Politics in New York

## ERIC HOMBERGER

John Reed, Harvard '10, settled in New York in March 1911. With the invaluable help of his father's friend Lincoln Steffens, Reed found work with the *American Magazine* and began to explore the metropolis. Steffens watched his young protégé with considerable delight:

> When John Reed came, big and growing, handsome outside and beautiful inside, when that boy came . . . to New York, it seemed to me that I had never seen anything so near to pure joy. No ray of sunshine, no drop of foam, no young animal, bird or fish, and no star, was as happy as that boy was.[1]

Read was soon expressing in verse his sense of wonderment at the city:

> This city, which ye scorn
> For her rude sprawling limbs, her strength unshorn –
> Hands blunt from grasping, Titan-like, at Heaven,
> Is a world-wonder, vaulting all the Seven!
> Europe? Here's all of Europe in one place;
> Beauty unconscious, yes, and even grace.[2]

For many of the younger poets at that moment, the discovery of the city was a crucial component of the 'modern'. But Reed's city was not that of the naturalistic novelists such as Crane or Dreiser, or that created in paintings by William Glackens (*The Shoppers*, 1907), John Sloan (*Election Night*, 1907) and Everitt Shinn (*Sixth Avenue Elevated After Midnight*, 1899).[3] Reed of course was not alone in seeing the apotheosis of romance in the harsh reality of the city.

Alfred Stieglitz found a monumental beauty in a train moving through New York on a calm evening (*The Hand of Man*, 1902). Alvin Langdon Coburn found something romantic, even exotic, in workingmen standing before the Williamsburg Bridge, and presented *The Tunnel Builders* (both New York, 1910) as the epitome of the heroic. To John Gould Fletcher, who left Harvard in 1907 and travelled to Europe to become a poet, the city presented with images of extravagant romantic beauty:

> Over the roof-tops the shadows of clouds;
> Like horses the shadows of clouds charge down
>     the street.
> Whirlpools of purple and gold,
> Winds from the mountains of cinnabar,
> Lacquered mandarin moments, palanquins swaying
>     and balancing
> Amid the vermilion pavilions, against the jade balustrades.[4]

Ezra Pound was even more extravagant in apostrophising New York as 'a maid with no breasts' in *Ripostes* (1912), and in William Carlos Williams' 'The Wanderer' (1914) the poet's quest brought him to look within the harsh ugliness of 'that filthy river', the Passaic, for Beauty.[5] Reed's Harvard contemporary, T. S. Eliot, was alone among his contemporaries in seeking to discover in the city metaphors of a quite different kind to express the spiritual state of modern man:

> The morning comes to consciousness
> Of faint stale smells of beer
> From the sawdust-trampled street
> With all its muddy feet that press
> To early coffee-stands.[6]

In 1917, at the age of twenty-nine, John Reed wrote an autobiographical essay, 'Almost Thirty', in which he described with lyric delight his memories of discovering New York in 1911, when he returned to America after a stay in Europe. 'New York was an enchanted city to me', he wrote.

Everything was to be found there – it satisfied me utterly. I wandered about the streets, from the soaring imperial towers of downtown, along the East River docks, smelling spices and the clipper ships of the past, through the swarming East Side – alien towns within towns – where the smoky flare of miles of clamorous pushcarts made a splendor of shabby streets; coming upon sudden shrill markets, dripping blood and fishscales in the light of torches, the big Jewish women bawling their wares under the roaring great bridges; thrilling to the ebb and flow of human tides sweeping to work and back, west and east, south and north. I knew Chinatown, and Little Italy, and the quarter of the Syrians; the marionette theatre, Sharkey's and McSorley's saloons, the Bowery lodging houses and the places where the tramps gathered in winter; the Haymarket, the German Village, and all the dives of the Tenderloin. I spent all one summer night on top of a pier of the Williamsburg Bridge; I slept another night in a basket of squid in the Fulton Market, where the red and green and gold sea things glisten in the blue light of the sputtering arcs. The girls that walk the streets were friends of mine, and the drunken sailors off ships newcome from the world's end, and the Spanish longshoremen down on West Street.[7]

There is much that is central to Reed in this passage, with its mixture of aesthetic impulses and things romantic and adventuresome. A year later, taking a brief moment from his deepening political involvements, he wrote an autobiographical poem, 'America 1918', which was a guided tour of New York. Only one section of this poem appeared during his lifetime:

> *By proud New York and its man-piled Matterhorns*
> *The hard blue sky overhead and the west wind blowing,*
> *Steam plumes waving from sun-glittering pinnacles,*
> *And deep streets shaking to the million-river:*

> Manhattan, zoned with ships, the cruel
>    Youngest of all the world's great towns,
> Thy bodice bright with many a jewel,
>    Imperially crowned with crowns . . .

> Who that has known thee but shall burn
>    In exile till he come again

To do thy bitter will, O stern
Moon of the tides of men![8]

New York for Reed was a terrain of magic and enchantment, of diversity, vistas and power; it was above all a terrain through which he moved with freedom. Unlike Fletcher and Eliot, for whom the city had ulterior meanings (aesthetic or moral), all Reed wanted to do was celebrate the glories of the city.

We can say, with equal certainty, what New York was not for Reed: it did not call out to a sense of mission or guilt-ridden social conscience. This is what most clearly marked the generational fissure which separated Reed from those such as Robert Hunter (1874–1942), who grew up in a small town in Indiana, trained as a social worker, lived in Hull House in Chicago, and then came to New York in 1902 as the head worker at the University Settlement on Rivington Street. Hunter's *Poverty* (1904) was a class of the progressive conscience confronted by urban conditions, and for a decade he was a leading intellectual in the Socialist Party. Ernest Poole (1880–1950), the son of a wealthy grain-broker, was raised in prosperity and strict Presbyterianism in Chicago. After graduating from Princeton in 1902 he too settled in the University Settlement in New York. Poole was assigned by Hunter to do a report on newsboys, bootblacks and messenger boys for the New York Child Labor Committee, and was persuaded by the radical lawyer Morris Hillquit to join the Socialist Party. Along with William English Walling, he organised a mass meeting at Carnegie Hall in support of strikes at Lowell and Lawrence, and wrote a novel describing the titanic efforts of one of Bill Haywood's Wobbly organisers on the New York waterfront (*The Harbor*, 1915). Like Hunter, Poole resigned from the Socialist Party over its opposition to the First World War in 1914. Hunter and Poole, and so many others of their generation who grew up in families dedicated to the most rigid Calvinist beliefs, but who were unable to accept the call to the ministry, found an outlet in social work and the urban settlements for their feelings of guilt and social responsibility. The city, and in particular the urban poor, offered an outlet for emotions which society seemed to have stifled elsewhere. The decision to live in the slums and to affirm the brotherhood of man was an expression of a need to serve, to 'do something'.[9]

What was most characteristic of their way of seeing the city was essentially derived from their puritan forebears: they saw the city

typologically as the field upon which good and evil struggled for
mastery; and they derived a literary strategy for their campaign
against the worst of urban problems through the allegorical reinterpretation of 'sacred' texts. *The Divine Comedy* in particular gave
people such as Robert Hunter ways of understanding the dilemma
of the urban poor:

> these men, women and children were, to my mind, struggling
> up that face of a barren precipice, – not unlike that up which
> Dante toiled, – sometimes in hope, sometimes in despair, yet
> bitterly determined; the abyss of vice, crime, pauperism, and
> vagrancy was beneath them, a tiny ray of hope above them.
> Flitting before them was the leopard, persistently trying to win
> them from their almost hopeless task by charms of sensuality,
> debauch, and idleness. The lion, predatory and brutal, threat-
> ened to devour them; the she-wolf (Greed), hungry for them,
> enriched herself by their labors. Some were won from their toil
> by sensual pleasures, some were torn from their footholds by
> economic disorders, others were too weak and hungry to keep
> up the fight, and still others were rendered incapable of further
> struggle by diseases resulting from the unnecessary evils of work
> or of living.[10]

Dante also suggested to American reformers a central metaphor
for their understanding of the city. With the guidance of his master
Virgil, Dante descended into hell. In the opinion of many Americans
the city, and particularly New York, was akin to hell on earth.
Reformers derived from Dante's journey a strategy to confront the
ignorance and suspicions of the public towards the one city which
above all dominated American attitudes to urban problems. If
entrenched fears and aversions were to be challenged, the true
conditions within the slums would have to be understood. To be
adequately understood, they would have to be experienced. It then
became an essential project of reformers to find literary devices to
carry their case to the public, and the foremost of these was the
Virgilian mode of social investigation. Named after Dante's guide
(and also Dante's chief model, the *Aeneid*), the guided tour of the
underworld became one of the great commonplaces of reform
journalism. The poet and traveller Bayard Taylor contributed an
article to the *Nation* in 1866 ('A Descent into the Depths') describing
a visit he made to the notorious Five Points slum on Center Street

in New York. His guide was a knowledgeable policeman from the Mulberry Street station. Taylor sought to shock his readers, and to warn the public of the pestilential conditions which existed in the city's slums. Clergymen, social reformers and journalists made similar visits to the 'lower depths' and recounted their experiences through use of the Virgilian mode. Jacob Riis, who worked as a police reporter in Mulberry Street in the 1870s, introduced the readers of his *How the Other Half Lives* (1890) to the slums and alleys below Chatham Street as though the reader were accompanying him upon his descent into hell. In both the presentation of the city slums and the inhabitants, the personal feelings of the writer jostled with his attempt to record the objective conditions of the slum. Some writers assumed that a description of the conditions alone would be enough to touch the conscience of the reader. Others, exploiting an elaborate rhetoric of social reform, sought more directly to manipulate the reader's emotions. The Virgilian mode was equally available for a factual as well as an emotional approach: both shared the same didactic intention, and were based upon the assumption that the task of reform was ultimately to arouse the concern and conscience of the general public. The way such men saw the city and all its complex problems came directly from their troubled consciences, and from the assumptions they made about the consciences of their fellow citizens, who they confidently believed shared their protestantism and (however loosely felt) their sense of social responsibility.[11]

Although he was baptised in 1887 in the fashionable Trinity Episcopal Church in Portland, Reed's biographers say nothing further of either his or his parents' religious inclinations. Perhaps they should have, for the public life of small American towns was dominated by the ethos of the business community and the protestant churches. Reed's family were prominent 'old' settlers in Portland, and his father was a well-known figure in business circles. Had they stood out against conventional opinions, some word of this surely would have reached Granville Hicks, Reed's biographer in the 1930s. His silence on this matter, and that of Robert Rosenstone in the 1970s, suggests that public observances were probably fulfilled, but without an internalised meaning for any of them. Reed was not plagued by a guilty conscience, nor did he carry into the city a missionary's need to reform conditions and thereby to save souls. He came to New York free from such feelings, and in this lies his modernity. The guilty feelings he

carried throughout his life were generated by his failure as a child
to measure up to the expectations he believed his father had of
him. Reed's repeated childhood illnesses, which led to the removal
of a kidney in 1916, drew him apart from his contemporaries. He
was able to evade difficult situations, and stay away from school,
with the active sympathy of his mother; he developed a personality
based upon the assumption that he was weak and unwell. His
mother decided that he was a sickly child, and Reed came to view
himself in such a light. He remained an outsider throughout his
school career at the Portland Academy.[12]

Reed's career at Harvard was a chapter in the long history of
social snobbery of that institution. Reed aspired to being accepted
by his social 'betters', but was decisively rejected by the New
England elite whose clubs on Mount Auburn Street dominated
college life. In compensation, Reed recreated himself not in the
image of a Harvard gentleman (as was the tactic of Berenson, an
outsider of an earlier generation), but as a Westerner, a rough
child of the frontier. It was an image singularly false to the reality
of his protected childhood. He achieved every success at Harvard
except that which he sought. No matter how famous, no matter
how active, he was still an outsider. In later years he wanted to
belong to Harvard and, like his friend Alan Seeger, an even more
extravagant Bohemian and aesthetic rebel, persistently cultivated
Harvard ties. Reed was hard hit when his political radicalism led
to his being cut by old acquaintances.

When he came to New York, living temporarily at the Harvard
Club, he found a place which neither excluded him nor which
enfolded him in self-images of weakness and inadequacy. In New
York he could be boldly independent. The real meaning of New
York for Reed was freedom – from his mother's love, from his
father's (imagined) expectations, from Harvard snobbery, and,
when Max Eastman welcomed him to the pages of *The Masses*,
from the stifling moralism and conservatism of middle-class American life. In the city he was free to be a rebel and an artist. The
central emotional relationship in this period in his life was a clear
demonstration that the autonomy of his selfhood had to be
defended as much from those who loved him as from those who
judged him harshly and condemned his inadequacy. Nowhere is
this clearer than in his romance with Mabel Dodge.

Since Christopher Lasch first discussed Mabel Dodge Luhan in *The New Radicalism in America* (1966), she has been a type not so much of the 'new woman' of Greenwich Village bohemia, but of the intellectuals' will to power.[13] Lasch notes the disappearance of patriarchal authority in the Ganson family as she knew it, the unfeeling relationship between her parents, the utter absence of any public dimension to the family's life, and the consequential emphasis on personal relations. She grew up believing the world she had been born into was corrupt. Middle-class life, with its hypocrisies, filled her with loathing. She experienced a succession of emotional crises: neurasthenia, boredom and ill-health combined to make Mabel intensely alive to the power relations submerged within sexuality. She saw in sex a way of domination, and throughout her life, in heterosexual and lesbian relationships, approached her emotional life as others might approach a war.

In 1912 Mabel and Edwin Dodge settled at 23 5th Avenue, after living for several years at the Villa Curonia, near Florence. Their son John was five and they wanted to send him to an American school; Edwin planned to open an architectural office. The apartment was redecorated under Mabel's expert guidance: the woodwork was painted white, heavy textured white paper was put on the walls, white curtains were hung from floor to ceiling, embroidered white shawls were placed as decoration on the walls, and – at a moment when middle-class opinion had swung decisively from gas to electricity – a decorated Venetian glass chandelier for candles was hung in the living-room. The effect was stunning. The apartment made a very large statement about herself, and about her relationship to the city to which she had just returned. The chandelier, she recalled,

> hung from the ceiling in the living room, fresh as morning while the streets outside were dingy gray and sour with fog and gasoline. It overcame the world outside those walls. It made exquisite shadows on the white ceiling and altogether it acted as a charm with which to conquer cities . . . when the apartment was all put together, it seemed, at first, to do the thing I meant to have it do. It diminished New York, it made New York stay outside in the street.[14]

Edwin Dodge, a debonair man not much given to feats of introspection, enjoyed the city, taking their son to the Polo Grounds to watch baseball. Nothing could have displeased Mabel more. She visualised the scene, 'the crowd of dingy, dusty men and boys sitting in huge circles all chewing gum and wearing derby hats', and shook her head in disapproval. It became another source of discontentment between them. Edwin's 'hard-shelled, American aplomb' annoyed her, as did his lack of concern for self-analysis. And when he was driven to examine his motives and inmost drives, and to explore 'the darks of his consciousness', Mabel found him even more tedious. She believed that he was blocking her growth. 'If I wanted to go ahead and *live* mentally, I had to send Edwin away – that was all there was to it' (*IM*, III, 13). Her few friends in New York (Carl Van Vechten, Hutchins Hapgood, Jo Davidson and Lincoln Steffens) brought some animation to her lifeless apartment, but most of the time she described herself as suffering from the malady of Oblomovism, named after the indolent and listless hero of Goncharov's novel (1859), symbol of the state of the Russian nobility before the emancipation of the serfs: 'I lay listless on the pale French gray couch, dangling a languid arm, eyes closed before the recurrent death of the sweet antiquities about me that lapsed lifeless between-whiles' (*IM*, III, 16–17).

In February 1913 she became involved with the planning for the great show of modern art to be held at the 25th Street Armory. Living in Europe, and knowing Gertrude Stein, gave her some familiarity with the artists and writers of Paris. Mabel gave financial support to the organisers, and helped them to choose pictures from New York collections. The involvement energised her. As she recalled that moment in *Movers and Shakers*.

> I felt as though the Exhibition were mine. I really did. It became, overnight, my own little revolution. *I* would upset America; I would, with fatal, irrevocable disaster to the old order of things. It was tragic – I was able to admit that – but the old ways must go and with them their priests. I felt a large, kindly compassion for the artists and writers who had held the fort heretofore, but I would be firm. My hand would not shake nor could I allow my personal feelings of pity to halt me. *I* was going to dynamite New York and nothing would stop me. Well, nothing did. I moved forward in my rôle of Fate's chosen instrument, and the show certainly did gain by my propulsion. The force was there in me – directed now.   (*IM*, III, 36)[15]

In her own eyes, she had emerged from the couch of languor to play a Napoleonic role in the city. Her friends – Carl, Jo, Hutch and Steff – began to bring friends and interesting people over to 23 5th Avenue in the evening for conversation (and a smart midnight supper). It was the first real 'salon' in the city in ages, the first time in living memory that someone with money was interested in ideas, politics and art. The newspapers took her 'Evenings' as quite important events, and when the Wobbly leader Bill Haywood and the anarchist Emma Goldman were present, the whole city was reading about it the next morning. With Edwin now out of the picture, Mabel was hungry for the experiences which New York could provide:

> I kept meeting more and more people, because in the first place I wanted to know everybody, and in the second place everybody wanted to know me. I wanted, in particular, to know the Heads of things. Heads of Movements, Heads of Newspapers, Heads of all kinds of groups of people. I became a Species of Head Hunter, in fact. It was not dogs or glass I collected now, it was people. Important people.   (*IM*, iii, 83–4)

But she remained largely passive and withdrawn, amidst the sparkling talk. On her own account, she did not enter into the discussions and confined herself to a remote greeting and a low goodbye. She had created the salon, but chose to allow others to shine. It was a demonstration of power and modesty.

The role which Mabel played in New York in 1913, between Oblomov and Napoleon, was rooted in her adolescent experiences. Three examples may suffice. She showed herself to be an imperious lover in Buffalo of 'a silent, rather haughty-looking girl' of sixteen named Margaret, who coldly and silently watched as Mabel demanded to see and fondle her breasts. She cared little for Margaret but discussed at length in her memoir her obsession with the female breast. 'They filled me with a delicious, thrilly feeling that I did not feel for Margaret Strane, that cold girl. Her breasts seemed to draw love from me, but she – never. I cared nothing for her at all' (*IM*, i, 208). While at the Chevy Chase School Mabel received a love-letter from a girl named Beatrice. The girl came to Mabel's bed one night and lay, undemonstrative, as Mabel made love to her. Beatrice was offering herself, almost as a ritual sacrifice, to Mabel's power. She also cultivated the affections of her piano teacher, Miss Murray, and wrested from her the details of a terrible

struggle the teacher was going through. She had fallen in love
with a young man whom Mabel thought 'coarse-visaged', and she
did her best, with high-flown talk of the 'great spaces of feeling
and mystical knowledge' of music at its highest, to persuade the
teacher to break off the relationship. Mabel felt a 'thrill of delight'
when the teacher came sobbing into her bedroom and confessed
her agonising decision to send her young man away. It was the
delight of power effectively exercised. She felt nothing for Margaret,
Beatrice or Miss Murray. Her power over them showed Mabel that
the truth behind sex had more to do with will and domination
than with mutually giving pleasure. Her conclusions were chillingly
clear: 'I knew I could always win people to me if I could be near
them often enough and demand, by endless silent maneuvers,
their interest or affection or whatever it was I wanted of them.'
She drew similar conclusions about her relations with men: 'My
interest in man was in discovering my affect upon them, instead
of in responding to their feeling for me' (*IM*, I, 275, 282).

Mabel's Evenings, so widely reported in the press, and her
involvement with the Armory Show in February 1913, quickly
made her famous and powerful. She was not slow to seize the
opportunities which came along. 'People attributed power to me
and by their bestowal I had it, so I was able to secure a singular
attention for anything any time and this made people eager to
have my name on committees and prospectuses, or to have me
associated with new movements' (*IM*, III, 140). But the boldness
of her success seemed to lack savour; it was living in the head at
the expense of the heart and the senses. She tried to make love to
a young man in her immediate circle, but instead of finding herself
melting 'into the joys of the flesh and the lilies and languors of
love', she was cold and unresponsive, 'my blood and nerves not
interested' (*IM*, III, 169). She wanted something out of experience
which was subtle, occult, secret and feminine, something which
she called 'la grande vie intérieure'. The phrase was given to her
by Violet Shillito, the sister of a friend from Miss Graham's School
in New York. She met Violet – known universally as 'Veeolette' –
in Paris when she was sixteen and stayed for part of the summer
with the Shillito family. Violet preached a doctrine of aesthetic
bliss, contemplation and introspection: whatever there was to be
experienced in life, it was of value principally for its inner effect.
The conscious turning inwards, the self-cultivation, the deliberate
search for the exquisite, makes Violet a child of the *fin de siècle*.

Mabel's relationship with her took on its supreme meaning when they slept together at the Shillito family's summer residence in France. Reaching out to touch Violet's breast, she heard 'a high, sweet singing' which ran from hand to breast through every cell of their bodies. The stone walls of their bedroom 'became vital with the overflow of our increased life, for we passed it out of us in rapid, singing waves – an emanation more fine and powerful than that from radium' (*IM*, I, 264). Mabel's attempts to describe such moments invariably tip over into cliché and hers is the language of the romantic novelists of the day, but the doctrine of 'la grande vie intérieure' remained as a powerful lodestone which served as a link between her moments of passivity and of furious activity. Oblomov and Napoleon were metaphors for her strategies for the enhancement and enjoyment of 'la grande vie'.

Mabel Dodge met John Reed in the early spring of 1913, when she was taken by Hutchins Hapgood to hear Bill Haywood talk about the silk-workers' strike in Paterson, New Jersey. A suggestion on her part that they 'bring the strike to New York' to break the embargo of newspaper coverage was enthusiastically taken up by Reed. He was twenty-six, and bursting with enthusiasm to stage a pageant. In this early period of their relationship Mabel slipped into a 'feminine' role which, in most circumstances, was far from congenial. 'I kept having ideas about what to do and he carried them out', she recalled. One imagines that she saw herself in those hectic weeks as wife and mother, the woman who was the power behind the throne, the woman who enabled her man to achieve things in the world (*IM*, III, 200, 205). Once, when Reed faltered and seemed to despair of ever succeeding with the pageant, she sharply rebuked him and sent him back to the fray. As a performance, her handling of Reed was masterful. When the strike pageant was over, and when she swept Reed off with her to Europe, their relationship began in earnest. She would not sleep with him on board the ship: 'something in me adored the high clear excitement of continence, and the tension we had known together that came from our canalized vitality' (*IM*, III, 213). It was a pre-emptive *coup*, a seizure of the high ground. If he assumed that he would remain the dominant male, she had a surprise for him. The relationship was consummated in Paris. When she made love to him, and when she didn't, the power relations within sexuality were Mabel's paramount consideration.

Things went wrong almost at once – not in bed, but when they visited old cities, churches and castles. Reed, who had travelled in Europe after graduating from Harvard, was interested in every-thing. Mabel, custodian of 'la grande vie intérieure', was interested in nothing except their relationship:

> I hated to see him interested in Things. I wasn't, and didn't like to have him even *look* at churches and leave me out of his attention. When we . . . found the Italians giving 'Aïda' at night in the amphitheater of Verona, I was inclined to force him to go on, drive all night, anything rather than submit to the terror of seeing his eyes dilate with some other magic than my own. Everything seemed to take him away from me, and I had no single thing left in my life to rouse me save his touch.   (*IM*, III, 217)

(Steffens, too, in the early days in New York feared that 'convic-tions' might spoil Reed's youthful high spirits. Like Mabel Dodge, he knew a thing or two about manipulation.[16]) While visiting Venice Mabel rather resented Reed's exclamation of 'The things *Men* have done!' and his wish to be among the doers now. She had no interest in those who did things, and jumped into her car to return to Florence, leaving Reed to make his own way back. 'I tried to wrest him away from Things, especially man-made things. He was sturdily loyal to his own wonder' (*IM*, III, 218). But there were reconciliations that summer. One was heralded by Reed's poem, 'Florence', which seemed to placate Mabel's feelings about history and Things. The Florentine air seemed to him to be 'choked with the crowding-up, struggling souls of the dead'. The landscape which once bred 'turbulent armies' now only yields 'olive and wine, wine and oil!' The poem ended with a plea for escape:

> O let us shake off this smothering silky death, let us go away,
> My dearest old dear
> Mabel! What are we living things doing here?[17]

But what seemed to reflect a calming of Reed's enthusiasm for Italy contained hints that he was still 'loyal' to energy and life – ominous signs, if she had cared to notice them, as they prepared to return to New York. Mabel had, for most of the summer, successfully cocooned Reed from political news. As late as 8 September, he had not heard anything about the fate of the Paterson strike, and knew nothing of its acrimonious aftermath.[18]

When they returned to 23 5th Avenue, the tension between them was scarcely disguised. [We reconstruct their relationship largely through her *Intimate Memories*, written two decades after the events of 1913, and with a very large and very visible axe to grind on Mabel's part. Reed's letters to her were burnt to ease her relationship with Maurice Sterne, Mabel's third husband (*IM*, III, 256). That imperious act denies us at least part of his view of their relationship.] Living openly with Reed was, even by the enlightened standards of the day, an invitation to social condemnation by 'respectable' New York. Mabel wanted to live quietly with him, and do simple things gracefully and slowly. But from the first day of his return to the city, Reed 'was eager to be off and *doing*'. He became the managing editor of *The Masses* in October, and with Art Young, John Sloan, Glenn Coleman, Stuart Davis and the writers, from Max Eastman to Floyd Dell and Louis Untermeyer, Reed was never more fully engaged with the rich variety of Manhattan. Mabel placed herself obstructively in his path. One day, when he planned a jaunt to the Lower East Side to collect material for the articles he was writing for *The Masses*, Mabel mischievously offered to summon up her chauffeur-driven limousine to take them there. Even simple matters were richly productive of conflict. Mabel liked to take her breakfast in bed, and she made calls to her friends to plan the day. Reed put his nose into a newspaper: 'He drank his coffee with the morning newspaper propped up before him,' she wrote,

> his honey-colored round eyes just popping over 'the news!' Any kind of news as long as it had possibilities for thrill, for action, for excitement.
>
> Now newspapers have never meant anything to me.
>
> I have never read the news in all my life except when it was about myself or some friend or enemy of mine. But what the morning paper said was happening in Mexico, or in Russia, or at the Poles, seemed to make Reed's heart beat faster than I could, and I didn't like that. I felt doomed.   (*IM*, III, 233)

Mabel experienced flashes of jealousy. One night when Reed came

back and told her of meeting a young prostitute, she threw herself
on the floor in a faint. She dramatically threatened several times
to commit suicide when he seemed to be neglecting her. As he
grew busier, Mabel yearned more and more for domesticity. This
was, again, a tactic to dominate Reed: 'I tried to hem him in, and I
grew more and more domestic except for the Evenings, when I sat
tragic and let It do what It wanted' (*IM*, III, 235).

It was about this time, in November 1913, that Reed confessed
to Hutchins Hapgood: 'Oh, Hutch, Mabel is wonderful, I love her,
but she suffocates me, I can't breathe.'[19] A break with Mabel was
now inevitable, and he left her a heartfelt note:

> Good-by, my darling. I cannot live with you. You smother me.
> You crush me. You want to kill my spirit. I love you better than
> life but I do not want to die in my spirit. I am going away to
> save myself. Forgive me. I love you – I love you. Reed.   (*IM*,
> III, 242)

Mabel fled to the Dobbs Ferry home of Hapgood and his wife
Neith Boyce, where she sobbed, and smoked cigarettes, and talked
the evening through, bitterly demanding the return of her lover.
That night she took an overdose of veronal.[20] Reed went to Harvard
to see his former teacher, Charles T. Copeland. (Mabel was
impatient with Reed's Harvard chums, regarding them all – with
the exception of Walter Lippmann – as overgrown adolescents).
Steffens and Hapgood soon effected a reconciliation of sorts, and
brought a chastened and repentant Reed back to 23 Fifth Avenue.
It was, he agreed, 'Your way, not mine' (*IM*, III, 245). With a clarity
which could sometimes be shattering, Mabel wrote to Neith Boyce
after her reconciliation:

> To him the sexual gesture has no importance, but infringing on
> his right to act freely has the first importance. Are we both right
> & both wrong – and how do such things end? Either way it kills
> love – it seems to me. This is so fundamental – is it what
> feminism is all about? . . . I know all women go thro this – but
> *must* they go on going thro it? Are we supposed to 'make' men
> do things? Are men to change? Is monogamy better than
> polygamy?[21]

Several weeks later Carl Hovey, managing editor of the *Metropoli-*

*tan Magazine*, asked Reed to go to Mexico to report the revolution. The *Tribune* was sending Richard Harding Davis. It was a challenge Reed instinctively reached for. Mabel tried to persuade him to give up the commission, but he remained loyal once again to his wonder. After his departure, Mabel felt a 'sudden compulsion' to go with him to Mexico. She wired ahead that she was going to join him in Chicago, but when she arrived she was disappointed to find that Reed looked 'rather glad instead of overjoyed. The man in him was already on the job. The woman's place was in the home!' (*IM*, III, 247). Hoist rather on her own petard, and upon her yearning for domesticity with Reed, she travelled awkwardly with him to El Paso. But with hundreds of Federales streaming across the Rio Grande in pell mell retreat, Mexico was no place for a gringo woman. She tried for a few days to make 'a little life' in a hotel in El Paso, but it didn't work, and she returned to New York.

To keep herself occupied, Mabel began an affair with the handsome young artist Andrew Dasburg. Almost as soon as Reed came back from Mexico, he was sent off to Ludlow, Colorado, to cover the labour troubles which had culminated in a massacre of striking miners and their families. While there he wrote a letter to Mabel, the only one to have survived, in which he describes a relationship he had with a young woman and her mother. The girl was a violinist from a family deeply respectful of tradition and law. The mother had wanted to get a divorce but in the end decided that the stain upon the family's character was too high a price to pay for her personal happiness. His years in Greenwich Village clearly arming him for such a conversation, Reed doubted whether 'moral standards' were such a great idea. Values change. If the daughter wanted to become a great violinist there were no rules to follow: 'There isn't any law you have to obey, nor any moral standard you have to accept, nor in fact anything outside of your own soul that you have to take any account of' (*IM*, III, 259–61). When the significance of his ideas sank in, the girl was transformed; life seemed at last something to be lived and not just something to endure. The conversations thrilled Reed, too, in part because he knew he was saying what Mabel would have said.[22] 'I wish it could have been you that told her, and could show her at the same time what a marvelous thing is the result of a soul. You are so beautiful to me for just that soul of yours, and so alive. You are my life.' He had learnt much from her. It is hard to think of the young man who left Harvard four years before writing such a letter. If in the end the cult of 'la grande vie intérieure' could not hold him, he had at least come to sense some of its richness of cultivation, some of its beauty.

It is hard to see Mabel having learnt much, if anything, from her relationship with Reed. She asked Neith Boyce: 'Are we supposed to "make" men do things?' but, in truth, the question was rhetorical: she had tried, and for a time succeeded in an attempt to 'hem him in'. But she didn't care for his ideas, and had little of his passion for social change: 'I wasn't dying to alter everything.' His imagination was fired by the struggles of ordinary people; hers was repelled by men who sat in bleachers and wore derby hats and chewed gum. She was a heroine looking for a tragedy in which she could dominate; Reed was a hero who searched for a community, a cause, to give his life meaning. Mabel craved submission and peace; he wanted freedom and excitement. They were happy together for a little while, but so fierce was the struggle between them that a victory for either one would have been disastrous for the other. It took them several years to understand this.

## NOTES

1. Lincoln Steffens, obituary of John Reed in *The Freeman*, 3 November 1920, reprinted in *Lincoln Steffens Speaking* (New York: Harcourt Brace, 1936) p. 313.
2. 'A Hymn to Manhattan', *The Education of John Reed: Selected Writings*, with an Introductory Essay by John Stuart (Berlin: Seven Seas Publishers, 1972) p. 257. This poem was first published in the *American Magazine*, February 1913, and was collected in Reed's *Tamburlane* (1917). For unexplained reasons it was omitted from Reed's *Collected Poems*, ed. and with a Foreword by Corliss Lamont (Westport, Conn.: Lawrence Hill, 1985).
3. See William Innes Homer, with the assistance of Violet Organ, *Robert Henri and His Circle* (Ithaca and London: Cornell University Press, [1969]) pp. 138–45.
4. John Gould Fletcher, *Irradiations Sand and Spray* (Boston, Mass.: Houghton Mifflin, 1915) p. 7.
5. William Carlos Williams, 'The Wanderer: A Rococo Study', *The Egoist*, I (16 March 1914) pp. 109–11.
6. T. S. Eliot, 'Preludes', *Blast*, II (July 1915) pp. 48–51. It is worth noting that Fletcher essayed an urban realism in certain sections of 'Solitude in the City (Symphony in Black and Gold)' in his *Goblins and Pagodas* (Boston, Mass.: Houghton Mifflin, 1916) pp. 32–3. Unlike Eliot, the

details of 'greasy' rain and 'dirty gutters' were at the service of an aesthetic perception.

7.  John Reed, *Adventures of a Young Man: Short Stories from Life* (San Francisco: City Lights, 1975) pp. 138–9. 'Almost Thirty' was first published in the *New Republic*, LXXXVI (15 April 1936) pp. 267–70.

8.  'Proud New York' appeared in *Poetry*, April 1919. The complete text of this poem was first published in *The New Masses*, 15 October 1935.

9.  The link between progressivism and the protestant mind has long been debated. See Richard Hofstadter, *The Age of Reform from Bryan to F.D.R* (New York: Vintage Books, n.d.) pp. 203ff.; Allen F. Davis, *Spearheads for Reform: The Social Settlements and the Progressive Movement 1890–1914* (New York: Oxford University Press, 1967) ch. 2; Robert M. Crunden, *Ministers of Reform: The Progressives' Achievement in American Civilization, 1889–1920* (Urbana and Chicago: University of Illinois Press, 1984) ch. 1. On Poole see his *The Bridge: My Own Story* (New York: Macmillan, 1940) and Truman Frederick Keefer, *Ernest Poole* (New York: Twayne, 1966).

10. Robert Hunter, *Poverty: Social Conscience in the Progressive Era*, ed. Peter d'A. Jones (New York: Harper & Row, 1965) pp. 325–6.

11. This paragraph emerges out of work I have been doing on Dr Stephen Smith, the chief organiser of the 1865 Council of Health survey of the sanitary condition of New York. Smith's *The City That Was* (New York: Frank Allaben, 1911) is a remarkable example of the controlled indignation possible within the Virgilian mode. For Bayard Taylor, see 'A Descent into the Depths: Sixth Ward', *Nation*, II (8 March 1866) pp. 302–4; and for Jacob Riis, *How the Other Half Lives*, ed. Donald N. Bigelow (New York: Sycamore Press, 1957). See also Robert H. Bremner, *From the Depths: The Discovery of Poverty in the United States* (New York: New York University Press, 1956) and Roy Lubove, *The Progressives and the Slums: Tenement House Reform in New York City 1890–1917* (Pittsburgh, Penn.: University of Pittsburgh Press, 1962).

12. The fullest account of Reed's childhood appears in Robert A. Rosenstone, *Romantic Revolutionary: A Biography of John Reed* (New York: Alfred A. Knopf, 1975).

13. Christopher Lasch, *The New Radicalism in America (1889–1963): The Intellectual as a Social Type* (New York: Alfred A. Knopf, 1966) pp. 104–40.

14. Mabel Dodge Luhan, *Intimate Memories*, vol. III: *Movers and Shakers* (New York: Harcourt Brace, 1936) pp. 5–6. The four volumes of *Intimate Memories* (hereafter cited as *IM*) have been reprinted in two bulky volumes by Kraus in 1971, which retain the pagination of the original editions. Further references to this edition will appear in the text. There have been two biographers: Emily Hahn, *Mabel: A Biography of Mabel Dodge Luhan* (Boston: Houghton Mifflin, 1977) and Lois Palken Rudnick, *Mabel Dodge Luhan: New Woman, New Worlds* (Albuquerque, NM: University of New Mexico Press, [1984]). Both follow *IM* closely, though Palken is based upon the more solid archival research.

15. The historian of the Armory Show gives Dodge only a walk-on role in the event. Of some $10,000 raised in New York to pay for expenses,

she and her mother donated $700. See Milton W. Brown, *The Story of the Armory Show* (New York: Joseph H. Hirshhorn Foundation, [1963]).

16. *Lincoln Steffens Speaking*, p. 313.

17. Reed, *Collected Poems*, pp. 89–91.

18. Reed to Walter Lippmann, 8 September 1913, Walter Lippmann Papers, Yale University Library. The political consequences of the strike appear in Melvyn Dubofsky, *We Shall Be All: A History of the Industrial Workers of the World* (New York: Quadrangle / New York Times Book Co., 1969) ch. 11, and Steve Golin, 'Defeat Becomes Disaster: The Paterson Strike of 1913 and the Decline of the I.W.W.', *Labor History*, xxiv (Spring 1983) pp. 223ff. For the view of one disillusioned participant, see Elizabeth Gurley Flynn, *I Speak My Own Piece: Autobiography of 'The Rebel Girl'* (New York: Masses & Mainstream, [1955]) pp. 143–59.

19. Hutchins Hapgood, *A Victorian in the Modern World*, ed. Robert Allan Skotheim (Seattle, Wash.: University of Washington Press, 1972) p. 353.

20. Rudnick, *Mabel Dodge Luhan*, p. 96, following Granville Hicks, *John Reed: The Making of a Revolutionary* (New York: Macmillan, 1936) p. 111.

21. Mabel Dodge to Neith Boyce, Yale University Library, quoted in Rudnick, *Mabel Dodge Luhan*, pp. 96–7.

22. This was virtually the programme of *The Masses*. 'So far . . . as I shaped its policy,' wrote Max Eastman in *Enjoyment of Living* (New York: Harper & Brothers, 1948) p. 420, 'the guiding ideal of the magazine was that every individual should be made free to live and grow in his own chosen way . . . Even if it can not be achieved. I would say to myself, the good life consists in striving towards it.' Mabel Dodge did not necessarily endorse all of the *Masses* ideals, but they – and many others – would have agreed on the imperative of self-fulfilment.

# 4

# John Sloan in New York City

## ALLEN J. KOPPENHAVER

John Sloan lived and painted in New York City in the early part of the twentieth century, and what he left behind was a human comedy, a portrait of the city done in satire and anger at times, but more often done with love and affection. Strongly influenced by Whitman, Sloan felt compelled to document the life of the city in his art, 'the crazy, wonderful, slamming roar of the street', as Carl Sandburg said of Chicago; or as Sloan himself said, 'I have never liked to show human beings when they are not themselves. I think it is an insult to their human dignity. . . . One of the things I so dislike about most socially conscious pictures, is that the artist is looking down on people'.[1] And Sloan never looked down.

He had a warm concern for the lives of the people he drew and painted, and he caught their 'animal spirits', as he liked to call them, in all sorts of situations from McSorley's Bar to the teeming streets and rooftops of the city, from the courtrooms to the parks, from the elevated trains to the ferries that traversed the rivers before bridges made the ferries obsolete.

Sloan found the life of the city exactly what his new-found talents required. He had been an illustrator for the Philadelphia *Inquirer*, the Philadephia *Press* and eventually for the New York *Herald* from 1904 to 1911, one of the richest periods of his city-life art. Like writers such as Whitman, Twain, Hemingway, Steinbeck and others, Sloan had his apprenticeship in the newspapers, and the effect upon him was to democratise his art as it had done theirs. The very nature of the American newspaper makes the contributor most conscious of the fact that everyone from the lowest street-cleaner to the president himself can claim a spot on the front page depending upon the circumstances of the news. When Whitman drew up his long catalogues of occupations in 'Song of Myself', he juxtaposed his people the way they might be

47

found on the pages of any American daily newspaper. In half a dozen lines taken at random, Whitman describes, in order, a pedlar, a bride, an opium-eater, a prostitute, the president, and three stately matrons. Whitman, the poet who democratised American poetry, had taken his early lessons from the various newspapers he served. So too Sloan. One might also note that America's finest nineteenth-century artist, Winslow Homer, also had his beginnings as an illustrator for *Harper's Illustrated* and *Ballou's Pictorial*.

Sloan's pedigree almost certainly ensured that he would be an artist of the common man. He studied with Thomas Anschuz, who was the most famous student of Thomas Eakins, and he met and became friends with Robert Henri, the guiding force behind the 'Ashcan School' of American painters, a number of whom served their apprenticeships as illustrators with newspapers. There is a major study to be done with the effects of this sort of apprenticeship on American art and literature, but that is for another time.

Sloan also illustrated for a number of socialist papers and magazines, such as *The Masses* and *The Call*, but he never regarded himself as a party-line artist. Called by some 'the American Hogarth', he was amused, but admitted that he hadn't discovered Hogarth until years after he had been doing his city works. He was impressed by the idea, however, since he called Hogarth 'the greatest English artist who ever lived . . . Hogarth painted life around him, with an illustrator's point of view, a very healthy thing for an artist'.[2] This American Hogarth had a broad view of the human comedy, and he saw it with penetrating sensitivity.

Some of Sloan's illustrations could be biting in their attack when he saw justice being violated, as in *The Great Subway Contractor: The Promised Loaf*, a 1911 scene of exploited workers being led to their graves by the greedy mismanagement of their employers, or in his *Picketing the Police Permit* (1910) when he protested the violent handling of shirtwaist-makers who were striking for decent wages, and Sloan noted the police brutality. He was outraged when the police entrapped New York prostitutes and treated them like cattle. *Before Her Maker and Her Judge* (1913) was his sarcastic illustration of what he had seen. He attacked the indifferent church with *Calling the Christian Bluff* (1914). Many of the hungry and unemployed were shown in front of St Alphonsus' Church demanding food and shelter. Later, when the police arrived, they arrested all those who wouldn't leave and threw them in jail. Sloan saw humans being violated and recorded it. His harshest picture is of police beating and trampling protestors with their horses in *The Constabulary Policing the Rural Districts*. Note the controlled sarcasm of the title. In several works he defends women who have been forced into prostitution, and describes the rag-pickers and old tramps going through rubbish bins, not unlike the homeless in any modern city today. Sloan, when he was angry, could dip his brush in acid.

But more often than not, Sloan celebrated the common people of New York. He caught the hustle and bustle of the city street with pictures of boys and girls sledding, boys playing leap-frog, building snowmen or swinging cans of hot coals in a brilliantly made etching, *Bonfire* (1920). This print shows a rich balancing of lights and darks in a night scene with three centres of light: the major bonfire in a box that one boy is leaping over, and the two bright lights of the boys spinning cans full of fire held by long wire handles.

Like any good artist, Sloan was a watcher, one who took in more than any of us might have seen, and he more than once framed his pictures of the city in his own window-frame. His 1914 print, *Village*, and *The City from Greenwich Village* (1922) are two of his finer oil paintings of the city from his window. In a number of entries in his New York diaries he mentions seeing scenes from his back window that later became works of art, and since he did all his scenes from memory, he took in everything. The most typical Sloan oil of this kind is *Stein at the Window*, a portrait of his good friend Zenka Stein, whom he regarded as the best professional model in New York. She looks out of the window at the city and the elevated railway, one of his favourite subjects, seen in the warm light of early morning. One is reminded of the earlier colonial formula for portraits where the sitter is balanced in the picture by an open window in the upper right or left corner which looks out on a scene related in some way to the subject of the work, in this case, Sloan's New York.

His subjects were numerous and tell us much about him. He did a number of pictures of the world of popular entertainment. There is the 1915 print of Isadora Duncan, 'a great dancer, she would bring tears to my eyes'.[3] One of his prints has interesting literary connections. He did *Frankie and Johnnie* from E. E. Cummings's play *Him*, done by the Princetown Players at MacDougal Street, New York in 1928. And he painted may other places of entertainment including the Haymarket, an old dance hall infamous for its underworld connections, the Carmine Theatre, and the 'Coburn Players' doing an open-air performance at Columbia University in 1916. He remarks amusingly, 'The mosquitos attended to our ankles while the Coburn Players kept our minds amused'.[4] One of the most joyous prints is *The 'Movey' Troup*, a 1920 print of 'a movie director, leading man, leading lady and camera man making use of the picturesque background to be found in Greenwich Village at that time'.[5] The 'picturesque' refers to the children and adults crowding around the scene being filmed on the street, framed overhead by women and washing at the windows. *Movies, Five Cents* (1907) may be the first painting ever done of people sitting inside a movie theatre. Sloan had observed the movies in their 'sordid infancy'.[6] Frequently Sloan caught the humour of the show going on all around him on the New York streets. He was a people-watcher and his prints reveal that he loved to do pictures of people watching other people as well, often being entertained unintentionally.

In *Sixth Avenue & 30th Street* (1918) several young girls watch a street-walker starting out on her evening rounds. In *Sidewalk* (1917) Sloan draws a mother helping her son relieve himself into the gutter while the passing crowd watches with amusement. Of the scene he said it was 'an everyday incident in New York's East Side. . . . They put up signs in the sweller apartment districts, "Curb Your Dog"'.[7] In the 1905 print *Monkey Man*, 'the one-man band with hand-organ accompanist furnished free entertainment to those who dropped no pennies. He worried the horse-drawn traffic of the time, but before many years the motor car and motor truck cleared him from the streets'.[8] In *Showcase* (1905) young girls laugh at a corsetted manikin while just behind them is a well-dressed woman with the same heavy bust, corsetted, escorted by her husband. In *Fifth-Avenue Critics* (1905) he shows us two sharp-nosed wealthy ladies casting a disdaining look a very lovely lady in another open carriage.

In other pictures young girls slide across the ice for the benefit of several vagrants on a bench, young women swing in the park watched by old men, a man watches himself in the mirror as a barber trims his hair and a pretty woman does his nails. Again and again, Sloan catches people watching other people. One of his frequently reprinted oils is the 1907 *Hairdresser's Window*. As Sloan described it, 'Sixth Avenue had a Coney Island quality in 1907. It was the Fifth Avenue of the poor'.[9] A crowd is being entertained as Mme Malcomb bleaches a customer's long hair in her window. Sloan had come upon the scene on the way to Henri's 6th-Avenue studio.

What is most impressive is that Sloan never did sketches in the street, but always did his work in the studio from memory, working on the canvas without preliminary drawing; yet his work has more life than many another's who worked directly from the subject. No one else in his group seemed able to capture the rich humour of the scene as well as Sloan.

Of all the 'Ashcan school', Sloan also ranged most widely in subject-matter, even travelling west to Santa Fe for pictures later on. It was the cityscape of New York, however that most excited him and which he kept reproducing in such variety. He said: 'While my work is sufficient evidence that the city streets and landscapes have afforded me a rich subject matter, there is the prevailing ideal that I am no longer painting "Sloans" because I am doing figures and portraits.'[10] Hardly true. He never left his 'people', continuing to paint and etch them into his plates and into our minds.

In all his rich variety, Sloan did have several subjects that he returned to with frequency, a continuing theme and variations on the scenes he loved most. The most famous and most often reproduced image of his, reminiscent of Whitman's 'Brooklyn Ferry', is *The Wake of the Ferry* (1907), a picture he did three times. The first version, showing a woman standing on the right of the picture brooding over the wake of the boat, was damaged soon after completion, so he did a second one. Of this second one he said, 'A melancholy day, when she, to whom the coming of the landing means nothing, seeks the sad outlook of the vessel's broadening wake. Such was the mood under which the picture was painted'.[11] In the first version, he painted the woman more clearly along with clearer images of the other boats on the river and of the New York skyline, thus softening the sense of loneliness in this scene. By the time he did the third one in 1949, years later, he had left the seriousness behind and turned to a parody entitled, *The Wake* on *the Ferry* (emphasis mine), peopled by a party of drunken Irishmen and women next to a horse-drawn hearse, somewhat like the satires the Greeks performed after the trilogy of tragedies.

Sloan made the Washington Arch in Greenwich Village his own personal icon, with his many different etchings and paintings which use it as a major backdrop. More than a dozen works show the arch, and he even did a lighthearted etching of a group of friends on top of the arch, a memory picture of the night Marcel Duchamp and others somehow got into the Arch and up on to the top of it for a midwinter party. There they drew up a document to establish the secession of Greenwich Village from the United States, with President Wilson's protection as one of the small nations.

The elevated railway led to a number of pictures, several of them well-known oils. *The City from Greenwich Village* (1922), *Jefferson Market* (1925) and *Snowstorm in the Village* (1925) are just a few of the better-known ones. The most famous is, of course, *Dust Storm, Fifth Avenue* done in 1906. This picture of adults and children blown by a dust storm that swirls around them below the dominant weight of the El won him his first public acclaim in New York and was eventually his first museum sale. The sad note was that Sloan, in the richest period of his creative life, was unable to sell many of his oils, and this major work of American painting was not sold until fifteen years after it was painted. It was purchased by the Metropolitan Museum of New York in 1921.

One of the subjects that appealed to him most was the life on the rooftops of the city in summertime. As Sloan said about his 1941 etching, *Sunbathers on the Roof*, 'the roof life of Metropolis is so interesting to me that I am almost reluctant to leave in June for my summer in Santa Fe'.[12] He pictured the sunbathers on Saturdays and Sundays, old men sleeping, a thief stealing washing, women gossiping as they hang out their washing. The subject, a woman putting out her wash, is one that never loses its charm for me'.[13] He loved to catch people watching other people, as shown earlier. In *Night Windows* (1910) he shows a man on the rooftop watching a woman in a window across the way undressing for bed, while just below him is his wife leaning out of their apartment window hanging out washed linen. This picture was in the 1913 Armory Show. *Love on the Rooftops* (1914) reveals a young man and an older woman in a passionate embrace under her blowing line of washing while her baby chews on the clothes still in the basket. 'Note the protest of the fluttering garments and the neglected child. The nightshirts and underwear belong to her husband. All these comments are deductions, I just saw it and etched it'.[14] This particular print was cited in a 1934 trial about the immorality of art. Today it would be regarded as an innocent event. His 1906 print *Roofs, Summer Nights* is one of his best rooftop prints; it shows families scattered over the rooftops sleeping, while one man, awake next to his sleeping wife, stares across the roof at another sleeping woman. Sloan is again watching people watching people.

Of the rooftop pictures, *Pigeons* (1910) has the most interesting background. All his life Sloan had difficulties selling his pictures. *Pigeons* was rejected by the National Academy in 1910, but was shown at the Independents Exhibition. Robert Henri said, 'That canvas will carry into future time the feel and way of life as it happened and as it was seen and understood by the artist' and indeed it was. Late in his life, Sloan put an announcement into the art journals to the effect that he was getting old and might die in the next few years, at which point the value of his pictures might go up. Consequently, he was selling them now at cut-rate prices. *Pigeons* was the only one bought; it is now owned by the Boston Museum of Fine Arts.

The final set of pictures to be considered is the McSorley's Bar group. The bar was visited by Sloan, Everett Shinn, George Luks, William Glackens, Robert Henri and many other artists, especially the ones who worked at Cooper Union. Van Wyck Brooks commented upon the importance of the saloon in America, citing the works of Jack London, Eugene O'Neill, John Dos Passos, Ernest Hemingway and John Steinbeck among others. 'The bar is undoubtedly what the drawing room used to be, the favorite locus of the literary imagination'.[15]

McSorley's was an artist's haven, and Sloan visited it many times over a period of eighteen years. In 1912 he did his first painting of it, *McSorley's Back Room*, which he described as a 'sacristy': 'Here Old John McSorley would sit greeting old friends and philosophizing. Women were never served, indeed the dingy walls and woodwork looked as if women had set neither hand nor foot in the place'.[16] Sloan did a second painting in 1912, *McSorley's Bar*, which has been frequently reproduced; it was shown at the Armory Show. McSorley's was known for its good ale, raw onions and no ladies. A woman would know where her husband had been by the distinct smell of McSorley's onions.

Sixteen years later he painted *McSorley at Home*, a group of old-timers in front of the bar. In the same year he did *McSorley's Cats*, which shows Bill, the bartender, feeding the cats at the foot of the crowded bar, eighteen at one time. He did a 1929 painting, again called *McSorley's Cats*, showing Bill in his 'regular ceremony of feeding the cats at the rickety old refrigerator'.[17] Seated at the table in the foreground are Hippolyte Havel – a Village anarchist, Art Young – a socialist cartoonist, George O. Hammlin, with pipe – a close friend of Sloan, and Sloan himself at the extreme far left corner.

The last version was *McSorley's Saturday Night*, painted in 1930. Sloan speaks of his picture with a sense of loss:

> Here is McSorley's during the dark days of prohibition. Had all the saloons been conducted with the dignity and decorum of McSorley's, prohibition would never have been brought about. Saloons would not have been closed. McSorley's never was closed [during prohibition] an example of the triumph of right over might.[18]

Sloan once mentioned the fact that he had only been in McSorley's about ten times and painted five pictures of it, and he remarked several times that 'No woman ever touched foot in there and no hard liquor was ever served'.[19]

From the children on the streets to the throngs of people in Washington Square, from the rooftops of New York City to the saloons and places of entertainment, John Sloan caught the life of the people of the city, his vision of the inhabitants living out their lives. He was like Whitman, showing us the city by showing us its people in their everyday activities close up and with affection.

He did an etching in 1911 called *Salute*, in which a worker stands on the steel frame of a building being constructed, hat off, saluting a woman and child in a window below. Over the rooftops we see the city. The man must surely have been Sloan himself on the superstructure of his rich body of city art, hat in hand, giving us all a welcoming salute, and saying, 'Come and love my people as much as I have loved them.'

NOTES

1. John Sloan, 'Introduction', *John Sloan's New York Scene: From the Diaries, Notes and Correspondence, 1906–1913*, ed. Bruce St John (New York: Harper & Row, 1956) p. xx. (Hereafter cited as *NYS*.)
2. John Sloan, *The Gist of Art* (New York: American Artists Group, 1939) p. 2. (Hereafter cited as *GA*.)
3. Peter Morse, *John Sloan's Prints: A Catalogue Raisonné of the Etchings,*

*Lithographs, and Posters* (New Haven & London: Yale University Press, 1969) p. 196. (Hereafter cited as *JSP*.)

4. *GA*, p. 223.
5. *JSP*, p. 222.
6. *GA*, p. 211.
7. *JSP*, p. 210.
8. Ibid., p. 139.
9. *GA*, p. 213.
10. Ibid., p. 16.
11. Ibid., p. 209.
12. *JSP*, p. 340.
13. *GA*, p. 229.
14. *JSP*, p. 176.
15. Van Wyck Brooks, *The Confident Years: 1885–1915* (New York: E. P. Dutton, 1952) p. 542.
16. *JSP*, p. 207.
17. *GA*, p. 301.
18. Ibid., p. 305.
19. *JSP*, p. 207.

# 5

# John Sloan's New York, 1906–13

## DEREK POLLARD

John Sloan, illustrator, print-maker, etcher, painter, modest gastronome and lover of stimulating conversation, could also write a little. Although he kept a journal for only two short periods of his long life (he died in his eighty-first year), he provides intriguing glimpses of his creative skills and of New York City at the beginning of the twentieth century. Bruce St John's edition of the Sloan diaries – regrettably the only one available – gives little explanation about editorial selection, though St John does admit to excluding whole days without ellipsis to keep the version short.[1] This compilation covers a period of eight years, of which the last two are a meagre record – a mere thirty pages, whereas each preceding year occupied ninety pages or so with an average of twenty-three to twenty-four days a month receiving comment. The editor tamely suggests that Sloan's increased endeavours on his art work accounts for the waning interest in his diary, and he fails to mention that Sloan began one again in 1948. Except for the dedicated keeper, diaries often tend to be desultory affairs, and one should first ask why Sloan kept a diary at all rather than criticise him for lack of continuity.

Helen Farr Sloan, his second wife, gave two reasons in her own Introduction to the edited version: first, that Dr Bower, the family physician, prescribed it as an antidote for Sloan's bouts of melancholy and second, that Dolly, his first wife, might take comfort in its carelessly left open pages, grow in confidence and perhaps become less alcohol-dependent. A third, unstated, reason becomes clear from the entries. The Sloans had moved from Philadelphia to New York in 1904, following several of his artistic friends from the days of the Charcoal Club and the studio at 806 Walnut Street, the most influential of whom was Robert Henri. It was in New York that Sloan's fascination with urban activity needed to be recorded not just visually, by means of sketchpad, plate and canvas, but verbally, describing in detail his encounters with friends and his peregrinations about the streets.

One is reminded of Alfred Kazin's *A Walker in the City* (1951) whilst reading a 1904 comment of Sloan's:

> New York had its human comedy and I felt like making pictures of this everyday world. On the whole, when finding incidents that provided ideas for paintings, I was selecting bits of joy in human life. I did not have any didactive purpose, I was not interested in being socially conscious about the life of the people.

Note that Sloan rarely had any sociopolitical axes to grind, was unconnected with the progressive movement and commented in 1950 that he considered any link between the artists he befriended and the realistic writers of the period to be a current fad. He had not read the work of Crane, Norris and Dreiser until well after their publication dates. Nor is it likely, as Oliver Larkin has posited, that the writings of O. Henry had any influence upon Sloan's work. The twenty-five stories published in *The Voice of the City* (1908) – one of four such collections – undoubtedly present an array of captivating characters ranging from bartenders to society ladies to police cops, and show especial affection for Irish-Americans, but Sloan's people have different attributes. Most of them are working class and there are far more children and very few elderly persons. Thus, any reading of doctrinaire motives into his art must give place to this primary concern in recording people as people, and providing 'slices' of their lives.

Jerome Mellquist referred to this aspect of Sloan's work as 'a nostalgia for humanity', and continued, 'whether it was pity, mockery or anger, always a beneficence seemed to temper his drawing'.[2] His print series *New York City Life*, originally ten in number when exhibited at Pisinger's Modern Art Gallery in April 1906 and later increased to thirteen, gave ample proof of this beneficence. Una Johnson commented more recently that these etchings were 'humourously anecdotal in their shrewd observations of city life', and they have a narrative quality as well.[3]

One can take up another question raised by the 1904 extract just quoted, namely: was Sloan a voyeur? Peter Conrad in *The Art of the City* (1984) seems to suggest this when he writes:

Sloan, for whom the female nude was – in spite of its physical
flagrancy – a symbol of the lofty Platonic spirituality of art,
anatomizes New York as a plumply appetizing woman's body.[4]

He later refers to Sloan 'spying' on women 'bathing in rooms
across the backyard' and uses as illustration *Looking Out on
Washington Square* (1933), where a plump nude is doing the spying
from HER window. It makes a provocative thesis, which might
have been better supported by his etching *Night Windows* (1910),
about which Sloan wrote on 12 December:

> The subject of the plate is one which I have in mind – night, the
> roofs back of us – a girl in deshabille at a window and a man on
> the roof smoking his pipe and taking in the charms while at a
> window below him his wife is busy hanging out his washed
> linen.[5]

Conrad relies too much on retrospective evidence. Yes, Sloan did
paint a great number of nudes in his later years, as did Renoir,
and probably for the same reason. The lost vigour of youth is
compensated for by rewarding the appetite of the eye. Evidence
from earlier years suggests that he tried to capture in his prints
and paintings people in their unguarded moments. Sloan was, as
Lloyd Goodrich noted in 1952, 'fascinated by the private life seen
through windows, and recorded many such glimpses of comedy
and tragedy.'[6] An excellent example of his getting behind the
façade occurred in April 1909 when Sloan began painting *Three
A.M.* His entry for 28 April reads:

> A good day's work, painting on the subject that has been stewing
> in my mind for some weeks. I have been watching a curious
> two room household, two women and, I think, two men, their
> day begins after midnight, they cook at 3 A.M.[7]

Later, in *The Gist of Art* (1939), which should be compulsory reading
for all students of Sloan, he wrote:

> Night vigils at the back window of a Twenty-third street studio
> were rewarded by motifs of this sort; many of them were used
> in my etchings. Some of the lives I glimpsed, I thought I
> understood. These two girls I took to be sisters, one of whom

was engaged in some occupation that brought her home about this hour of the morning. On her arrival the other rose from her slumbers and prepared a meal. This picture is redolent with the atmosphere of a poor, back, gaslit room. It has beauty, I'll not deny it; it must be that human life is beautiful.

How much attention should be paid to that last comment? 'It must be' suggests an acceptance by Sloan, whether in 1939 or earlier in his career, that every detail is worth recording, and the more intimate it is, the more revealing to the unobserved observer. What is voyeuristic about that? Beauty, it has been said, is in the eye of the beholder.

What were Sloan's working methods? Taking the period June–July 1907 as an example one discovers that he began work on *Hairdresser's Window* on 5 June. He noted in his journal:

Walked up to Henri's studio. One the way saw a humorous sight of interest. A window, low, second story [sic], bleached blond hairdresser bleaching the hair of a client. A small interested crowd about.[8]

The next day Sloan returned to take another look and then went home and started to paint. As in *Three A.M.*, one should note that he painted chiefly from memory and rarely made preliminary sketches. He worked on it again on the 7th. Three days went by and then more work was done on the 10th and 11th. The painting was not mentioned again until 19 January 1908 when he added 'a few touches'. Then on 11 April he decided to enter it with some others that he had worked on the previous June for an exhibition in Cincinnatti. The final reference comes on 15 April, when he changed his mind and withheld the picture.

The life of his next painting, begun on 13 June, is also interesting. The first references are to the 'tenderloin' district off 6th Avenue, where there were abbatoirs and small butcher's shops. A week passed before he put in a full day's work upon it 'till tired out'. On 21 June Sloan commented:

Worked on the 'Tenderloin Sixth Avenue' old girl in white with beer kettle, etc. . . . and have it about finished – and I think a right 'good one'.[9]

Before tracking this painting further, one should record that he started a third painting on 24 June and a fourth on the 30th. The pattern here is of a weekly picture on which he might work for about three days, though not necessarily on consecutive dates. This, however, was not standard practice. For example, a painting of the Greenwich Savings Bank begun on 20 January 1908 was not completed until 1911, and others, too, had long gestations. The 'Tenderloin' picture, now officially titled *Sixth Avenue & 30th Thirtieth*, turns up in his diary again on 23 December 1907 as a possible entry for the National Arts exhibition to be opened a week later. But that is not the end of it. It is reconsidered in April 1908 alongside *Hairdresser's Window* for exhibition in Cincinnati. In August, Sloan requested J. H. Gest in Cincinnati to send the picture on to Chicago. Then there was a gap of four years and the last mention of it was when a private dealer came to call on 27 January 1912 with a view to purchase.

Sloan did not sell a single painting until 1913 when an old classmate, Albert C. Barnes, bought *Nude in the Green Scarf*. Thus, Sloan survived until his forty-second year by illustrative work, print-making, sending regular 'word charade' puzzles to the Philadelphia *Press* and a modest amount of teaching. Even that first sale did not start a flood of enquiries: it was 1916 before he sold a second one.

The fourth picture of June–July 1907 referred to earlier was entitled *Moving Picture Show*, and Sloan worked on it for a couple of days. He had seen some silent Kinematograph pictures on 28 June for five cents. How interesting not that he started the painting but that on 6 July he took some photographs of 'some of the things I've been painting on'. The next day (7 July) he made a lot of prints which turned out 'a little yellow'. On 10 July he went to see Gertrude Kasebier, who gave him three more prints of his photographs, and the next day he sent off these, including one portrait photograph of himself by Mrs Kasebier, to Pittsburgh. These entries reveal that Sloan did get the bit between his teeth once inspiration caught hold of him. The visit to the picture house had rekindled his interest in photography. There was no further reference until 1908 when Mrs Kasebier again helped him. Sloan consistently undervalued photography chiefly because he never satisfactorily mastered the technique of developing prints.

The spate of activity during the summer of 1907 was almost certainly prompted by the decision in the preceding May that the

'Eight Independent Painters' were to hold an exhibition of their work at the Macbeth Gallery in February 1908. George Luks had had some pictures hung there in March which were favourably received and all of them had previously experienced difficulty in getting shown in regular galleries. Such was the opposition from juries of selection that even Robert Henri had failed as a panelman to alter the conservatism of his fellow twenty-nine, as Sloan noted on 3 March:

> Henri came to dinner after the third day of jury work. He found it advisable to withdraw two of his paintings. The puny, puppy minds of the jury were considering his work for # 2, handing out # 1 to selves and friends and inane work and presuming to criticize Robert Henri. I know that if this page is read fifty years from now it will seem ridiculous that he should not have had more honour from his contemporaries.[10]

The newspapers soon learnt of their intentions and there was an interesting comment from Sloan on 15 May: 'Altogether there is no lack of incentive for plenty of hard work between now and the time of the exhibition'. Sloan did not realise just how involved he would become with practicalities for Henri was absent in Wilkes-Barre for part of January 1908, leaving Sloan to take care of secretarial duties, buy stamps, pay printer's bills, ensure that all pictures reached the gallery on time, and substitute for some of Henri's classes at the New York School of Art.

The exhibition, totalling sixty-three paintings and sketches, opened on 3 February and closed on the 15th. A good crowd were attracted on the opening day, including 'young Du Bois, the artist and critic of the *American*', and visitors kept coming through most of the first week. There was an offer from Rowlands Galleries in Boston to take the show. As the gallery would not pay the transfer expenses and insurance, the offer was declined. The newspaper articles that the exhausted Sloan mentions in the New York *Sun* on 9 and 10 February, written by James Huneker, gave encouragement, and Sloan's entry for the 17th suggests that everyone, including William Macbeth, was well pleased with the exhibition. Sales amounted to nearly $4,000 and five of the 'Eight' had sold seven paintings between them. Only Prendergast, Glackens and Sloan failed to part with a sample of their work.

The New York Evening *Post* in its preview of the exhibition gave a fair account of the intentions of the painters 'who thought it would be a good idea to let art lovers see that there is a group of men in the city that, to quote one of their numbers, are "doing something" '; the New York *World* saw in it 'a new and distinctive movement towards Americanism' with emphasis given to New York scenes and types. Of the hostile critics of Robert Henri and his 'revolutionary black gang' there were no signs in the edited version of Sloan's diary. However, one learns of his personal dislike for Charles De Kay, the art critic of the *New York Times*, from unpublished material. Sloan intimated sarcastically that 'his patronym is a compliment to him for decay implies some original quality gone by'.[11] The phrase 'Ashcan', which Sloan disliked, was not used until 1916 when the cartoonist for *The Masses*, Art Young, criticised them for not turning their art into socialist propaganda, at which point Sloan resigned from the magazine.[12]

Although the show did not travel to Boston, it did proceed to Philadelphia in March with substitutes for the sold pictures. On its return, Sloan and his friend C. B. Lichtenstein arranged a nine-month tour through eight cities, beginning at the Chicago Institute in September, going on via Toledo, Detroit, Indianapolis, Pittsburgh, Bridgeport, and winding up in Newark in May 1909. Little mention was made in the diaries of the first stage in these proceedings. Sloan was ill with rheumatic neuritis at the beginning of March and only able to pay the show in Philadelphia fleeting visits on the 6th and again on the 19th. But Sloan's concern about lack of acceptance continued long after Henri's interest in the galleries appeared to waver. In March 1909 Sloan had a long discussion with Henri about NAD jury decisions and the possibility of establishing a permanent independent gallery. In December the National Academy returned three of Sloan's four entries and hung the remaining one, *Chinese Restaurant*, in a poor place. But Sloan was not only upset on his own account, he frequently objected to the neglect shown to others, and, on this occasion, he felt for Jerome Myers, with whom he had sketched in the summer of 1906. Myers had, since the 1890s, expressed a similar interest to Sloan's in painting 'common people'.

In January 1910 Henri proposed the title 'Independent American Artists' but preliminary discussions on the 10th came to nothing. A stalemate of inactivity ended in March when the National Academy again rejected entries by Henri and Sloan. The diary entry for 9 March was, in the circumstances, quite droll:

Back rejected! from the N.A.D. jury came *City Pigeons* and *Three A.M.* The latter I sent them as much as a joke like slipping a pair of men's drawers into an old maid's laundry, so that its refusal I expected surely. The first, *Pigeons*, I rather thought had a chance to pass but I evidently under-rated it.[13]

The next ten days are filled with references to an Exhibition of Independent Artists in the 35th-Street building to open on 1 April with Sloan acting as treasurer and general factotum. Each contributor put up $200 and some 103 artists delivered 627 works of art by 25/26 March. The opening, according to Sloan, was sensational:

> the three large floors were crowded to suffocation, absolutely jammed at 9 o'clock the crowd packed the sidewalk outside waiting to get in. A small squad of police came on the run. It was terrible but wonderful to think that an art show could be so jammed. A great success seems assured. Three small pictures have been sold.[14]

The last sentence may have been unintentionally sardonic for the sales were poor, and the investors only got back 33.8 cents on a dollar. Nevertheless, the interest of those that attended persuaded the artists to hold another show in 1911, but in the event plans were changed and some fifteen painters held their own show at the Union League Club in April 1911. A breakaway group led by Rockwell Kent also held an exhibition in March and this divergence of activities caused Sloan to comment in February 1912 that there was an insufficient audience for so many conflicting shows.

Although Sloan did not receive public recognition until 1916, he had by that time, according to his second wife, etched sixty pictures of the city on metal, produced seven lithographs and over sixty paintings. Almost one hundred works are referred to in his journal, even though about half of them receive only one or two mentions. Some twenty works attract remarks on six or more occasions. The St John edition also contains thirty-six illustrations by Sloan, of which all but seven are cited in the text. By any measure this is a substantial written record of his work over the period, yet it is clear that his efforts were not wholly concentrated upon the cityscape. Indeed, his reference to *Hudson from the Palisades* on 24 November maintains that this is the first landscape he had tried to exhibit. As so often, the jurymen at the National Academy were not impressed. Among the one hundred works there are at least a dozen portraits, including one self-portrait. This is notable for two reasons: first, one does not usually associate Sloan with portrait painting (he only did four commissions during his entire career) and second, the fact that he made no serious attempt to earn a living by such means may reflect upon the growing supremacy of the photograph.

Which of his paintings referred to in his journal give most insight into the interior and exterior life of the city and its people? There are six excellent examples. *Sunset, West Twenty-Third Street* was begun in the autumn of 1905 before Sloan embarked on his writings and thus his commentary is very brief – two entries only. On 11 January he did some work on it as his model had not arrived. The next day after breakfast at 2 *p.m.* he mentions a rooftops picture, which is almost certainly the etching *Roofs – Summer Night* referred to again on 26 February. On 13 January he worked on *Twenty-Third Street Roofs, Sunset* and then the picture drops from view. This is not unusual, for Sloan is often caught up with several things of the moment and often had two or more creations on the go. The result, however, is rewarding since we have a roofscape (reminiscent of later work by Edward Hopper) where interest is divided between the woman and her washing-line, the street below and the substantial building commanding the middle distance.

*Dust Storm, Fifth Avenue* is mentioned six times over a space of four years. On Sunday 10 June 1906, while walking on 5th Avenue, Sloan noted: 'we were on the edge of a beautiful wind storm, the air full of dust and a sort of panicky terror in all the living things in sight'. On Monday 11 June he began to paint, but was distracted by witnessing across the backyards the death of a child in its mother's arms while several men watched helplessly. The next day, by contrast, he walked up from West 10th Street along 7th and 8th Avenues and saw lots of 'children dancing to the music of street pianos'. He returned to the picture on Thursday (nothing was recorded for Wednesday 13 June) and one is led to speculate whether more children now appear in the painting than he originally intended, as if to wipe out the painful visual memory and replace it with livelier images. The work was not mentioned again until the end of the year, when the National Academy placed it on their reserve list. Sloan then entered it for the Carnegie Institute, Pittsburgh on 7 February 1907. Eighteen months went by before there was another reference. On 18 August 1908 Sloan retrieved the picture from the Macbeth Gallery where presumably it had been hung since the exhibition of the 'Eight' in the previous February. There was a brief mention of *Duststorm* and another painting when both were taken to be photographed for *Sunday Sun* on 25 April 1910. The final reference comes on 12 June, when Sloan hoped to sell it for $350 to the art collector John Quinn. Although Quinn bought a number of his prints, he did not acquire the painting. It was eventually purchased by the Metropolitan Museum of Art in 1921 and has the distinction of being the first sale Sloan made to a museum. The scurrying movement of the people captured by Sloan ensured its success.

*The Picnic Grounds* also has quite a catalogue of mentions. Its genesis is absorbing. On 24 May 1906 Sloan, his wife Dolly and cousin Nell, together with Robert Henri, crossed New York Bay to Bayonne – he and Dolly had been earlier in the month – and evidently all enjoyed the outing. A third visit on 30 May (Decoration Day) prompted a specific comment on the picnic grounds, where there was a dancing pavilion and 'young girls of the healthy lusty type with white caps jauntily perched on their heads'.[15] Three days later Sloan started his painting and over the next three years there were regular references to it. He entered it for the Fellowship Exhibition of the Pennsylvania Academy of Fine Arts the following October. In February 1907 he did some more work on it for the National Academy. Sloan often reworked his paintings though comments thus far on *The Picnic Grounds* do not suggest that he was dissatisfied with it. A few days later he sent it off to the jury. It was accepted and on 15 March he attended a private viewing. Six months later it was selected for the Dallas, Texas, State Fair, though this western excursion elicited no special comment from Sloan. In April 1908 it went with the travelling exhibition of the 'Eight' to Cincinnati, and finally, in March 1909, it was sent to the Carnegie Institute along with two others; all were rejected. One becomes aware even in discussion of these *three* paintings that a pattern of rejection had emerged. Yet *The Picnic Grounds* did meet with some success and gives clear indication of Sloan's pursuit of innocent merry-making. His delight in people enjoying themselves knew no bounds – as witnessed by the shy young couple embracing behind one of the trees on the right.

The 'pursuit of happiness' can also be sensed in *South Beach Bathers* begun during that heady and productive summer of 1907.

After it had lain dormant for about a year Sloan worked on it again for a week in July 1908 before entering it for the Chicago exhibition. Sloan seems to have taken particular care over this painting. Perhaps this is not surprising given its unusual composition, in which so little of the skyline from Staten Island is visible and nearly all the attention is focused on human activity. The three couples in the foreground are deliberately balanced so that the couple on the left, with the girl standing and holding on to her hat in the breeze, receives some attention from the two couples on the right in prone or semi-prone positions. Sloan may have been troubled by the self-conscious and schematic poses that are reminiscent of the 'tableaux' effect sought by one of the popular photographers of the day, Frances Benjamin Johnston, though there is no specific indication of this worry in the diary.

Meeting places feature frequently in Sloan's work and the history of two such paintings illustrates this. There are five references to *Haymarket* during its initial stages in September 1907. One morning he and Dolly witnessed some vaudeville acts at the New York Theatre where he was impressed by a 'troop of Spanish dancers'. In the afternoon of the same day Sloan began work on his picture of the Haymarket Theatre on 6th Avenue. Much later, in *The Gist of Art*, he recalled that 'this old dance hall . . . famous through infamy, was a well-known hangout for the underworld. Ladies whose dress and deportment were satisfactory to the doorman were admitted free. Gents paid'. Sloan worked right through 7 September, pausing only to take another look at the building. Nine days went by before he again mentioned the painting. He considered it finished on the 20th and allowed the editor of *McIntosh Monthly* to reproduce it alongside a work of Everett Shinn's. The following month it was exhibited in Philadelphia and the National Academy followed suit in March 1908. Seven months later Sloan agreed that the Kansas–Nebraska Art Association might show it and the last reference is to its return in March 1909. The painting requires little elucidation beyond Sloan's comment except to draw attention to the magnetic properties of light which attract people like moths to a candle flame. In this sense this painting shares similar properties with *Hairdresser's Window*.

*Chinese Restaurant* might be regarded as the first in a series that continues with Sloan's studies of McSorley's Bar on East 7th Street, with two paintings in 1912 and a further three studies in 1928–9. Interspersed is an unusual etching of 1917 entitled *Hell-hole*, which shows the backroom at Wallace's on West 4th Street and 6th Avenue. Sloan is mildly satiric about the Greenwich Village inmates that included a celebrated toper, Eugene O'Neill. Several of the 'Eight', especially Glackens and Luks, enjoyed café meetings and local hostelries and Sloan, a little belatedly, also engaged in their pictorial representation. The first journal reference to *Chinese Restaurant* occurred on 23 February 1909. Sloan had been over to Bayonne again and, feeling restless, went into a Chinese restaurant where he saw 'a strikingly gotten up girl with dashing red feathers in her hat playing with the restaurant's fat cat'.[16] Almost a month went by before he mentioned the painting again, on 18 March when he revisited the restaurant to refresh his memory. 'Just in time,' he remarked, 'for tomorrow they move to the corner below' (on 29th Street).[17] Sloan considered the picture finished by mid-April. Compared with some of the others we have looked at, this painting was slightly longer in the making, mainly because Sloan was busy on other projects. These, included, rather surprisingly, several portraits (Miss Converse, W. S. Walsh and Dolly) as well as drawings for *Century* magazine. *Chinese Restaurant* was one of four paintings mentioned earlier that Sloan sent to the NAD jury on 22 November and the only one they accepted. This success encouraged the Pennsylvania Academy of Fine Arts to show it; in March 1910 Sloan commented on the poor reproduction of it in *Craftsmen* since the girl's face was 'badly scratched'. Almost a year passed before the next reference, when Sloan touched up several pictures for an exhibition in Newark library and there was a further mention about a possible showing in Pittsburgh. Evidently this was one of Sloan's more successful and satisfying pieces, and it is not difficult to see why. The cat and the girl steal the show despite the presence of three men, one of whom is much more concerned with his dinner, but taken together a harmony of ordinariness is achieved.

In summary, one must admit that Sloan's journal is tantalising. The amount of comment here on the creative process is small – more can be gleaned from *The Gist of Art* – yet the fortunes and misfortunes that his work encountered, the details about the preparations for exhibitions, the shows themselves, especially in 1908 and 1910, the 'rent money' work he did for the press, the remarks about his fellow artists, even his passing comments on disparate events such as the Triangle fire, the loss of the *Titanic* and the death of King Leopold of Belgium, combine to establish an intricate mosaic of his life in New York. One wishes for fuller commentary, especially when he was in difficulty with his work, but one has to be content with partial revelations.

Understandably Sloan was caught up with the pulsating life of the city, in much the same way as was the photographer Lewis Hine, and he was at times so busy, particularly in 1907, that there was little time for reflection. David Scott, in his 1975 biography, noted that there were no less than fourteen 'scene' paintings completed that year. Thus, in his full-time role as spectator he did get, as he desired, 'into contact with real things'. Certainly his etchings and paintings speak far greater volumes than ever his journal can. Perhaps the highest tribute to Sloan's work during this period was paid by Robert Henri, who, in his manual *The Art Spirit* (1923), wrote of *Pigeons* that the atmosphere of the painting was 'steeped in the warmth of sunlight', and would, in his opinion, 'carry into future time the feel and the way of life as it happened'.[18] How fortunate that there are both words *and* pictures, for it would be an incurious student who would dispense with the additional knowledge that Sloan's journal can give.

NOTES

1. John Sloan, *John Sloan's New York Scene: From the Diaries, Notes and Correspondence, 1906–1913*, ed. Bruce St John, with an Introduction by Helen Farr Sloan (New York: Harper & Row, 1956). (Hereafter cited as *NYS*.)
2. Jerome Mellquist, *The Emergence of an American Art* (New York: Charles Scribner's Sons, 1942) p. 132.
3. Una E. Johnson, *American Prints and Printmakers* (New York: Doubleday, 1980) p. 41.
4. Peter Conrad, *The Art of the City* (Oxford: Oxford University Press, 1984) p. 90.
5. *NYS*, p. 486.
6. Lloyd Goodrich, *John Sloan* (New York: Whitney Museum of American Art, 1952) p. 20.
7. *NYS*, pp. 308–9.
8. Ibid., p. 133.
9. Ibid., p. 137.
10. Ibid., p. 109.
11. 17 May 1907, unpublished diary.
12. 7 April 1916, unpublished diary.
13. *NYS*, pp. 395–6.
14. Ibid., pp. 405–6.

15. Ibid., p. 38.
16. Ibid., p. 292.
17. Ibid., p. 300.
18. Robert Henri, *The Art Spirit* (Philadelphia, Penn.: Lippincott, 1923) p. 222.

# 6

# The New York Art Scene in the 1960s

## JOHN OSBORNE

### I CONSUMER CAPITALISM AND THE ART MARKET

With the rise of Fascism in the 1920s and 1930s, many of the leaders of European modernism emigrated to the United States, thereby freeing American artists from their traditional feeling of inferiority. The result was an uprush of creativity, as American art first assimilated and then moved beyond the European inheritance. In the Abstract Expressionism of the 1940s, such as one associates with the names of Jackson Pollock, Willem De Kooning and Mark Rothko, and in the 1950s assemblage art of Louise Nevelson, Robert Rauschenberg and Jasper Johns, American art acquired a confidence, an inventiveness, a largeness of ambition, that matched the nation's assumption of the custodianship of the western world. The USA replaced France as the country towards which international avant-gardists gravitated; New York replaced Paris as the art capital of the world.

The United States was slow to realise its cultural pre-eminence. In 1947, the art critic Clement Greenberg bemoaned the fact that, out of a population of 140 millions the audience for a Pollock or De Kooning was perhaps fifty.[1] It was only in the last few years of his life – he died in a car crash in 1956 – that Jackson Pollock achieved celebrity; and when it came it was frequently crass and uncomprehending, as when *Time* magazine did a feature on him under the soubriquet 'Jack the Dripper'.[2] In 1950, the Museum of Modern Art in New York refused its director's request to purchase a Mark Rothko; and when the director, Alfred J. Barr, arranged for the architect Philip Johnson to *give* the picture to the Museum, the trustees prevaricated for two years before reluctantly agreeing to accept it – whereupon one of the Museum's founders, A. Conger Goodyear, resigned in disgust.[3] Rothko was 57 years old when in

1960 he was at last able to give up teaching and concentrate on his painting. Another of the masters of Abstract Expressionism, Franz Kline, was living on a paltry $5,000 a year at the time of his death in 1962. The same was true of the 1950s assemblage artists. After one show in Florence, from which not a single work was sold, Robert Rauschenberg threw the entire exhibition into the River Arno, for lack of the money to either house the pictures in Italy or transport them back to the USA.

This neglect of its modern masters was not new. Throughout the twentieth century, the United States had provided a philistine and financially unsupportive environ for its leading painters and sculptors, whether they were traditionalists or innovators. The Realist painter Edward Hopper was 42 before he had a successful show: prior to that time, he had sold only one picture – and that by the expedient of knocking $50 off the asking price. Similarly, avant-gardists such as Charles Sheeler and Stuart Davis had to earn their livings by some other means than their painting – the former as a professional photographer, the latter by teaching. It was therefore justifiable for American artists to perceive themselves as lonely, heroic individuals struggling for aesthetic values in a brutally materialistic society.

By 1960 this situation was reversed. American capital suddenly woke up to the high esteem in which the nation's art was held by others, and began to recognise the capacity of art to convert business power into social prestige. The kind of capitalism involved was 'consumer capitalism', rather than the industrial capitalism of an earlier historical phase. If the industries that best symbolise the latter mode of production are those associated with iron and steel – shipbuilding, say, or the construction of the railways – then those that exemplify consumer capitalism might be advertising, fashion, pornography, cosmetics, pop music or the movies. If the necessary prop of industrial capitalism, and in that sense its purest creation, is the worker, then the necessary and perfect creation of the later phase is the consumer. This consumer is a *tabula rasa*, an infinite blank, an endless Third World to be repeatedly colonised with needs it never knew it had and which capitalism can maintain itself by fulfilling. The products of consumer capitalism are not manufactured to satisfy a need, but to create one. And, of course, every such needless need locks one back into the system in pursuit of the money with which to fulfil it.

It was the new bourgeoisie presiding over this ad-mass consumer capitalism that now discovered American art. The idea of social improvement through contact with high culture struck a responsive chord, and throughout the 1960s the wealthy poured hundreds of millions of dollars into the construction and endowment of museums bearing their name. The federal and state governments can claim some credit for this, partly because of the example they set (as late as 1965 the total direct public support for the arts was a mere $20 million; by 1970 it had reached $85 million; by 1975, $282 million – a more than thirteenfold increase in one decade), but more literally by facilitating laws that made gifts to museums tax-deductible, as they are not in Britain, Germany or France.[4] No other country has made it possible for a donor to register actual cash gains from giving by deduction from tax liability the current market value of donated assets, such as paintings, originally purchased at much lower prices. It has been estimated that by 1974 the reduction in tax liability enjoyed by donors because of such 'gifts' to art institutions amounted to more than $700 million.[5]

'Part of their reward', Tom Wolfe has claimed,

is the ancient and semi-sacred status of Benefactor of the Arts. The arts have always been a doorway into Society, and in the largest cities today the arts – the museum boards, arts councils, fund drives, openings, parties, committee meetings – have completely replaced the churches in this respect. But there is more!

Today there is a peculiarly modern reward that the avant-garde artist can give his benefactor: namely, the feeling that he, like his mate the artist, is separate from and aloof from the bourgeoisie, the middle classes . . . the feeling that he may be *from* the middle class but he is no longer *in* it . . . the feeling that he is a fellow soldier, or at least an aide-de-camp or an honorary cong guerilla in the vanguard march through the land of the philistines. This is a peculiarly modern need and a peculiarly modern kind of salvation (from the sin of 'Too Much Money').[6]

What Wolfe is describing is that contract in which the avant-garde artist, who had sometimes been for the people and sometimes against, but who had always claimed to be opposed to the bourgeoisie, unashamedly bedded down with the 'enemy'. When did the consummation take place? The year is perhaps 1958, when

Jasper Johns had an exhibition in New York, and a taxi-cab mogul named Robert Scull attempted to purchase the entire show.

The point at issue is not simply that the wealthy began investing in New rather than Old Masters, but that in the process they remade the art world in the image of the consumer capitalism which had made them rich. Art for the first time was marketed on the same basis as fashion or pop music: with the characteristic jargon of the 'new', the 'latest', the 'trendy', the 'with it'; the overnight elevation of 20-year-olds, fresh from art school, into superstardom; the accelerated turnover in movements, yesterday's avant-garde becoming today's derrière-garde; and the disabling of promising talent with an over-liberal application of bank notes, a succession of artists collapsing, like bloated Elvises, into silence or fatuousness after a mere four or five years of genuine creativity. Henceforth, the problem for the American artist would not be one of evolving survival tactics in an unheeding or hostile society, but of evolving survival tactics in a society whose limitless capacity for consumption could be trivialising and cannibalistic.

As the navel of western art and western capitalism, New York was the locus of this remarkable transformation. From the perspective of the aspiring artist, the ladder of success could be measured out, rung by rung, in a geographical progression from down-town to up-town. The artists' colony was in the Soho district of Manhattan's Lower East Side. Here they rented as their studios vast lofts at the top of crumbling tenements. Having acquired a 'loft' reputation amongst their peers, these young artists might hope to win a one man or woman show at such down-town venues as the Tanager Gallery on 10th Street, or the nearby Reuben and March Galleries. If the show proved a success, they might be taken up by one of the more fashionable mid-town galleries, such as the Judson, the Green, the Martha Jackson or the Sidney Janis. However, for the truly ambitious artist such venues were but a stepping-stone to their real destination, Leo Castelli's gallery, further up-town still at number 4 East 77th Street. To be represented by Castelli was to have 'arrived'. He, it was, who hosted the 1958 Jasper Johns exhibition. The show was a sell-out, the New York Museum of Modern Art buying four of the works. It was this that led Castelli's friend, the Abstract Expressionist painter Willem De Kooning, to remark that if Leo put his mind to it he could sell a pair of old beer cans. Two years later, Jasper Johns made a $5\frac{1}{2}$-inch high, hand-pointed bronze sculpture of two Ballantine Ale cans;

Castelli auctioned it in 1973 for $90,000. By 1980, the Rauschenbergs and Jasper Johns that Castelli had for sale were priced at upwards of $250,000 – a quarter of a million dollars each.[7]

As Andy Warhol said: 'To be successful as an artist you have to have your work shown in a good gallery for the same reason that, say, Dior never sold his originals from a counter at Woolworths. . . . You need a good gallery so the "ruling class" will notice you and spread enough confidence in your future so collectors will buy you, whether for $500 or $50,000.'[8] Warhol was devastated when Castelli initially declined to represent him. In 1964 Castelli changed his mind; two years later, Warhol was rich enough to consider retirement.

Though most artists represented by Castelli were happy to remain with him, there was one further rung of financial success to which they might aspire: Marlborough Fine Art, the world's biggest chain of showrooms, whose American operations were controlled from 57th Street, New York. Marlborough offered its artists a complete package deal: a substantial, steady income for life; help with financial investments; advice on maximising tax deductions; worldwide showrooms; monographs by well-known critics; and unrivalled contacts with private collectors and public museums. Marlborough Fine Art sold to the Pope, to Giovanni Agnelli (the head of Fiat), the the American banker Paul Mellon, and to film tycoons such as Otto Preminger. In return, Marlborough claimed exclusive rights to the sale of works by their contract artists, and at huge rates of commission. By the 1960s, Marlborough represented Henry Moore, Barbara Hepworth, Francis Bacon, Oscar Kokoschka, Naum Gabo, the estates of Jackson Pollock and Franz Kline, Robert Motherwell, David Smith and younger artists such as Larry Rivers. But as the owner, Frank Lloyd, was fond of reminding his staff: 'Remember, I don't collect pictures. I collect money.'[9]

When economic interests as organised and powerful as those associated with Marlborough moved into the New York art scene, pressures were exerted that, without necessarily being corrupt or fraudulent, involved a thousand little compromises, equivocations and betrayals throughout the existing system for marketing, exhibiting and studying contemporary art. In 1967, for example, New York's Metropolitan Museum belatedly opened a department of contemporary art with Henry Geldzahler as its curator. This innovation was celebrated two years later when thirty-five galleries of the Museum hosted 480 works by forty-three artists in a mammoth exhibition entitled 'New York Painting and Sculpture: 1940–1970'. Despite its size, however, the show offered a peculiarly skewed and unrepresentative chronicle of the period it was purporting to document. Why? Because much of the exhibit was for sale, Geldzahler covertly using a supposedly impartial survey to shop-window goods currently on offer from dealer friends such as Frank Lloyd, Leo Castelli and Sidney Janis. The historical record was being travestied to suit purely commercial ends.[10]

The boom in monographs on living artists carried further potential for abuse, since even reputable art presses found the cost of colour reproductions sufficiently prohibitive to require subsidy from the gallery representing the artist in question. This inevitably led to a spate of books that were virtually promotional literature, for what picture dealer would underwrite a hostile text that might devalue his or her product? Maurice Tuchman, curator of the Los Angeles County Museum, accepted a $5,000 honorarium from Marlborough Fine Art for a monograph on Soutine and later recommended that the Museum purchase several Marlborough-owned works. When this became known there was a public outcry and Tuchman was reprimanded (but not dismissed) by the Museum's trustees.[11] In 1969, Mark Rothko named his friend and fellow artist Theodoros Stamos as one of the executors of his estate. Within three months of Rothko's death in 1970, Stamos had played his part in signing the estate over to Marlborough at bewilderingly low prices (Frank Lloyd later sold some of them for fifteen times the sum paid). Early in 1971, Stamos, whose career was conspicuously flagging, was signed up by Marlborough. In 1974 Marlborough underwrote the publication (at $32.50 per copy) of a glossy study of Stamos by his friend Ralph Pomeroy, who had earlier been employed as a restorer by the Marlborough Studio on 69th Street.[12] Even if no malpractice were entailed, it is difficult not to believe that in cases such as these the services of art critics were being co-opted at the expense of their independence and probity.

One small but unmistakable symptom of this malaise was the invasion by hyperbole and triumphalism of the rhetoric of the art historian. High-minded formalists such as Clement Greenberg had already prepared the way for this linguistic collapse by portraying the history of modern art as a sort of relay-race in which the baton, formerly passed from Courbet to Manet to Monet to Cézanne to

Picasso, was, *circa* 1948, snatched by Jackson Pollock on behalf of the virile young American team. This same heroic, progressivist, chauvinistic note is struck, ever more emphatically (as even the titles declare), in the art histories of the period: Sam Hunter's *Modern American Painting and Sculpture* (1959); Barbara Rose's *American Art Since 1900* (1967); Irving Sandler's *The Triumph of American Painting: A History of Abstract Expressionism* (1970); and E. A. Carmean's *The Great Decade of American Abstraction: Modernist Art 1960 to 1970* (1974). Moreover, the prevailing metaphors required a steady succession of new Pollocks to receive the baton from those who, for whatever reason, were about to retire from the race. Spotted in 1959, as a 23-year-old fresh out of art college, Frank Stella was signed up by Leo Castelli the following year. A decade later, when Stella was still in his early thirties, Robert Rosenblum, Professor of Fine Art at New York University, wrote a monograph proclaiming him 'the finest painter of his generation anywhere in the world'.[13] Rosenblum is a distinguished critic, but not even he is in a position to assess the entire artistic output of the world in a given generation and then bestow the laurels on the head of a single, sky-towering genius. This is not the undeluded lexis of the art critic. This is the high-pressure patter of the salesman.

## II   POP ART: THE AESTHETICS OF CONSPICUOUS CONSUMPTION

The first movement to benefit, and suffer, from this change in the circumstances of art production was Pop Art, whose American version emerged in 1960, three or four years after its British equivalent. The five leading American Pop Artists were based in New York and all had backgrounds in commercial art: Andy Warhol was an award-winning fashion illustrator of shoes before entering the world of fine art; James Rosenquist was a billboard painter who claims to have covered by hand every billboard in Times Square; Roy Lichtenstein worked in design and window display; Claes Oldenburg in magazine illustration and display; and Tom Wesselmann studied cartooning as a trade. Perhaps because of this commercial training, the Pop Artists accept it as a given that at the centre of our conception of 'reality' there is a void which languages strive to fill, and that the language which presently fills that void to repletion is the language of consumer capitalism. The typical Pop artifact is therefore a site where the language of high art and the language of commerce meet and contend. Consequently, the city of New York is both entirely present and entirely absent from these works. As a place, it is characterised by the ubiquity of its absence, being less an actuality charged with its own presence than a storehouse of images, slogans, neon, billboards, movies and mirror windows. This absent presence of New York, the city as a crucible of signs, presides over much of the art of the 1960s.

The first distinguishing trait of Pop Art is its appropriation of images that have already been processed by the urban mass media: newspapers, magazines, advertisements, films, record covers, television, comics, and the like. For all its surface realism, therefore, Pop Art is not an unmediated transcription of reality: rather it offers a picture of a picture of reality. Second, the sorts of processed images selected for recycling are icons or archetypes of the popular culture generated by consumer capitalism – Coca Cola, Marilyn Monroe, Elvis, Campbell's soup, hamburgers. In this sense, Pop Art is extroverted rather than introverted, appearing to accept the urban environment rather than disdaining it. Much of the success of the movement stems from its accessibility, the annexing of forms available to all through the mass media instantly establishing a shared world of reference with the spectator. Hence, the 'Pop' in Pop Art means 'popular', as in pop music. A third characteristic is the attempt to mime in the painting process the mechanical production of those media that provided the appropriated images. Roy Lichtenstein uses a slide projector to project on to his canvas, ready for copying, the cartoons he has stolen from comic books. He also mimics the dot colour-printing of the originals by using as a stencil sheets of plastic with regularly spaced holes. Similarly, Andy Warhol used photo-silkscreens to stamp out versions of newspaper pictures, thereby echoing the presses' own methods of duplication. This use of mechanical aids gives Pop Art a pristine, untouched-by-human-hand quality entirely appropriate to an art concerned with consumer objects which are themselves packaged to have no past. As the decade progressed, art became ever more skilled at hiding the hand of its creator; as we shall see, the immaculate surfaces that Pop parodied would later be used to lend art itself an unused, 'buy me' glamour.

The Pop tactics of selection, appropriation, isolation, magnification and replication are well displayed in the works Roy Lichtenstein produced between 1960 and 1965. By isolating and magnifying for our better analysis cartoons from popular comic strips, Lichtenstein uses the grammar of fine art to unveil the ideology inscribed in the vernacular. Such images tease out the ways in which, if we create language, it also creates us. We are born into a world where sign systems already exist, and in teaching us the alphabets of these sign systems society simultaneously imbues us with its preferred values. Lichtenstein's 1960s deconstructions of 1950s comics lucidly expose the ways in which American kids were encouraged to define themselves differently on the basis of gender. For girls, there were romance comics in which femininity is equated with love, domesticity and longing for an often absent male. For boys, war comics defined masculinity in relation to aggression. Girls become women by loving members of the opposite sex; boys become men by killing members of the same sex. The female sex organ is most commonly symbolised by a wedding ring; while for the boys, the pistol replaces the penis as the symbol of virility.

Comic strips, like a garrulous ribbon, hasten the viewer from frame to frame by the urgency of the narrative drive. By detaching key images from their narrative context, blowing them up on to a huge scale, and placing them in an art environment – where people are used to giving protracted contemplation – Lichtenstein creates the conditions in which their uglier ideological functions can be excavated. The magnification of scale exposes the language of the cartoon to the viewer's gaze: the limited but brilliant colour range; the thick black outlining; the speech bubbles; the contradiction between the volumetric drawing and the flat colouring, etc. By thus exposing the image-making process, Lichtenstein implies that the media landscape, of which comics are but one part, can more easily be grasped in terms of lexical patterns than as a material phenomenon.

However, these paintings depend for their high tension on a two-way transmission: the viewer would quickly lose interest if all we had here was fine art condescending to popular culture. Lichtenstein's best work shows a magisterial talent for creating unified, powerful and coherent structures. The fact that he is able to generate designs of an almost classical simplicity out of the most vulgar sources, amounts to an act of homage to the vitality of commercial art. It is because the two language systems are so well-matched that their interaction on the canvas provokes laughter in the audience. This humour of incongruity, or irony, may well constitute Pop Art's most subversive aspect; for by introducing laughter into the hushed, pious, chapel-like atmosphere of the art gallery and museum they effected a small revolution. Nothing is more anti-authoritarian than laughter.

By 1966, Roy Lichtenstein was rich, famous and bankrupt of ideas. Having exhausted the semantic and ideological analysis of comics, he could think of nothing better than to superimpose the formal language of the cartoon on previous art works by other hands. At first, this had a certain cheeky subversiveness to it. His Pop Art replicas of Abstract Expressionism are witty and complex visual puns: what looks like a thick and succulent daub of paint is actually applied flatly in comic book style; what appears to be spontaneous is the result of painstaking labour; what appears to be the product of human gestures is mechanically reproduced; what appears to be abstract is in fact a realistic depiction of abstraction. And, of course, by translating the supposedly profound calligraphics of a Pollock or De Kooning into a sequence of Ben Day dots, Lichtenstein jokingly suggests that Abstract Expressionism's much-prized intensity and uniqueness is bogus: a machine can do it.

Soon, even this degree of impishness was gone. One of his paintings is based on Picasso's *The Woman of Algiers*. That, however, is by no means the whole story: for the Picasso was one of a series of fifteen which redefined in Cubist terms a painting by the nineteenth-century French Romantic artist Eugene Delacroix. What we have here, then, is a Lichtenstein of a cartoon of a Picasso of a Delacroix of a Woman of Algiers. The linguistic systems do not really comment on each other: instead, they engage in an endless lexical slide; a vacuous semantic slither.

Lichtenstein has spent the last twenty years applying these sorts of visual strategies to different phases of art history: Ancient Greek ruins; North American Indian artifacts; nineteenth-century American realism; the Impressionism of Claude Monet; the Fauvism of Matisse; German Expressionism; the Cubism of Léger; Italian Futurism; Surrealism; Purism; the abstractions of Mondrian; Art Deco bric-à-brac . . . and so on. In every case, the comic-strip language is no longer there to throw other lexical codes into analytical relief: rather, it is used to stamp Lichtenstein's imprimatur – 'made in America' – on the totality of known world culture. Unwittingly, his *œuvre* has thus come to resemble the private collections of American millionaires, such as J. Paul Getty, who in the mid-century vacuum-cleaned Europe of its cultural treasure. Both are facets of the cultural imperialism of a newly aggrandised USA. The fact that Lichtenstein's painting is far less capable of sustaining attention than either the Delacroix or the Picasso which it assimilates perhaps testifies to the debilitation that this form of imperialism, like any other, entails.

Andy Warhol's career trajectory is almost identical. His early silkscreens of Hollywood stars, such as Elizabeth Taylor, apply colouring in a random colour-chart manner that parallels the occasional non-alignments, or slippages, of mass-produced newspapers and magazines. Such tactics not only call attention to the image-making process by means of which Hollywood constructs 'stars', but also calls into question the gender stereotypes of the mass-media: *Liz* looks like a transvestite, a person whose original monochrome identity is only rendered 'female' by a garish use of lipstick, mascara and false eyelashes. Similarly, his multiple images of *Marilyn* mimic the strips of celluloid and endless newspaper photographs that invested her with star status. His *Campbell's Soup Can* series parodies the 'bigger-is-better' philosophy of consumer capitalism: surely, if one can of soup is good, one hundred cans are one hundred times as good, and two hundred cans of soup are two hundred times as good. Yet Warhol shares Lichtenstein's awareness of the visual panache of the commercial arts. His multiple images are not just a parody of media mass-production techniques, but also a means of distancing the subject-matter in the interests of a formal geometry. His serial pictures demonstrate how a fine art image of essentially abstract character can be salvaged from commercial sources without denying what those sources were.

Warhol called his New York studio 'the Factory', and employed a team of assistants to help him manufacture silkscreen prints. However much he satirised the mass-production methods of consumer capitalism, he also benefited from them, producing 2,000 saleable art works in a two-year period from August 1962. (Warhol once estimated that, working flat out, he could manufacture in eight months the 4,000 pictures Picasso produced in his entire career. 'It was disillusioning', he added, 'to realize it would take me that long.')[14] For a time, the audience benefited too: as late as 1965, Warhol was producing silkscreen prints in editions limited to 300 at a mere $10.00 each – a bargain by any standards. (One day the story will be told of how, beginning in the 1960s, the limited edition print, whose original function was to use mechanical reproduction to bring fine art within the reach of the average wage-packet, became yet another means of accruing status to a financial elite. At the 1986 International Print Biennale in Bradford the Lichtenstein was so expensive one had to make a special application to learn the price; a Hockney lithograph cost £9,760; and a Frank Stella print, in an edition of sixty, was priced at £12,500. When all sixty copies are sold, this one image will have grossed – I won't say earned – approximately $1,000,000.) Soon, however, he was running the Factory like any other absentee boss: collecting the profits from the labours of his employees. His movies were farmed out to sex-and-violence director Paul Morrissey, who has since become an outspoken neo-conservative and supporter of President Reagan (I see no contradiction there). In 1968 he started allowing Brigid Polk to manufacture Warhols for him, his sole contribution being the signature that ensured the work's 'authenticity' and guaranteed its sale. At the height of his celebrity he placed an advertisement in the *Village Voice* stating that he would sign anything for money: as portraitist to Campbell's soup and Coca Cola he understood perfectly the allure of a brand name.

Latterly, his main project was *Andy Warhol's Interview: The Monthly Glamour Gazette*, in which our hero featured alongside other glitterati: the Hollywood Borgias, minor royalty, couturiers, disgraced presidents, pop singers, murderers, society hostesses, and other media personalities whose fifteen minutes of fame one might reasonably hazard had long since expired. He still occasionally topped up his bank balance with a run of screen prints (such as the 'Dollar Sign' series of 1981 – no one could accuse him of stooping to subtlety) or a commissioned portrait ($30,000; $50,000 a pair), but essentially he had reached that level of celebrity where he no longer had to *do* anything to maintain his reputation; he just did fame by itself.

The one diversion of his later years was to go 'shopping' every day in the hour before noon, Warhol sometimes spending a million dollars in a single year. And just as the artist who began with a genius for targeting consumer icons later became an indiscriminate adulator of the coke-sniffing classes, so his collecting involved one hundred per cent non-discrimination. Vito Gialto, a New York antiques dealer, said: 'He was liable to buy *anything*. . . . He would just say, pick out a hundred for me – he loved multiples.'[15] After his death, in February 1987, a vast trove of objects was discovered, most of them unused and uncherished, some still in unopened wrappers, others dumped in identical cardboard boxes with a dated label on the side – what Warhol called his 'box-of-the-month'.[16] It took Sothebys of New York ten days to auction 10,000 of these objects in 3,000 lots for a grand total of $25 million. Looking at the superb Art Deco items, or the American furniture from the Federal and Classical periods, one was inclined to accord Warhol the status of a great collector; but as one's eyes fell on the plastic monsters, the cardboard replica of a Marlboro' cigarette carton, the hundred or more biscuit jars, the stockpile of cheap saucers, the disintegrating feathered necktie . . . a great hoarder, perhaps, but not a great collector. Warhol once said, 'Buying is much more American than thinking.' Then he disarmingly added: 'And I'm as American as they come.'[17]

## III  EYE CONFECTIONS, EPIDIASCOPES AND THE DEMATERIALISED ART OBJECT

Even those New York art movements of the 1960s that appear not to be representing commercial imagery, that appear not to be representing, that appear to be thoroughly abstract, are replete with a sense of their own commercial value. The most influential of these movements was the Colour Field school of painting. This style, with some justice, was hailed by critics such as Clement Greenberg and Robert Rosenblum as the triumphant amalgamation of modernist principles evolved since the advent of Cubism in 1907: for instance, the principle that the painted surface is flat and should not lie about it (as Matisse said, 'The more flat, the more art'); the principle of all-overness – that is, that every part of the picture should be as important as every other; and the principle that every painting is essentially abstract, being but an arrangement of lines and colours on a flat surface – the function of abstract art being to persuade one that such is the case. So considered, Colour Field painting is the synthesis of sixty years of radical experimentation, avant-garde agitation and aesthetic high-minded-ness.

   This is all true, but it is not all of the truth. For it is impossible now to contemplate the bland perfection of Kenneth Nolands, such as *April's Equal*, without seeing in them ritzy carpet designs for an aristocracy of wealth; Larry Poons's vast canvases, with their all-too-appropriate 'pennies from heaven' motif, remind one of nothing so much as up-market wallpapers – unrollable to the desired length at thousands of dollars a yard; Morris Louis's acrylics, in enticing candy-floss colours, can easily be interpreted as eye-confections for jaded art gourmands; while Frank Stella's shaped canvases invoke the chevron designs on the front of consumer durables such as juke boxes and cars. Modernist principles that had been used to create profoundly disturbing and subversive images were now employed to manufacture images expressly designed for easy consumption by the rich. The huge scale of these works, their optical allure, their modish allusions to the then fashionable psychedelia, their lack of any conscience-pricking content – all seem to predispose this art for installation in luxury penthouse suites.

At the end of the decade, a considerable stir was caused by a movement which came to be known as Photo-Realism, and which employed the same tactics as Pop Art at a higher level of gloss but a lower level of analysis. These painters used epidiascopes to project on to their canvases photographs whose glossy surfaces they then copied with the aid of mechanical tools such as the spray-gun and the air brush. Most of the artists concerned were born in the 1940s, were famous by the end of the 1960s, were rich by the mid-1970s (in 1975, a Richard Estes would cost a cool $80,000), and were more or less forgotten by the 1980s. What had appeared to be the latest thing in 'unsentimental' urban imagery – New York as a peopleless city of mirrors – quickly came to seem like an arduous, indiscriminate enumeration of surface fact.

Richard Estes and Robert Cottingham still repay attention. Estes uses the intervention of the photograph to help delineate multiple reflections that the unaided human eye could never keep in focus. Cottingham is likewise fascinated by New York's reflective skin, but also employs the camera to snap sights the jostled pedestrian would miss. Both artists produce work of such technical refinement that viewers invariably find themselves asking some such sequence of questions as the following: Is this a photograph? Or is this a painting? If it is a painting, is it based on a photograph? If this painting is a copy of a photograph, is not its value as an artistic statement robbed of its uniqueness? And so on. In short, the conventions of painting and the conventions of photography are made to highlight each other. Cottingham underlines this semantic debate by concentrating on signs, and by cropping them in a punning self-reflexive manner: 'Odeon' is cropped to 'Ode'; the word 'Art' is isolated from a larger vocable.

Yet beautiful and witty though these paintings are, the lack of ideological incisiveness renders them akin to the *later* works of Lichtenstein or the abstractions of the Colour Field painters. All three engage in lexical games that feed the eye but leave the mind famished. Photo-Realism is essentially a decorative art, its immaculate sheen as desirable as that of a consumer durable.

Two movements of the 1960s attempted, by dematerialising the aesthetic object, to break the bourgeois capacity to convert art into just another commodity. Both, wrongly in my opinion, have been much praised by critics. The first of these involved the Happenings of New York artists such as Allan Kaprow, Jim Dine, Red Grooms and Yoko Ono. By using the art gallery to stage an event, rather than to exhibit artefacts, these artists sought to convert their audiences from passive consumers to active participants. The result was a sort of 'theatre without walls' that was meant to overlap with the everyday flux of existence. As Kaprow said: 'The line between art and life should be kept as fluid, perhaps as indistinct, as possible.'[18]

It is just here, with the supposed lowering, or even removal, of the threshold between art and life, that the paltriness of the Happening is exposed: for any art that throws off its artifice and simply merges with the surrounding panorama of human activity is bound to be beggared in the process. I take it as axiomatic that happenings happen everywhere except at Happenings. The assassinations of John F. Kennedy, Bobby Kennedy and Martin Luther King; the Civil Rights marches and the legislation they provoked; the corruption of Spiro T. Agnew and Richard Nixon; the Vietnam War – these, assuredly, were happenings of some moment. In comparison, a small middle-class audience persuading itself that it is 'really living' by flinging paint about or taking its clothes off in the safely corralled space of the Martha Jackson Gallery, is as nearly fatuous an event as even the 1960s' New York art scene had to offer.

Nearly, but not quite. For the decade closed with Minimalist or Conceptual Art. Robert Morris's piles of felt and rows of steel blocks; Carl Andre's metal plates, blocks of styrofoam and heaps of bricks; and comparable works – if that is the right word – by

Don Judd, Sol LeWitt or Walter de Maria, stop just short of the complete erasure of the art object. Instead, by reducing it to a bare minimum, they seek to provoke in the spectator a philosophical debate as to the minimal conditions required before an object is invested with aesthetic significance.

Even if the artifacts themselves are excruciatingly tedious, here, at last, it might be thought, is an avant-garde gesture sufficient to thwart the limitless appetency of consumer capitalism. Sadly, the opposite is true: consider the case of the New York artist Walter de Maria. At the Documenta 6 exhibition at Kassel, West Germany, he had a hole drilled in the earth to a depth of one kilometre, a brass rod of the same length inserted in the hole, and the hole capped with a metal plate. This invisible object cost in excess of £150,000 – paid for by a New York organisation called the Dia Foundation. The Dia Foundation is one of a set of interlocking trusts set up to function as a tax-loss for one of the wealthiest families in Texas, the de Menils. The de Menil fortune in part derives from the manufacture and rental of oil-drilling equipment. The head of the Dia Foundation was an art dealer named Heiner Friedrich, who had galleries in New York and West Germany. It is not a coincidence that one of the artists his galleries represent is Walter de Maria. The media fuss surrounding Maria's *Vertical Kilometre* pumped up the value of his other works, available from Heiner Friedrich, and was good publicity for the de Menil drilling-bits that made the hole in the German soil. The £150,000 bill de Menil's had to pay was offset against tax. In effect, American taxpayers footed the bill for the export to Germany of an art work that is inaccessible to the human eye.[19]

## IV  ROTHKOGATE AND THE DISAPPEARING AVANT-GARDE

On the night of 24 February 1970, Mark Rothko committed suicide by slashing the crooks of both arms and bleeding to death. However, as Ambrose Bierce is fond of reminding us, death is not the end; afterwards there is the litigation over the estate. Within three months, Rothko's executors had granted control of the almost 800 paintings in their charge to Frank Lloyd of Marlborough Fine Art, directly contravening the artist's known wishes. There followed nearly eight years of litigation as Kate Rothko, the painter's daughter, sought to expose the scandal and to honour her father's intention that the sale of his lesser works be used to finance the display of his masterpieces and the granting of endowments to impoverished painters. Finally, in a series of judgements handed down between 1975 and 1977, Marlborough was ordered to return the 658 unsold estate paintings in its possession and to pay $9 million in damages and fines. Frank Lloyd was further charged with two counts of tampering with the evidence – he conveniently found it unnecessary to ever again set foot in the United States and run the risk of being jailed for eight years. It is the consensus amongst commentators that Marlborough got off exceedingly lightly.

Rothko belonged to the last generation of American artists seriously to espouse the mythology of avant-gardism. According to its own mythology, the avant-garde was international rather than national, experimental rather than traditional, abstract rather than representational, spiritual rather than materialist, and generally given to rocking the boat rather than becalming it. The artists perceived themselves as the antennae of the race, an intelligentsia which already had one foot in the future and which therefore would not be understood until after an appreciable time-lag (by when, of course, they would have forged still further ahead into the day after tomorrow).

Despite its oppositional ideology, however, avant-garde art remained bourgeois in certain regards. First, the nearest it comes to being tolerated, let alone honoured, is in the very liberal-bourgeois democracies it affects to despise. Second, artists are themselves in the business of producing consumer luxuries. Moreover, painting and sculpture are typically time and labour intensive; simply in order to earn a living, the artist will usually have to price the artifact beyond the means of the lower-income groups. Even if it is later rather than sooner, the bourgeoisie has therefore always been able to reclaim innovative art and turn it into a new form of academicism. With the advent of consumer capitalism the whole process of neutralising the avant-garde was ruthlessly accelerated, the *nouveau riches* recognising that the best way to stifle dissent is not to suppress it, but to market it.

The very avant-garde ideology which had sustained the Abstract Expressionists through the dark days of the Depression, the Second World War and the McCarthyite era, rendered them hopelessly vulnerable – mastodonic – when the new ruling class started competing for their wares and according them guru status. It is pitiful to note the speed at which the Rothko generation destroyed itself when success finally came its way. The disarray in which Rothko left his affairs, a disarray which Frank Lloyd sought to exploit, was symptomatic of his total inability to cope with the merchandising which is an inevitable aspect of art production in a capitalist economy.

In comparison, the Pop Artists seem wonderfully sane in their easy acknowledgement that anyone who these days makes as if to ignite bourgeois trousers is simply a poseur. There is also something peculiarly liberating about those Pop artifacts that manage to celebrate the stupefying creativity of consumer capitalism whilst reserving the right to satirise its grosser manifestations. And even if most of the Pop Artists quickly succumbed to banality or inanition, it could yet be claimed that (contrary to the avant-garde view) more people's lives are corrupted by poverty than by wealth and that, having been born into one condition, an Andy Warhol has a perfect entitlement to aspire to the other. In this sense, his most blatantly commercial works may be praised for honestly unveiling the system of values which undergirds all contemporary art production, most paintings preferring to efface their status as consumer luxuries by invoking spiritual or aesthetic codes that supposedly raise them above such tawdry considerations.

The issue is therefore not moral, and may well not be qualitative. It is just that as one examines the customised cars that Rauschenberg, Lichtenstein, Warhol and Stella produced for BMW; or the tapestries that Frank Stella designed in 1986 for Pepsi Cola's New York headquarters; or the 68-foot painting Lichtenstein created especially for the new Equitable Life Tower on 7th Avenue; or the carpet designs Lichtenstein, Hockney, Sol LeWitt and others have recently produced for the Vorwerk company, it is impossible not to recognise that in the 1960s an entire disposition of self was lost to the painter, and with it any hope that visual art could act as an independent barometer of our times. Little of the art produced in that decade was sufficiently abraded by the world outside the gallery to stand comparison with that ill-focused photograph of a South Vietnamese officer shooting a Viet Cong prisoner in the head; or that equally affrighting photo of a napalmed girl running naked and in tears from a nearby bomb-blast. To put it another way, the New York art scene of the 1960s witnessed the demise (or, rather, the wholesale purchase) of a tradition in art capable of imagining revolutionary alternatives to the status quo. This, then, was the time and this the place where the concept of the avant-garde finally collapsed before the commodifying power of consumer capitalism.

NOTES

1. Clement Greenberg, 'The Present Prospects of American Painting and Sculpture', *Horizon*, October 1947, pp. 28–9.
2. 'The Wild Ones', *Time*, 20 February 1956, pp. 70–5.
3. L. Seldes, *The Legacy of Mark Rothko* (New York: W. Holt, 1978) p. 26.
4. D. Netzer, *The Subsidized Muse* (New York: Cambridge University Press, 1978) p. 4.
5. Ibid., p. 242.
6. Tom Wolfe, *The Painted Word* (New York: Farrar, Straus & Giroux, 1975) p. 22.
7. J. Kosciuszko, 'Marketing Rebellion', *Chrome*, vol. III (Winter 1987) pp. 45–58.
8. Andy Warhol and P. Hackett, *POPism: The Warhol '60s* (New York: Harper & Row, 1980) pp. 20–1.
9. P. Deeley, 'The Million-Dollar Art Wrangle', *Observer*, 30 December 1973, p. 17.
10. C. Tomkins, 'Moving With the Flow: Henry Geldzahler', *New Yorker*, 6 November 1971, p. 58; Seldes, *Legacy of Mark Rothko*, pp. 93–6.
11. See Clark Polak's series of articles in the Los Angeles *Free Press*, 17 January 1974–3 January 1975.
12. Seldes, *Legacy of Mark Rothko*, pp. 259–60.
13. Robert Rosenblum, *Frank Stella* (Harmondsworth, Middx: Penguin, 1971) p. 52.
14. Andy Warhol, *The Philosophy of Andy Warhol (From A to B and Back Again)* (New York: Harcourt Brace, 1975) p. 148.
15. V. Giallo, quoted on 'Review', BBC2 television, 22 April 1988.
16. Warhol, *Philosophy of Andy Warhol*, p. 145.
17. Ibid., p. 229.
18. H. Adams, *Art of the Sixties* (London: Peerage, 1978; new edn, 1984) p. 76.
19. Kosciuszko, 'Marketing Rebellion', pp. 45–58.

# 7

# Andy Warhol's Velvet Underground

## JOHN SIMONS

This essay is a reading which articulates two texts: a record, *The Velvet Underground and Nico*, and a body of images produced by Andy Warhol. It is a critical analysis of two unwritten (i.e. not written) texts and a demonstration of the mechanisms by which they come to stand for a still unwritten text: New York City in the late 1960s. Let's go back to Roland Barthes. In 'Myth Today', an essay which inhabits very much the same cultural environment as the texts under discussion here, he produced the following diagram:[1]

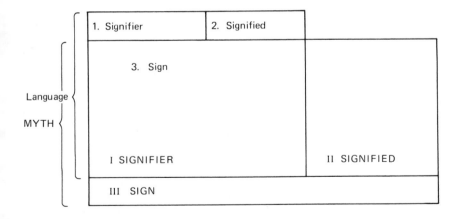

To use this ancient rebus marks me out, I suppose, as a fellow-traveller from an antique land but what I want to say about the Velvet Underground, Warhol's art and New York City will, to some extent, disclose the avant-garde's necessary dependence on tradition, within the economic processes of the art world. In this case an elementary semiotic model which permits a generalisation of the particular operations of the text may not be out of place. In the examples which Barthes himself uses to show his model in action he argues that the phenomenology of the image as concrete utterance or representation constitutes, in the bound structure of the sign, the beginning of a secondary level of signification in which the mythic structure of the signified experience, that thing of which the utterance (or image) is superficially silent, is made manifest. Let us then redraw Barthes's diagram and replace its general semiotic terms with the subjects which form the subject of the present essay:

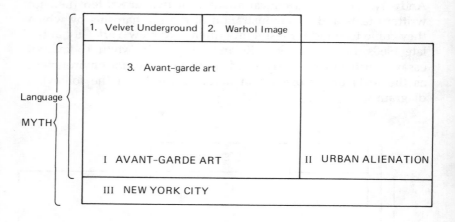

In explication of his work, Barthes points out that while the first term of the first level is strictly a signifier, the sign of which it constitutes a part may be more properly designated *form* as it takes its place in the secondary order of signification.

Thus, avant-garde art becomes the form through, which and by which the *mythic* experience of New York City is spoken. At the second level, Barthes uses the term 'signification' to designate the place of the sign. He is, therefore, able to suggest the ubiquitous, if covert, presence of myth throughout the semiotic system and the mechanism by which it is pushed back up through the signifying chain as the signified becomes apparent through the signifier. The sign as *form* is:

at the same time meaning and form, full on one side and empty on the other. . . . The meaning is already complete, it postulates a kind of knowledge, a past, a memory, a comparative order of facts, ideas, decisions. When it becomes form, the meaning leaves its contingency behind; it becomes impoverished, history evaporates, only the letter remains.[2]

These are poignant phrases, and to anyone familiar with Warhol strangely resonant. They seem redolent of his protestations of automatism and championship of the boring and redundant, the flippant side of existential seriousness, to which we may return.

The above brief disquisition and presentation of a semiotic model is here because of the position and placing of his essay. On the one hand, it is part of a larger text which celebrates a particular urban space and, as such, it will find its way into many different hands; on the other, it is travelling towards the specifically delineated environment of that sector of the academic world which concerns itself with American Studies. Before I continue with the analytic section of the work I want to provide it with an *envoi* which will safeguard it on its perilous journey.

American Studies is a curious and composite beast. It has developed a simultaneous progressivism and a conservatism which hang together in a roughly coherent whole, the institutional validations of which enable the containment of its potentially disintegrative contradictions. When we compare American Studies with one of its chief points of origin, English, there is little doubt that it has largely failed to develop any complex or advanced theoretical base for its work which rises above the fairly loose and no longer schismatic assumption that it is 'inter-disciplinary'. However, those Mayflower pilgrims who left English and History departments, etc., two decades ago and more to set up an American Studies culture complete with chairs and a learned journal have definitely advanced very far down an alternative road which has always presented itself for the radical development of any cultural studies programme – changing the canon. Thus, while English critics of the 1980s may be eavesdropped upon talking Derrida over Dickens and the other texts canonised by the famous dead (at the time of writing, for Derrida substitute Bakhtin or Baudrillard), one may read a humanistic Mickey Mouse, Lone Ranger and, germane here, Campbell's soup tin on the walls of American Studies. My own position on this interesting state of affairs may appear contradictory but I must confess that, while my inclination and training is for the theoretical movements of English, I find in American Studies a genuine commitment of the will to change. This will may perhaps even be exemplified by the kinds of material submitted to this volume. I realise that this is not, in itself, anything new, but in American Studies the aesthetic of mass culture can be taken seriously and not merely as an eccentric appropriation of the ephemeral or a crude attempt to popularise the war horses of traditional critical practice. My own approach to the material here, through conventional semiotics, is not, incidentally, to be construed as an attempt to build a bridge across the gap which I have indicated between two academic discourses. I am trying to provide a species of mnemonic for the difficult process of articulating sound, sight and space in print, bereft as I am of the cassette player and slide projector which are my amanuenses when I lecture on this material in an American Studies department.

*The Velvet Underground and Nico* was released in 1967 and, quite literally, may be seen as the record of a multimedia event: the 'Exploding Plastic Inevitable' and its forerunner 'Andy Warhol, Up-Tight'. This was conceived out of Warhol's 47th Street 'Factory', the ashram of New York pop culture, and taken on a tour of the USA in 1966 and 1967.[3] Little remains as a visual record of the show though there are copious verbal memoirs. Its mix of light-show, dance, film, sculpture and the complex 'deconstructive musicality' (remember that 1967 was the year that Derrida's first wave of publications appeared) of the Velvet Underground led Marshall McLuhan to see in it something of his prophecy of a technologised, mediaful world, the show's polymorphous perversity genuinely becoming an extension of city culture.[4] The McLuhanite dictum that the medium is the message is, it will be noted, strikingly analogous to Barthes's semiotic plan of form as the signifier of myth:

> Electric circuitry profoundly involves men with one another. Information pours upon us, instantaneously and continuously. As soon as information is acquired, it is very rapidly replaced by still newer information. Our electrically-configured world has forced us to move from the bait of data classification to the mode of pattern recognition. We can no longer build serially, block by block, step by step, because instant communication insures that all factors of the environment coexist in a state of active interplay.

We have now become aware of the possibility of arranging the whole human environment as a work of art.[5]

I shall be taking account of McLuhan's implication that serialisation is impossible as it manifests itself in the Velvet Underground's music and Warhol's art, but more generally I want to suggest, provisionally, here that the point about environment as art is expressed in my texts as the microcosmic organisation of an aestheticised and, consequently, mythicised New York City.

To remain faithful to the spirit of the album and to show how the music and the structure of the lyrics constitute a text produced out of New York culture at the time it will be necessary to refer the reader to music that s/he will not hear and to images that s/he will not see and, to an extent, the force of the mixed media is enchained in the act of writing: 'only the letter remains'. Postwar art in New York City had been predominantly characterised, with the notable exception of the 'Boogie-Woogie' paintings of Piet Mondrian, by the New York school, with Jackson Pollock's Abstract Expressionism on one side and the austere classicism of Mark Rothko on the other. By 1963 Roy Lichtenstein, generator of archetypal comic-book images such as 'BRAT', was able to define a new type of art, Pop Art, as 'the use of commercial art as subject matter in painting'.[6] At this time, and in this phase of his many developments, Andy Warhol was the most notable exponent of his type of art, and it is my contention that in the musically serious and heady sounds of the Velvet Underground we hear at work 'Pop Music', that is the use of commercial music as subject-matter, as the band joyfully dissects the chimeral aspirations to romance, love, freedom and beauty of late 1960s commercial pop and subjects the pieces to parody, ironic comment and direct reversal.

The seriousness of Pop Art as art, that is as a medium the dissemination of which is legitimised through the disguised business organisation of salon and gallery, and the ironic paradox of its use of commercial art as subject is brought out best by Warhol himself. Here he is taking part in a three-way discussion with Roy Lichtenstein and Claes Oldenburg:

The young people who know about it [Pop Art] will be the people who are more intelligent and know about art. But the people who don't know about art would like it better because it is what they know. They just don't think about it. It looks like something they know and see every day.[7]

By 1967 he identified the process as having gone one step further:

When Thomas Hoving, the director of the Metropolitan, talked about an exhibit there that included three busts of ancient Egyptian princesses, he referred to them offhandedly as 'The Supremes'. Everybody was part of the same culture now. Pop references let people know that *they* were what was happening, that they didn't have to *read* a book to be part of culture – all they had to do was *buy* it (or a record, or a TV set, or a movie ticket).[8]

Still keeping one eye on McLuhan, note that Warhol did not say that people were part of what was happening but that they 'were' it. This cross-fertilisation of high culture and mass culture is nicely symbolised in Warhol's own mass-production (but not too 'mass') of the image of the Mona Lisa, icon of all that is good and great in western civilisation but now transposed, turned round and tinted, its evanescent smile becoming a sardonic smirk at the commercial bases of fine art.

The bridge between the salon and the street was always illusory and constituted only by temporary combinations of personality. All art is ultimately commercial and Warhol's most characteristic position is a refusal to cover his tracks on the question of economics, summed up in his nose-thumbing reproductions of dollar bills. In one sense, Warhol's work both on the production of *The Velvet Underground and Nico* and on the design of its cover meant that most people could own a Warhol (though, not surprisingly, copies of the original pressing with the vinyl banana skin still stuck to the front change hands at high prices) but it would be naive to see the Pop Art movement as in any sense a democratisation of art, even if it is visually demotic. Remember that Lichtenstein saw Pop Art not as commercial art but as 'the use of commerical art as subject matter in painting'. An indication that this fine humanistic distinction leads to strange bedfellows may be seen best in the career of the late Edie Sedgwick, heiress and descendant of Massachussetts aristocrat R. G. Shaw (Colonel Shaw of Lowell's 'For the Union Dead') and, simultaneously, underground movie star in the 'Factory' and *Vogue* 'Youthquaker'.[9]

The 'it' of which Warhol speaks in his dialogue with Lichtenstein and Oldenburg includes, of course, the commodities which form the subject-matter of his most notorious images (soup cans, Coca Cola bottles) and it is in these images, with their subtle variations of tone and detail, perfectly in the tradition of classical *nature morte*, that we may find enshrined at the base of the art and the organisation of the Velvet Underground's music the metaphor that 'every picture tells a story'. This is a cliché apt for Warhol's relentless exploitation and exploration of the conventional and hackneyed visual detritus of modern consumer culture. In New York City he inhabited its temporary capital and the streets surrounding him constantly replenished the imaginary stock.

In a trivial sense, all prints and paintings may be said to tell the story of their own production through the marks which designate them as having unique status as art, or in the sense that images such as the soup can may be seen as a term in an artistic meta-language which forms the base of a crude and quasi-allegorical fabulation: telling tales on New York City. Warhol, though, is a subtle storyteller. Take, for example, his image of fellow Pop artists Robert Rauschenberg, sometimes known as 'A Texan'. Here the multiply-reproduced scenes from the subject's life are organised in such a way as to stand in a straightforward temporal sequence, the piece presenting us with a clear and unproblematic narrative which it imposes firmly on its imagery. As his work developed Warhol proceeded to distort time in order to place the burdens of constructing a narrative on the viewer, to abdicate the responsibilities of authorship. Thus, in *Sixteen Jackies* (1964) or *Jackie* (1965) natural temporal sequence is disturbed and subtle tonal variation in a multiply-reproduced image gives a sense of movement and change. The technique is analogous to that employed in the eight-hour record of the Empire State Building made with a fixed camera in 1964 or series such as '13 Most Beautiful Women', '13 Most Beautiful Boys', or '50 Fantastics and Personalities' in which 100-foot sequences from a fixed camera are edited together in series of barely changing portraits.

The impulse to narrative which does not operate on a principle of simple causality or 'natural' temporal sequence is exemplified in the structure of the Velvet Underground's album. I propose to see the text as a dismembered song-cycle which offers the reader a variety of possible reassemblies. It depicts the passage of time and the potential of life in New York City through a variation of modes. Notably, the narrative proceeds through contrasts of gender and the switching between musical styles which I shall characterise as 'rock' and 'lyrical'. There is a unity but this is, characteristically, imposed by an ambiguity, a pun on the polyvalent nature of heroin / heroine represented by the strong female figure who stalks through the album.

The lyrical 'Sunday Morning' opens the narrative and appears to fix it in a conventional time-scheme serving as a preface to the unlyrical ballad 'Waiting for the Man'. The text switches abruptly from female to male and from lyric to rock. The reader, seduced by the dreaminess of 'Sunday Morning', is plunged into the exciting violence of the quest for heroin in Harlem. In his remarks recorded on *Live at Max's Kansas City* (1970), Lou Reed characterised this song ironically as 'a tender folk song from the early '50's about the love between a man and a subway'.[10] Through Reed's remarks during this session we have confirmed the idea that the mood of 'Sunday Morning' and its content does not necessarily imply a front-stopped temporal sequence: 'This is a song about . . . oh when you've done something so sad and you wake up the next day and remember it.'[11] The album refuses the easy strategy of beginning with the morning alarm bell. The world is, literally, all before it and the reader must take the responsibility of engaging with a structure which is disarticulated both in itself and with its 'natural' external referents.

In 'Femme Fatale' the encounter with heroin as a woman who has 'come by her reputation through cool deliberation rather than an accident of fate' is consummated and the ambivalence of the representation – literal or allegorical – is continued into what is certainly the Velvet Underground's masterpiece, 'Venus in Furs'.[12] Named after Sacher-Masoch's novel and performed live in the 'Exploding Plastic Inevitable' with Factory person (and, subsequently, historian of the Velvet Underground) Gerard Malanga kissing the boots of another Warhol actress, Mary Woronov, this song in many ways sums up the Velvet Underground's assault on popular music: their use, to go back to Lichtenstein, of commercial art as the subject. The Velvet Underground derived their name from a pornographic book, the cover of which made the following claim:

Here is an incredible book. It will shock and amaze you. But as a documentary on the sexual corruption of our age, it is a *must* for every thinking adult.[13]

Such disingenuous disclaimers are a typical strategy of pornography but the choice of the name (apart from the practical spin-off of using the then mantra word 'underground') is also typical of the Velvet Underground's constant exploration of the kinds of relationship marginalised by society. Compare 'Venus in Furs' with the interactions lyricised by the Beatles on *Sergeant Pepper* or even by The Doors on *The Doors*, both albums that struck out new ways for rock music and both also released in 1967. In both cases the drama seems placed in the domain of teenage rebellion, familial discomfort and, quaint phrase, the 'generation gap'. The adolescent fantasies of both contrast strikingly with the harsh and lonely world of the Velvet Underground, conditioned as it was by the alienation and isolation of a huge city. Perhaps the album's packaging bespeaks this difference of *Weltanschauung* most eloquently. How callow seems the psychedelic Gothic of Peter Blake's montage for the cover of *Sergeant Pepper* compared with Warhol's pristine banana offering the consumer the chance to peel away its vinyl skin and expose the flesh.[14] It is essentially that difference which has been recently been pointed out by Robert Pattison: 'While the Turtles's sappy love song 'Happy Together' topped the charts in 1967, the Velvet Underground were recording their homage to Sacher-Masoch, "Venus in Furs".'[15]

The cycle continues with 'Run Run Run', a song about buying drugs in Union Square, Manhattan. While this song is, to my mind, one of the least musically interesting items in the cycle and adds only perfunctory support to an already established vocabulary of themes and procedural modes it is important for the general fact of the album's articulation with New York City. It is not just a question of specific topography – the movement of speakers around the city could be traced with almost the accuracy of Bloom's stroll round Dublin – nor is it that the celebration of street life and the driving rhythm create an almost naturalistic surface; it is the song's unambiguous introduction of that milieu into the cycle at a point where, to return to our original semiotic model, the mythic level pushes through the work as the expressive content of the formal strategies of the test. The Velvet Underground are unashamed celebrants of New York:

They were the only band who spoke for the city, delineating so accurately the love–hate relationship it inspired. New York was for the Velvet Underground what Paris was for Baudelaire. In each case the city provided an existential justification for their creations.[16]

When the 'Exploding Plastic Inevitable' appeared in Chicago in June 1966 the *Chicago Daily News* recognised the experience's roots in both Baudelaire and McLuhan:

> Warhol has indeed put together a total environment, but it is an assemblage that vibrates with menace, cynicism and perversion. . . . The flowers of evil are in full bloom with Exploding Plastic Inevitable.[17]

Nowhere is the sense of New York City and the Velvet Underground protagonist as amphetamine-loaded *flâneur* on 42nd Street clearer than in 'Run Run Run'. The important point is that in 1967, when *The Velvet Underground and Nico* appeared, young men went west (some in more ways than one), and while San Francisco became the spiritual metropolis of the Age of Aquarius the Velvet Underground sweated it out in New York celebrating not love and peace but sadism and heroin, not beauty and the environment but concrete and cars. Their foray to the San Francisco Fillmore makes amusing reading:

> Paul was saying everything he could to offend Bill Graham's San Francisco sensibility, but in the end it was dropping the tangerine peels on the Fillmore floor – which he had done totally unconsciously – that brought on the showdown . . . I don't remember his exact words but he started yelling – things like: 'You disgusting germs from New York! Here we are trying to clean up everything, and you come out here with your disgusting minds and *whips* – !'[18]

As Paul Morrissey said on the way home: 'There's a lot to be said for the hardcore New York degenerates.'[19] This fierce attachment to the idea and ethos of New York, to its myth, marks their music out from another, specifically West Coast, bands of the time. The Velvet Underground did not participate in 1967: they made it the subject of their art. For the children of a City State which wears alienation as a medal of honour what other course was there?

Against all this it must also be said that art has an effect on its consumers and that the album undoubtedly contains an element of moral ambiguity which provides an ironic commentary running against the grain of the urban *Songspiel*, converting it from a paeon to underground life into a salvationist homily on the dangers of the street. The catalogue of the young and beautiful dead among Warhol's associates of this time makes depressing reading and Warhol himself almost fell victim to his system when he was shot. Edie Sedgwick, who died at 28 years old, probably told the truth when she observed that: 'Warhol really fucked up a great many people's – young people's – lives.'[20] It could also be said that this kind of damage always results where art is confused with life. As Sterling Morrison, one of the Velvets, said:

> The real damage, particularly in New York, has been done through the cult of personality. Rock fans have taken heroin thinking Lou Reed took heroin, forgetting that the character in the song wasn't necessarily Lou Reed.[21]

Perhaps it comes down to saying that only good literary critics survive on the street and, taking literary criticism to mean a wide competence in disparate sign systems, this is probably true. Even so, it seems that in his role of director of the 'Exploding Plastic Inevitable' Warhol shifted out of Pop Art and into Performance Art, using other human beings as his material: a Stewart Brisley drowning his own audience. Warhol's absolute refusal to take responsibility for his art dates from very early in his career. Here he is in conversation about 'Race Riot' an image of violence against black demonstrators:

OLDENBURG: When I see you repeat a race riot, I don't see it as a political statement but rather as an expression of indifference to your subject.

WARHOL: It is indifference.

GLASER: Isn't it significant that you chose that particular photograph rather than a thousand others?

WARHOL: It just caught my eye.

OLDENBURG: You didn't deliberately choose it because it was a 'hot' photograph?

WARHOL: No.[22]

As an aside on this debate it is curious to see, given McLuhan's imminent intervention as a commentator on the underground, the conscious appropriation by a Pop Artist of the seminal McLuhanite term 'hot', and his apparently using it in a McLuhanite fashion.

From 'Run Run Run' the album shifts back into lyrical mode with 'All Tomorrow's Parties': time here chopped into the future. This song further establishes the detailed urban ambience. Warhol himself found time to comment on his song quite explicitly:

> 'All Tomorrow's Parties' was the name of a song the Velvets used to do at the Dom when the Lower East Side was beginning to shake off its immigrant status and get hip – 'What costumes shall the poor girl wear / To all tomorrow's parties. . . .' I really liked that song.[23]

At a superficial level, the narrative concerns the inability of the alienated New York poor to burst into the argent revelry of the counter culture, partying 'in a subway . . . in the Statue of Liberty', but in fact there is a complex irony at work, for those who understand the text's place in a particular sector of city life at the time:

> In those days everything was extravagant. You had to be rich to afford pop clothes from boutiques like Paraphernalia or from designers like Tiger Morse. Tiger would go down to Klein and Mays and buy a two-dollar dress, tear off the ribbon and flower, bring it up to her shop and sell it for four hundred dollars. She had a way with accessories too. She'd paste a ditsy on something from Woolworth's and charge fifty dollars for it.[24]

This is precisely the kind of culture which William Burroughs prophesied two years after the event:

> The chic thing is to dress in expensive tailor made rags . . . loud cheap pimp suits that turn out to be not so cheap the loudness is a harmony of colours only the very best Poor Boy shops can turn out.[25]

Here there is a contradiction between popular culture and its milieu: the Factory drawing together an eclectic gathering of New York society under the aegis of commercialised high art. This seems an inevitable phenomenon when the images of mass consumption became specifically aestheticised. Take, for example, David Oxtoby's portraits of rock and roll singers: the heroes of a proletarian culture in a world which their admirers cannot afford to enter. There is, however, an essential difference between Warhol and Oxtoby: while the latter's portraits of Elvis Presley retain, through their painterliness, the charismatic uniqueness and the maximised commodity value of the gallery painting, the smooth images generated by Warhol appropriate the technique and style of the mass-produced while losing none of their fetishised value. It is the cheap dress sold dear all over again. Some might see this as dishonest. Personally I think that we should understand it as a rational development of the role of the artist in a consumer society. The work of art becomes an ergonomic icon for a frenetic urban market where the unique talismanic value of the painting creates commercial cynicism among buyers who are investors rather than connoisseurs. In *Bomb Culture*, a book which is very much of its time, Jeff Nuttall tried to explain the difference in these matters between Britain and the USA:

> He (Warhol) stood for all the qualities which marked off the American Underground from its English counterpart, for hip exclusiveness, for huge commercial success set against the English firm socialist attitudes.[26]

This is terribly pious but, in some ways, it is an accurate summation. It is also naive, for whatever socialist attitudes may or may not have been held by the working-class painters emerging from, say, St Martin's in the 1960s, the economic base of British art can hardly said to have been changed by them. Speaking of Warhol's critique of the urban image Peter Conrad makes much the same point as my own but from a different perspective:

> His paintings are death notices for the image, which he despoils of aura and individuality – which he metaphorically slays as nature and resurrects as mechanism. The face of Marilyn Monroe is to him as potentially plural as a box of soap flakes or a Campbell's soup can. No single life matters, since humanity can be mechanically reproduced and mechanically exterminated.[27]

In 'Heroin' the album's structuring theme comes to the fore.

Heroin as a drug becomes totally confused with the female figure: it becomes 'a wife'. The text begins its slow wind-down to death and silence. The rock and lyric modes become increasingly intermingled and a new element enters which appears radically to deny the possibility of any reality principle. When we look back through the narrative we discover this in other alternately celebratory and mournful songs. As we reassemble the narrative we find the death instinct encased, from the beginning, in the pleasure principle, like a ruby in the skull of a toad.

'There She Goes Again' has been characterised as a 'tough song about a tough chick'.[28] In isolation it is a solid piece of rock and roll which well deserves such laconic praise. In juxtaposition with 'Heroin' however, the quasi-moral element to which I have just alluded becomes clearly apparent. The sense of a potential identity between the white drug and the elusive (allusive?) seductress is further enforced by the lyrical 'I'll Be Your Mirror' in which the main thrust of the song and the voluntary disintegration and self-annihilation which the title promises, together with the implication of a collapse of gender difference, is counterpointed by a refrain 'reflect what you are'. A play on the reflexive possibilities of the verb 'reflect' offers the inhabitant of the cycle's textualised New York a moment of pause before the drop into the final catastrophe.

The disaster begins with the extraordinary 'Black Angel's Death Song', where musical complexity strives with increasingly garbled lyrics which aspire to the condition of white noise. As in the urban environment, the senses are so loaded with information that the resulting text is silent: 'We are surrounded by emptiness but it is an emptiness filled with signs.'[29] This peculiarly urban 'silent noise' is developed in the culminating 'European Son', a song dedicated to Delmore Schwartz with whom Reed had a close relationship when he was a student at Syracuse University – 'My Daedalus to your Bloom' – another example of the peculiar contact between high culture and mass culture which the Velvet Underground achieved, if only in illusory fashion.[30] The song has the fewest words of any on the album yet at eight minutes long it is by far the most extensive piece. The words are punctuated by a crash which ends all vocal participation and leaves the world to the drum and guitar. The cycle comes to an end on a paradox of noisy silence. It does not settle for the lyricism of 'Sunday Morning' and its offer of a comfortable finish with all loose ends happily tied. Instead it cuts free of any imposed structure and achieves an unhappy quietude forged by its own distorted logic, significant of loneliness in the street and idiotic alienation in one of the world's most populous cities.

The text offers a narrative which pulls the audience in contrary directions. It operates through contrast and through the generation of a cut-up time-scheme. It is simple to take the idea of the city and to read the text as a fundamentally topographical celebration of a morally duplicitous New York City but this kind of reading cries out for insertion into a wider scheme. The question 'what does it mean?' is capable of being clearly answered by resort to hermeneutic paraphrase, but if that is all we want then analysis is superfluous and inferior to the experience of the art work itself – *si monumentum requiris circumspice*. In tackling the more significant question 'how does it mean?' I have attempted to integrate the text (through a very lightly imposed analysis) into a general semiotic model of the culture in which it is embedded. It thus becomes an almost undifferentiated meaning in itself and detailed interpretation of its parts does not add to our sense of its significance. In Barthes's semiotics, as I have said, the idea of the signified as the form of mythic discourse seems neatly coterminous with McLuhan's medium as message. In writing about a text which is so rooted in the 1960s I have found that these rather outmoded theories fitted like a long-discarded glass slipper.

Nietzsche wrote that: 'Only as an aesthetic phenomenon can the world be eternally justified.'[31] If the Velvet Underground are seen as the mythographers of a world then their sceptical aestheticisation of New York becomes, together with Warhol's images, a peculiarly accurate and poignant reflection of their culture. In Nietzsche's terms we might wish to see the text as the dynamic representation of Apollo's struggle with Dionysus turning to nausea in the crash of 'European Son'. The album achieves its integrity through this dynamism and its projection of the culture of which it forms a part. It becomes a critique of New York City and the consumer capitalism for which the city itself acts, at a third and highly general level of semiosis, as both form and signifier. Plainly, the analysis of Pop Art and the representation of a mythic New York might be seen as an analysis of a post-modernist text, not least at those points where the strategies of the narrative are to collapse the positive terms of gender and 'normal' sexuality into a plethora of difference, where the chief discursive mode operates only through its reference to another discourse which it parodies and undermines, and where the sense of historical development (presented here through narrative time) is broken up. However, although *The Velvet Underground and Nico* might appear to exemplify post-modernist textuality it might also be said to refuse post-modernism's assumptions about the eclipse of high art by mass culture. On the contrary, mass culture is slyly dragged into the realm of high art by a text which hides like a chameleon on a market stall. If post-modernist logic is truly the cultural logic of capital then perhaps, and most unexpectedly, the Velvet Underground appear more subversive than even they believed and New York becomes a meeting place for all those tendencies which might collectively construct an oppositional culture.[32] If post-modernism privileges difference and destabilises canonical meaning it does so in the interest of creating out of the social margin a newly homogenised market-place and of bringing a previously recalcitrant public of 'individuals' into the fold of consumerism. The broken life of New York as depicted by the Velvet Underground, and the drug addicts, paupers, sado-masochists, *femmes fatales* and 'hard core degenerates' who throng its mythic streets and refuse the erasure of difference in their demand for the wholly personal and antisocial, may coexist with Wall Street without being fetishised (ironic word!) by it. Twenty-one years on (I am writing in 1988) this possibility may very well have vanished, even as a myth, but the Velvet Underground testify to its existence and to the difficulty of controlling, even through electronic media, the modern urban environment as the global village becomes the global market and the insignificance of centre makes even New York City dispensable.

NOTES

1. Roland Barthes, 'Myth Today', in *Mythologies*, trans. A. Lavers (London: Paladin, 1971). The diagram is reproduced on p. 115.
2. Ibid., p. 117.
3. The best monograph on Warhol is J. Coplans, *Andy Warhol* (New York: Weidenfeld & Nicolson, 1971). His analyses of Warhol's techniques are intelligent and sound. V. Bockris and G. Malanga, *Up-Tight, The Velvet Underground Story* (London: Omnibus, 1983) provides a mass of documentation of Warhol's connection with the Velvets.
4. D. Hill, Obituary for Nico, Independent, 25 July 1988, p. 26; Marshall McLuhan, *The Medium is the Message* (New York: Routledge & Kegan Paul, 1967).

5. McLuhan, *The Medium is the Message*, quoted from Bockris and Malanga, *Up-Tight*, p. 42.
6. G. R. Swenson, 'What is Pop Art?', in *Roy Lichtenstein*, ed. J. Coplans (London: Penguin, 1973) pp. 52–5, p. 52.
7. B. Glaser, 'Oldenburg, Lichtenstein, Warhol: A Discussion', in *Roy Lichtenstein*, ed. Coplans, pp. 55–66, p. 65.
8. Andy Warhol and P. Hackett, *POPism* (London: Hutchinson, 1981) p. 207.
9. On Edie Sedgwick see J. Stein, *Edie*, ed. G. Plimpton (London: Jonathan Cape, 1982).
10. Bockris and Malanga, *Up-Tight*, p. 120. The recording was made on 23 August 1970 but not officially released until 1972.
11. Ibid., p. 120.
12. Hill, Obituary.
13. Bockris and Malanga, *Up-Tight*, p. 21.
14. George Melly, *Revolt into Style* (Harmondsworth, Middx: Penguin, 1972) pp. 127–8 speaks of Blake's work in rather more complimentary terms and also draws attention to Warhol.
15. Robert Pattison, *The Triumph of Vulgarity* (New York: Oxford University Press, 1987) pp. 116–17.
16. Bockris and Malanga, *Up-Tight*, p. 76.
17. Ibid., p. 50.
18. Warhol and Hackett, *POPism*, p. 170.
19. Ibid., p. 171.
20. Stein, *Edie*, p. 302.
21. Bockris and Malanga, *Up-Tight*, p. 74.
22. *Roy Lichtenstein*, ed. Coplans, pp. 65–6.
23. Andy Warhol, *From A to B and Back Again* (London: Cassell, 1975) p. 25.
24. Ibid., p. 25.
25. William Burroughs, *The Wild Boys*, quoted in D. Hebdige, *Subculture: The Meaning of Style* (London: Methuen, 1979) p. 23.
26. Jeff Nuttall, *Bomb Culture* (London: Macgibbon & Kee, 1968) p. 170.
27. Peter Conrad, *The Art of the City* (New York: Oxford University Press, 1984) p. 221.
28. Bockris and Malanga, *Up-Tight*, p. 74.
29. H. Lefebvre, *Everyday Life in the Modern World*, quoted in Hebdige, *Subculture*, p. 117.
30. Pattison, *Triumph of Vulgarity*, p. 205.
31. F. Nietzsche, *The Birth of Tragedy*, trans. W. Kaufmann, in *Basic Writings of Nietzsche* (New York: Random House, 1968) variations on the remark are on pp. 22, 52 and 141.
32. On post-modernism see F. Jameson, 'Postmodernism, or the Cultural Logic of Late Capitalism', *New Left Review*, 146 (1984) pp. 53–92 and F. Lyotard, *The Post-Modern Condition* (Manchester: Manchester University Press, 1984).

# 8

# Harlem Street Speakers in the 1930s

## ROMA BARNES

Strolling through Harlem one summer's evening in 1931, journalist Henry Lee Moon came upon a familiar sight: 'Here on the corner of the highways and back alleys you may hear lectures on such sundry subjects as religion, politics and race relations. For with the coming of summer we have again with us the perennial soapboxer.'[1]

By then, street speakers addressing crowds from boxes, auto-fenders and step-ladders, were an accepted part of Harlem life. They were, according to out-of-town newspapers, 'part of that general air of cosmopolitan liberalism that is peculiar to Harlem'. They symbolised that 'freedom, independence!' that a migrant generation of Southern Afro-Americans and Caribbean blacks had come to New York City to find.[2]

The 1930s were to be the heyday of street speaking. In the midst of the Depression, these self-educated orators mobilised Harlemites to march, picket and demonstrate on local, national and inter-national issues. According to a contributor to a periodical published by a local tenants' league, they gave Harlem a 'courageous and practical type of leadership' that the black establishment could not provide.[3]

It was, though, a short-lived heyday. By the following decade, street speaking was in decline. Journalists and novelists acknowl-edged its former importance but portrayed it unsympathetically. The speakers who attracted most attention in the 1940s were nationalists whose chauvinism was tinged with anti-Semitism and who were linked, largely unfairly, with pro-Japanese and pro-Nazi sentiment.[4]

The virulent ethnocentrism of the nationalist speakers, although shorn of any fascist sympathies, is most vividly described in Ralph Ellison's *Invisible Man* (1952) in the figure of the flamboyant Ras

106

the Exhorter. Ras appeals to Harlemites to 'organise black, BLACK'. He cries for vengeance against whites – 'Blood calls for blood'. And he enacts his pledge in a night of rioting, when he appears, transformed as 'Ras the Destroyer'.[5]

In this novel, and in Carl Offord's *The White Face* (1943), the street speakers are shown harping on Harlem's social and economic ills and exposing the nerve ends of ethnic relationships in the community. They address crowds that are volatile and on the verge of violence. They are the harbingers of catastrophe.[6]

This alarming picture had a basis in reality. Harlem in the 1930s was racially sensitive and turbulent. There were riots in 1935 and 1943, in which crowds, aroused by rumours of white brutality against blacks, fought and stoned the police and smashed and looted local stores. After the riots, official investigations fixed, for the first time, the image of the ghetto as a proscribed and deprived world in a state of 'emotional tension'.[7]

To this extent, the speakers were seen by their contemporaries, for good or ill, as voicing Harlem's grievances and reflecting Harlem's mood. But they may have done more. Reverend Adam Clayton Powell Jr, an important participant in Harlem agitation in the 1930s, saw the events in which the speakers had played a part as the stirring of a militant black populism. He wrote, in *Marching Blacks* (1945), that in the Depression black people had 'learned as a group to move under their own power'.[8]

August Meier and Elliott Rudwick, in a historical survey of Afro-American non-violent direct action, recognise the 1930s both as a time of an unprecedented scale of activity in northern cities and as a time of black working- and lower-class participation. Although they accept the influence of 'outside' radical organisations, notably the Communist Party, they too argue that black direct action was 'essentially an indigenous creation of the Negro community'.[9]

This present essay, by examining street speaking, especially the nationalist speakers, looks at the origins and development of this independent movement – 'the rise of the black common man', as Powell put it – in Harlem, one of the black communities involved. It sheds light on a tenacious Afro-American cultural form which was a link in a plebeian black nationalist tradition that stretched from Marcus Garvey to Malcolm X.

Harlem streets were not, except in winter, just a means of getting from one place to another. They were important venues for social life, as in other poor districts of the city. Women met and talked on the stoops, men 'hung out' on the corners and children used the streets as their playground. The streets were a means of livelihood for pedlars, entertainers and folk doctors, whose numbers were increased by the privations of the Depression.

Not all street life was legal or desirable: 'numbers runners' collecting bets and traders in 'hot stuff' (stolen goods) were tolerated; but prostitution, drunkenness and robbery made some streets uncomfortable and dangerous, especially at night.[10]

Yet there was considerable pride in Harlem that was also expressed on the streets. Black churches, clubs and lodges held frequent parades with bands, uniforms and regalia, which, along with funeral processions, were not only spectacles that invited the participation of onlookers but an informal way of celebrating the community and marking its boundaries.[11]

During the 1910s and 1920s these boundaries had been set ever wider as Harlem revelled in its reputation as the 'race capital': a showplace of Afro-American social mobility with its own social, business and civic life.[12] These formative years fixed the hub of the black community at a group of blocks around 135th Street, where New York's major black institutions had their premises: the YMCA, the YWCA, the New York Urban League and the Harlem branch of the New York Public Library among them.

It was here, on street corners on Lenox and Seventh Avenues between 134th and 137th Streets, that Harlem's first secular speakers held forth on the eve of America's entry into the First World War. Although they were radicals, they shared the prevailing faith in self-improvement and racial progress.[13]

The previous form of street speaking in black New York had been religious. Churchmen sometimes preached on the streets or held tented revivals on empty lots. But those who relied on the streets for their congregations were typically wandering preachers or members of millenarian sects, for whom street speaking was an expression of their hostility to the established black churches and their commitment to the salvation of the poor.[14]

Although the radical speakers of the 1910s were equally antagonistic to Afro-American leadership and intent on the conversion of black working people, their grounding in street oratory took place in the ranks of New York's socialists.

The founder, and the acknowledged greatest exponent, of secular street speaking in Harlem was Hubert Harrison, an immigrant from the Virgin Islands. He served his apprenticeship as an orator with the Socialist Party and 'electrified' his audiences with anti-capitalist lectures on down-town street corners on Wall Street and at Madison and Union Squares. He was employed by the Socialist Party as an organiser in Harlem, but he left them in 1914 and, on Harlem street corners, called for a 'New Negro Manhood Movement' that would free blacks from the 'grip of the old time leaders', who were prepared to use only muted protest and litigation to secure black rights.

In 1920 Harrison joined Marcus Garvey's Universal Negro Improvement Association (UNIA) and served as editor of the organisation's newspaper, *The Negro World*, from 1920 to 1921. After 1923, he worked as a part-time lecturer for New York City's Board of Education until his death, at the age of 44, in 1927.[15]

Harrison was largely self-educated but he could talk, and write, on 'philosophy, psychology, economics, literature, astronomy or the drama' as well as social and political issues. Race pride and self-assertion were his common themes. As a contemporary said of Harrison's lectures: 'he told the Negro to think for himself'; he urged black people to release the 'mighty spring of power' that they had within them; he eulogised black women; and he delighted in exposing 'the countless fallacies of the white race about the Negro and itself'.[16]

He was joined on the Avenues by other young 'New Negro' orators, many were Caribbean-born and some were authors, editors and pamphleteers like himself. But the New Negro movement split into two camps in the 1920s. One emphasised black nationalism and spoke on behalf of the UNIA. The other was socialist and communist.

Garveyites favoured black business and sought to build separate black economic and political institutions. They advocated the creation of an international racial homeland in Africa freed from white domination but did not adopt an aggressive attitude to the existing political economy. The black socialists and communists advocated an alliance with the white working class, trade unions and radical political parties to reform or overthrow international capitalism and free its colonies.[17]

The UNIA had by far the greater influence among Afro-Americans in the 1920s. But the socialists and communists introduced ideas that must have been a revelation to many ordinary blacks who, at this time, relied on the Bible and a body of folklore and 'common sense' as their most familiar guides to the world and their place in it.

In its emphasis on propaganda, debate and popular education, the 1920s was street speaking's formative period. It established the broad character of black street oratory: criticism of middle-class leadership; a concern with the black economic condition; race assertiveness and a rejection of the passivity of black religion ('that stuff about "he who humbleth himself shall be exalted"', as Harrison put it).[18] These traits were carried forward into the different conditions of the next decade.

After Garvey's deportation in 1927, the UNIA disintegrated and, by the early 1930s, many former Garveyites in Harlem were acting as independent speakers. By then, the great debators of the 1920s had left the Avenues to the care of more rough and ready voices: 'a crop of oratorical aspirants' that the black press charged with an 'utter disregard of history, economics, politics, logic and all other sciences' and with 'brutally butchering the English language'. Eloquence and erudition were now out of place, as the acute distress of the Depression caused education to be replaced by agitation.[19]

The communists were the first to act. They formed the Upper Harlem Council of the Unemployed in 1930 and organised mass demonstrations, eviction resistance and sit-ins at the relief bureaux. They held street meetings and rallies in defence of the 'Scottsboro boys', nine black hobos accused of rape in Alabama, who were being represented by the communist legal organisation, the International Labor Defense. The Communist Party made a determined effort to act on a strategy of interracial solidarity but its important rank and file agitators in Harlem were black. Some were recent defectors from the UNIA.[20]

By 1932, the communists had helped to create a 'radical street culture', through which Harlemites had become willing to confront authority on racial and economic issues and demand a response. However, for the next three years, they remained uncomfortably on the periphery of a street campaign which brought together race and employment with powerful immediacy: a boycott of Harlem's white-owned stores to secure black employment as sales assistants.

Most of the businesses in Harlem in 1930, as in other ghettos, were owned by whites and very few employed blacks other than as cleaners, porters and lift attendants. The 'Don't Buy Where You Can't Work' campaigns began in Chicago in 1929 and spread to other cities, including New York, as the Depression deepened.[21]

The instigator of the boycott in Harlem was Sufi Abdul Hamid, a peripatetic street speaker who had been prominent in the Chicago events. His past was obscure. 'A huge, statuesque figure', habitually dressed in a turban, Sam Browne belt, cape and high boots, he dramatised his militant racial attitude by his adopted 'Egyptian' identity, his religion and his military dress.[22]

The Sufi, with the eclecticism of the autodidact, combined elements of street speaking that had previously been discrete: the black millenarian pursuit of a racially assertive religion, the persona of the conjure-man and the tactics of a labour organiser. In New York, he set up the Oriental, Occidental, Scientific and Philosophical Society and began picketing on Harlem's main shopping thoroughfare, 125th Street, in 1932. His speeches were a blend of sacred references, street profanities and fierce invective. He urged blacks to organise themselves into a 'gigantic and cohesive body' and to make use of 'the weapon of labor, picketing, as the best and quickest means of obtaining results'.[23]

He made little progress. His greatest achievement was to shame more prominent New York City blacks into action. In 1934, a community coalition was formed – the Citizen's League for Fair Play (CLFP) – with the young Rev. John H. Johnson of St Martin's Protestant Episcopal Church at its head.[24]

The CLFP decided to picket Blumstein's, a prestigious family business on 125th Street: and, to organise the picketing, it turned to the street orators. It avoided the Sufi and recruited two nationalist speakers, Arthur Reid and Ira Kemp of the African Patriotic League (APL). In July 1934, after nearly two months of picketing, Blumstein's agreed to appoint thirty-four black sales staff in the following two months and to add others as 'business conditions will warrant'.[25]

But jubilation among the boycotters did not last long. The Sufi continued to picket Blumstein's because he had been excluded from the CLFP boycott and agreement: and the CLFP Picket Committee, led by Reid and Kemp, broke away from the CLFP when the CLFP's leadership recommended light-skinned middle-class young women for the new positions at the store.[26]

The CLFP leadership then withdrew from the campaign, leaving both the Picket Committee and the Sufi mounting pickets throughout Harlem to secure employment for the unemployed members of their own organisations, until, within a year, their activities were stopped by court injunctions which ruled that the picketing was not part of a 'bona fide' labour dispute. By then, Reid and Kemp had achieved notoriety on Harlem streets.[27]

Arthur Reid, a man of Harrison's generation, was a Barbadian, who came to New York in 1917. He was a veteran street speaker and a former youth leader in the UNIA. He founded the APL with Kemp in 1932 to persuade blacks to establish and patronise their own businesses.[28] He taught a strident Harlem parochialism.

Reid believed in Harlem as a black people's 'territory' where 'their chests were well expanded'.[29] He had a vision of Harlem as a 'great Negro industrial city'. And he welcomed the Depression: 'the old methods of getting jobs', he remembered, with distaste, 'was to approach the so-called good white people . . . and proceed to beg for what was termed "Negro jobs" . . . so-called domestic jobs'. The economic collapse had made even these jobs hard to find and so Reid hoped that, for the sake of survival, blacks would set up in business and create 'work and opportunities for themselves instead of waiting on others'.[30]

To Reid, the Jobs Campaign was a fight for control and independence: for economic power in Harlem. He saw the sales assistant posts as a means to acquire business experience which would enable blacks to compete against and eventually oust white business in the ghetto.[31]

The boycott's critics, including the communists and socialists, saw its encouragement of black parochialism as the main danger. They pointed out that most blacks were employed outside Harlem. They would not be helped by the boycott and, if whites replied in kind, might even suffer as a result of it. The critics also feared that the boycott would incite violence between black and white and would inflame hostility to other ethnic groups.[32]

It was hard for the nationalist speakers to avoid inter-ethnic hostility, since business in Harlem was concentrated in the hands of Italian, Greek and Jewish Americans. Even before the boycott, the APL had fought, sometimes literally, to break Italian-American domination of the local pushcart markets and install black hucksters.[33] But it was the Sufi, with his unrestrained racist slurs, who caused panic among black community leaders.

The Sufi reserved his worst abuse for the Jews. Allegations of his anti-Semitism were published in New York's Jewish papers and were raised in court when he was tried on a charge of breach of the peace in October 1934. He was acquitted but branded as the 'Harlem Hitler' – a name of which, to begin with, he was not too ashamed.[34]

Inter-ethnic antagonism was expected. But the appointment of the new employees at Blumstein's exposed divisions in the black community itself. The CLFP leadership wanted the employment of 'race ambassadors'. The young women it recommended were not only well educated and well connected but least obtrusive in appearance, as the street speakers bluntly pointed out. Few, if any, of the new employees had walked the picket line.[35]

Reid and Kemp had a personal interest at stake: their followers expected some reward for their vigil on the streets. It was also a matter of principle. For, as Kemp once said, they had taken to the streets because of 'the suffering that was the lot of the people'.[36] Now the middle class was using a community struggle for its own advancement.

The street speakers saw themselves as the voice of the black man in the street. They were also the voice of youth. Ira Kemp, a migrant from Georgia, had come to New York in 1922. He was 32 in 1934.[37] The Sufi was much the same age and, according to Claude McKay, had a following among high-school graduates.[38]

The militance of youth found another expression on the night of 19 March 1935, when a rumour that a black boy had been assaulted in a 125th Street store caused a riot. The speakers were not directly responsible but there was a feeling in Harlem that they had contributed to a sense of resentment among Harlemites.[39] The pattern of the rioting showed some affinity with the parochialism of the nationalist orators, for it was the immediate symbols of white power and intrusion in the ghetto, the police and the stores, that were the targets of the crowd's assault.

When the Sufi began a picket of Lerner's on 125th Street in June 1935, claiming to be part of a fictitious Afro-American Federation of Labor, the merchant sought an injunction against him, arguing that to deny the injunction 'may tend to lead to further race riots'.[40] Of all the street speakers, the Sufi was most readily identified by the white merchants, conservative black opinion and the communists as dangerous, because of his anti-Semitism.[41] Following his trial in January 1935, on a charge of preaching atheism, and a deportation hearing in June 1935 as a suspected illegal immigrant, he finally gave way and abandoned the boycott.[42]

The riot helped to curb picketing but it gave the speakers unprecedented platforms at the hearings of two commissions that were set up in response to it: the Mayor's Commission on Social and Economic Conditions in Harlem (1935) and the New York State Temporary Commission on the Condition of the Urban Colored Population (1935–8). These hearings, by publicly examining the ramifications of discrimination in Harlem and in New York City as a whole, indirectly encouraged both the nationalist and communist speakers, broadened their interests and suggested some common ground in their struggle to improve conditions in Harlem.[43]

In 1935, Italian aggression against Ethiopia presented itself as an issue on which the communists could form a 'united front' with the nationalists and yet hope to avoid the provocation of the boycott campaign.

Ethiopia had long been eulogised by Afro-Americans as the cradle of civilisation. The phrase from the Psalms, 'Ethiopia shall soon stretch forth her hands unto God', had been interpreted as a biblical promise of liberation for all black people, in Africa and the New World.[44] And, in the twentieth century, Ethiopia's name was kept alive by historical journalism, commonly used by the street speakers to arouse blacks to pride in their racial heritage.[45]

In March 1935, the communists, in alliance with the Central Division of the UNIA, set up the Provisional Committee for the Defense of Ethiopia (PCDE). They deferred to the UNIA's request that only blacks should attend the PCDE's meetings and Captain A. L. King of the Central Division was elected the committee's chairman. In the following months, pro-Ethiopian groups mushroomed in Harlem; in November 1935, a new federation, United Aid for Ethiopia, was formed. This, like the PCDE, was heavily reliant on the communists.[46]

Both committees, supported also by black professionals and churchmen, lobbied Washington DC, European governments and the League of Nations and collected funds for medical supplies. They emphasised alliance with white anti-fascists, particularly

Italian-Americans. More influential on the streets, however, were the nationalist orators led, once again, by Reid and Kemp.

The APL was a part of the PCDE until May 1935 when it began a boycott of Italian-American ice dealers and introduced the local ethnic hostility that the PCDE had sought to avoid. Reid and Kemp argued that the Italian assault was the final step for the white race to complete its control over an enfeebled 'colored race'. Money given to local Italians went directly into Mussolini's hands. It was resist or die: and the best way to resist was for blacks to seize economic control of their own communities.[47]

Throughout the summer of 1935 there was loud polemic on the streets: 'Gum beatin' is at its height', wrote Roi Ottley in the *Amsterdam News*, one of Harlem's black weeklies. At the invasion of Ethiopia in October 1935 and the fall of Addis Ababa in May 1936, street audiences were numbered in hundreds. There were flying pickets, scuffles in front of Italian-American businesses and fights with the police.[48]

The police, in the wake of the riot, brought in reinforcements and broke up communist and nationalist meetings alike. There was outrage in the black press and condemnation of the boycott and of Kemp in particular, who was seen as the cause of most of the disturbances.[49] Matters came to a head in July 1936 with a street battle between the crowd and the police in front of the Bella Restaurant on Lenox Avenue and the arrest of a nationalist speaker, Carlos Cooks.

For over a month, the nationalists had been holding meetings outside the restaurant. Not only was it Italian-owned, it was also, the speakers alleged, the scene of gambling and prostitution for white clients. It was another instance of predatory white activity in Harlem according to the speakers.[50]

After the altercation, the police presence in Harlem, that the *Amsterdam News* had already dubbed an 'occupation', became overwhelming.[51] A Harlem delegation demanded urgent action from Mayor LaGuardia. The delegation was headed by a representative of the American Civil Liberties Union and included representatives of the Urban League, the NAACP, the Communist Party and communist-supported organisations; and Reid, Kemp and Cooks.

The delegation wanted curbs on police activity, freedom of assembly and picketing, an end to instances of police intimidation and brutality in Harlem, a clean-up of vice and, among other

demands, the publication and implementation of the recommen-
dations of the report of the Mayor's Commission on the Harlem
riot. LaGuardia agreed to set up a grievance committee to examine
complaints about the police. The speakers, in return, agreed to
close their meetings at 11.15 p.m.[52]

The delegation was a recognition by the speakers that they had
a common interest in protecting their rights, resisting police
suppression and in achieving municipal reform.

In the early 1930s, there had been frequent violent clashes
between speakers over pitches. By the middle of the decade,
despite continuing ideological differences and some heckling and
disruption, more civilised relations seem to have prevailed. The
speakers generally respected each other's right to a hearing and
there was even an informal timetable, with certain speakers
expected to speak at set times at particular locations. The most
prominent nationalists, notably the APL, could now afford to rent
headquarter premises on the Avenues, publish newspapers and
run supporting programmes, such as the APL's Sunday children's
'black history' hour.[53]

In March 1936, at the beginning of a new speaking season, Adam
Clayton Powell Jr offered his own lighthearted advice on the
conduct of street meetings. There should be a 'standard uniform';
a minimum audience of 200; police and fire protection; 'cooperation
with the street cleaning department'; and 'no soapboxer allowed
to speak on atheism, Negro business, "de masses", police brutality
or Ethiopia more than two nights running'. He concluded: 'Failure
to observe all this will result in a walkout. Imagine warm nights
and no soapboxers. The Avenue desolate, broken hearted wives
not knowing on which corner to find their husbands; men plodding
home wearily from work, no place to go.'[54]

To the APL, of course, the Ethiopian campaign was the Jobs
Campaign in another guise; in November 1936, Kemp and Reid
gained a charter for a black trade union – the Harlem Labor Union
(HLU). It was intended to open jobs for blacks in Harlem stores
and act as the black employees' representative.[55] But, for the next
three years, it was in sharp competition with the Negro Labor
Committee (NLC), led by socialist Frank Crosswaith.

A Virgin Islander, Crosswaith had been a trade union organiser

Mama says, "you bring that ladder right home!"

'An inexperienced speaker none too sure of his "platform": E. Simms Campbell's gentle comment on the popularity of street speaking during the Italo-Ethiopian War'.

SOURCE: 'Harlem Sketches' by E. Simms Campbell, New York, *Amsterdam News*, 26 October 1935.

for twenty years and an associate of the New Negro radicals of the 1920s. The NLC was formed in 1935, with backing from the International Ladies Garment Workers Union, to recruit blacks into existing unions and to challenge racial discrimination in the labour movement. It intended to build fraternal links between black and white workers throughout New York and to ensure that jobs won for blacks in Harlem would not be at the expense of white workers in Harlem or Afro-Americans working outside the black community.[56]

The HLU, denounced by Crosswaith as 'spurious', 'racialist' and 'racketeering', was adamantly opposed to organised labour. At his street meetings, Kemp accused the AFL of 'indifference' to black workers and he argued that the CIO was 'more dangerous' still because it organised blacks in their existing jobs and fossilised patterns of job discrimination. In order to obtain jobs for blacks, the HLU was ready to strike-break, to underbid white labour and to offer 'no strike' contracts. These were policies that appealed both to unemployed blacks who knew the past record of white trade unions and to the beleaguered white store-owners.[57]

It was a measure of the HLU's success that Kemp was invited to stand as Fusion–Republican candidate, on LaGuardia's ticket, for the New York State Assembly in 1937. Reid served as Kemp's manager. Kemp pledged that, if elected, he would secure jobs for blacks in 'American industries such as bread corporations, milk corporations'. He would improve the working conditions and wages of black women domestic workers. And he called attention to the Bronx 'slave market', where black women lined up on the streets everyday to be employed as day workers at cut-rates by lower-middle-class Jewish-American housewives.[58]

Kemp came within two hundred and fifty votes of winning the election. It was the first time that a step-ladder orator had come so close to public office. A month later he suffered a fatal heart attack. The Abyssinian Baptist Church was packed for his funeral: and Adam Clayton Powell Jr's funeral oration showed how Kemp had won the admiration even of those, like Powell, who disliked his anti-white and anti-union stance. Powell said: 'If greatness is measured in daring, in leadership – then Ira Kemp died a great man. . . . Here was a man who was called a cheat and a savior . . . but no one ever called him a coward. . . . He did not trust the white man beyond the white of his eyes . . . and ever he sounded the tocsin for black men and women to unite for their own benefit.'[59]

Shortly after Kemp's death, the United States Supreme Court overruled the New York courts and decided that picketing against racial discrimination in employment was legal. The Jobs Campaign was revived by the Greater New York Coordinating Committee led by Adam Clayton Powell Jr. The committee had been organised in February 1938 to protest against employment discrimination throughout New York, particularly by the public utilities. But, once the Supreme Court decision was announced in April, it turned its attention to 125th Street and co-opted Arthur Reid and the HLU.[60]

What followed was almost a repeat of 1934. After extensive picketing, an agreement was reached with the Uptown Chamber of Commerce, the organisation of the larger merchants, in August 1938. It was agreed that a minimum of one-third of any store's workforce should be black, and that a 'placement bureau' for new black employees should be run by the Urban League and the Harlem YMCA and YWCA, black middle-class institutions. No time-limit was set for the implementation of the agreement's provisions.[61]

Disgusted by the agreement, Reid and the HLU continued picketing, creating, according to the *Amsterdam News*, 'a condition of uncertainty and fear among the merchants'. In November, Powell and Reid reached an accord. Reid accepted that the HLU should limit its activities to stores that did not employ blacks in sufficient numbers and to stores that employed blacks that were not members of a union. In effect, the accord left the enforcement of the August agreement in the hands of the HLU.[62]

Powell had little choice. For, although his committee included the communists, black churchmen and social service agencies, the HLU was the only effective picketing group. For the next three years, the HLU's willingness to challenge discrimination wherever it found it, even among left-wing trade unions, made it the Coordinating Committee's cutting-edge.[63]

But in 1939 the HLU was investigated, at the insistence of the NLC, by the Assistant District Attorney and the New York State Labor Relations Board. In December 1939, after he had been convicted of assaulting a store detective, Arthur Reid was forced to resign.[64] The new executive committee of the HLU, without compromising its stand on discrimination, accepted the place of white workers, unions and employers in Harlem: it disowned the nationalism that had given the HLU birth.[65] Then both the HLU and the NLC could claim a victory: a majority of the employees in Harlem's retail stores were black and the Afro-American trade union population in New York had increased by over 50,000 in five years.[66]

By the time of Reid's resignation, street speaking was on the wane. Kemp was dead and the Sufi was the leader of an esoteric religious sect when he was killed in a plane crash in 1938.[67] Nationalist oratory had become identified with demagoguery, racketeering and violence.

Although some speakers had jobs and spoke in their leisure,[68] the most prominent speakers depended on their street activity for their living. Some communist organisers were paid a salary by the Party: but nationalist fund-raising was more obviously open to abuse.

The nationalists depended on collections at their meetings; payments from businesses or political parties for speeches made on their behalf; and the establishment of dues-paying organisations such as the HLU. The self-interest of the nationalists was never separate from their activity on behalf of 'the race'. They lived on their wits, through their facility with words, never far away from the semi-legal world of the hustler.[69] In this world, deception and intimidation were ugly but sometimes necessary means of survival.

Some speakers were unalloyed demagogues. General St William Grant of the Tiger Division of the UNIA fought with the Sufi and with the communists in the early 1930s. In one fracas, a communist died. Even other divisions of the UNIA regarded Grant as an embarrassment.[70]

In the early 1940s, some street-speaker groups were proto-fascist. Samuel Daniels, who had been active in the APL, the Ethiopian campaign and the Jobs Campaign, edited a magazine, *Negro Youth*, dedicated to the 'racial purity' of blacks, which inveighed against 'mulattoes' and 'mongrels', and 'lousy, greasy, degenerate, diseased, rapacious Italians'. Arthur Reid himself was reported to be making anti-Semitic diatribes in 1941.[71]

In 1939, the editor of the *Amsterdam News* expressed a widespread unease about the street speakers: Hubert Harrison had been 'erudite and controversial' but some of his successors had become 'a serious menace to the peace and safety of Harlemites'. They should be taken off the streets and given a separate area – a 'Hyde Park'.[72]

Protest letters soon arrived. Typical was one from Enoch Bond, 'an old soapboxer', who, like many other unaffiliated speakers, had spoken on behalf of a variety of racial causes: 'with the UNIA, then with Sufi's job campaign, release of the Scottsboro boys, more home relief, lower rents, slum clearance'. He concluded: 'Freedom of speech is indeed a sacred thing. The soapboxer marches on.' Captain A. L. King of the UNIA agreed: 'those very people, ignorant as they may be . . . made it possible for many of the changes which have occurred in Harlem.'[73]

There was truth in King's words. Communist and nationalist speakers had confronted Harlem's social and economic problems. They had built on the propagandist rhetoric of race assertiveness of the 1920s and pressed for improvements in relief, housing and health provision. They had achieved a major change in employment patterns through mass direct action. But, even as agents of change, the speakers had their weaknesses.

The Communist Party in Harlem experienced changes of ideology and tactics at the behest of the Comintern or through local political expediency in the 1930s, which caused it to neglect, expel or lose some of its most capable black working-class organisers.[74] The nationalists failed to discover a coherent Afro-American nationalism and retreated into sterile racial abuse.

The UNIA had been Pan-Africanist and the Ethiopian campaign demonstrated that this sentiment was still alive in Harlem. But the Pan-African movement that developed from the Ethiopian war was based in London: an alliance of Caribbean and African radicals that, for the first time in Pan-African history, excluded black America.[75] The anti-imperialism generated in New York in the late 1930s went in two directions: into an expatriate West Indian agitation for Caribbean independence,[76] and into the ghetto nationalism of Reid and Kemp.

The APL's parochialism had considerable limitations. It could not dismantle white ownership of business and property in Harlem. It could not help those blacks who worked outside the ghetto – except perhaps in giving a boost to their morale. And it made itself redundant by the change it did achieve: the capture of ghetto jobs. The experience of the HLU made this clear. For, once the AFL and CIO unions were made more responsive to blacks, partly by competition from the HLU, the interests of black workers, in terms of wages and conditions, were better served by the national unions. CIO unions recruited blacks who had been placed in work by the HLU. There was little future for a sequestered union.[77]

In a sense, the argument between the nationalist and socialist wings of the New Negro movement of the 1920s was acted out on the streets of Harlem in the 1930s. For the time being at least, it was the socialists who were proved right. Paradoxically, it was the nationalists who had done most to make it possible.

The nationalist speakers were unlikely radicals. Like Garvey and Booker T. Washington, they were social and economic conservatives. They stressed property and business ownership; hard work, sacrifice and thrift; and conventional behaviour, morality and family life. They spent as much time berating blacks for their failings as whites for their injustice. Reid said, 'Most of the men in Harlem are no good. All they do is hang around and try to live off some woman.' As for the women, Reid told them, 'Get out and marry a good pushcart peddler and get behind him and help him up. In a few years he'll have a big business.'[78]

Kemp and Reid were failed businessmen, whose experience had taught them that it was not possible to create a black business world without challenging white economic power, even if it was just the street pedlar or the family corner shop.[79] They spoke also for those, including skilled workers, whom the discrimination of employers and trade unions had relegated to marginal employment and unemployment, and for whom small business was a means of independent survival.

They despised the black professional classes as 'go-betweens' for the 'white man' – 'house Negroes': schoolteachers who taught only 'what the white man wants you to know'; and social workers, strutting around 'with their briefcases' reporting to the white man 'so that he can decide when he will let you eat again'.[80]

Kemp and Reid retained of the dream of the black metropolis a sense of black territory and community. They rejected the faith that education, property, culture or social graces were a passage to acceptance in white America. Reid told his audiences that 'they were born black and were going to die black. . . . "Even when you die you will go to the 'black department' of the cemetery."' Blacks would have to stop 'doing "the truck" and praying' and fight for their share.[81]

From this basis they fought for control of the pushcart markets, then to place black clerks on 125th Street, then to be elected to the state legislature and then to end employment discrimination in the city's public utilities. Responding and reacting to the Depression, to communist and trade union activities in Harlem, to the liberal reform policies of the New Deal and the LaGuardia administration, and to the willingness of younger members of the black middle class to take part in direct action, the nationalists were drawn far from their roots.

'Practical economic necessity', as McKay said, was their main motive;[82] through Harrison, there was an unacknowledged socialist influence on street-speaker nationalism. Yet, beyond that, there was a moral conviction, whose religious origins were made explicit by the Sufi, and a sense of black community that was experiential rather than ideological.

It was in these terms that Ralph Ellison described the brand of black nationalism which he used for his portrayal of Ras the Exhorter: an elemental morality and racial loyalty based on the 'simple principle that Negroes deserve equal treatment with all other free human beings'. This was a morality that would have fitted all the speakers. A white communist wrote of his black comrade, Solomon Harper, that he was 'part vagabond, part saint, with an inextinguishable fire'.[83]

But it was the nationalists, unrestrained by any ideological consideration except justice for black people, who best fitted the prophetic role. They incited their audiences to self-respect, to personal and community rebirth; they wanted blacks to purge themselves of demoralisation and their community of exploitation. The middle class reacted to them with public anxiety and some private admiration.[84]

A nationalist instinct (generally called 'race consciousness' in the 1930s) – a sense of community and an indignant assertion of its rights, characterised the Harlem constituency that the speakers addressed.[85] Both the communists and the nationalists struggled and failed to give this sentiment an ideological shape. Adam Clayton Powell Jr, a man of the same generation as the Sufi and Ira Kemp, confirmed its political reality.

Powell courted both the nationalists and the communists in the 1930s. In his weekly column, 'Soapbox', in the *Amsterdam News* from 1936, he developed a black populism that combined calls to black solidarity and vigilance, indictments of white injustice and a recognition of the need for blacks to make alliances with progressive whites. A showman and a crusader, he possessed a mass following in the Abyssinian Baptist Church and impeccable black middle-class connections. He was elected to the New York City Council in 1941 and then to the United States Congress in 1944 as an advocate of racial egalitarianism and social and economic reform.[86]

Events moved on, but the street speakers stood still. As black leadership used Afro-American participation in the Second World War as a lever for greater democracy at home, the rump of the nationalist speakers decried the conflict as a 'white man's war' in which they would take no part. This was an attitude which Ellison fairly described as 'of one who, driven into a corner, sees no way of asserting his manhood, except to choose his own manner of dying'.[87]

For the next twenty years, nationalism had no friends among the black leadership and its contribution to earlier struggles was largely forgotten. But the ghetto and its bitterness remained; in the 1950s, as a new wave of Southern migrants arrived and a ghetto-bred generation grew up, the street corners of New York were the training ground of Malcolm X, the most influential black nationalist since Garvey.[88]

It is easy to discount the contribution of unlettered popular leaders. The excesses and specious arguments of the nationalist speakers of the 1930s are plain enough. But, after all, as Myrtle Pollard wrote in 1937, people 'believe the speakers actually have something to say. . . . They mean to turn the world upside down to see the Negro gets a fair break. They talk about bloodshed and sacrifice. They make the white man appear such a ridiculously comical creature. In other words, they adjust the black man's *Ego.*'[89] The heirs of the New Negro, of Harrison and Garvey, were also, in their plebeian tone and their preoccupation with the ills of the ghetto, the forerunners of the Black Power movement of the 1960s.

NOTES

1. New York *Amsterdam News*, 8 July 1931.
2. Norfolk *Journal and Guide*, 25 June 1932; Pittsburgh *Courier*, 28 April 1934.
3. F. W. Jiles, 'Reaping the Whirlwind', *Education* 2 (July–August 1936) p. 4.
4. See, for instance, R. Ottley, *New World A'Coming: Inside Black America* (Boston: Houghton Mifflin, 1943) pp. 116–21. More sympathetic, but

not typical, was C. McKay, *Harlem, Negro Metropolis* (New York: E. P. Dutton, 1940) pp. 181–219.

5. Ralph Ellison, *Invisible Man* (Harmondsworth, Middx: Penguin, 1965) pp. 292–305, 387–90, 447–53.

6. Carl Offord, *The White Face* (New York: McBride, 1943).

7. New York City Mayor's Commission on Conditions in Harlem, *The Negro in Harlem: Report on the Social and Economic Conditions Responsible for the Outbreak of March 19 1935* (New York: 1936) p. 4; typescript in Schomburg Center for Black History and Culture, New York City.

8. Adam Clayton Powell Jr, *Marching Blacks* (New York: Dial Press, 1945) p. 5.

9. August Meier and Elliott Rudwick, 'The Origins of Non-Violent Direct Action in Afro-American Protest: A Note on Historical Discontinuities', in *Along the Color Line: Explorations in the Black Experience*, ed. August Meier and Elliott Rudwick (Urbana, Ill.: University of Illinois Press, 1976) pp. 314–44, 380, 386, 388–89.

10. See, for instance, McKay, *Harlem*, pp. 22, 29–30, 101–2, 106–7; Ottley, *New World A'Coming*, pp. 1–2, 120–3, 129.

11. J. Anderson, *Harlem: The Great Black Way 1900–1950* (London: Orbis, 1982) p. 320; J. W. Johnson, *Black Manhattan* (New York: Alfred A. Knopf, 1930) pp. 168–9.

12. Anderson, *Harlem*, pp. 59–71, 92–100, 117, 137–44, 225–31, 319–23.

13. Ibid., pp. 106–7; J. Anderson, *A. Philip Randolph: A Biographical Portrait* (New York: Harcourt Brace Jovanovich, 1973) pp. 68–9.

14. For instance, Rabbi Wentworth A. Matthew: H. M. Brotz, *The Black Jews of Harlem* (New York: Schocken, 1970) pp. 1–59 *passim*; and 'The Barefoot Prophet', Elder Clayborn Martin: A. Harris, 'Barefoot Prophet', in WPA in New York City, *Negroes of New York*, microfilm reel 1 in Schomburg Center.

15. For Harrison's life, see Anderson, *A. Philip Randolph*, pp. 79–80, 87, 120–3; *The Marcus Garvey and the Universal Negro Improvement Association Papers*, vol. 1, ed. R. A. Hill (Los Angeles: University of California, 1983) pp. 209–11. For his socialist career, see P. S. Foner, *American Socialism and Black Americans* (London: Greenwood Press, 1977) pp. 206–18. His oratory is described in H. Miller, *Plexus* (London: Weidenfeld & Nicolson, 1963) pp. 500–1.

16. From obituaries in Chicago *Defender*, 24 December 1927; *Negro World*, 31 December 1927; New York *Amsterdam News*, 28 December 1927; New York *News*, 31 December 1927; Pittsburgh *Courier*, 31 December 1927.

17. This simplifies a complex situation in which black communists and socialists were opposed to one another and the nationalists; all three groups remained 'race conscious'; and there was continual debate between the views. See Anderson, *A. Philip Randolph*, pp. 68–150; Anderson, *Harlem*, pp. 106–7, 186–91; Foner, *American Socialism*, pp. 265–336; M. Naison, *Communists in Harlem During the Depression* (Urbana, Ill.: University of Illinois Press, 1983) pp. 3–10.

18. *Clarion*, August 1919.

19. New York *Age*, 5 August 1933; New York *Amsterdam News*, 13 August 1930; see also *Negro World*, 17 January 1931.

20. Naison, *Communists*, pp. 34–5, 40–1, 57–89.
21. *Along the Color Line*, ed. Meier and Rudwick, pp. 315–32.
22. Ottley, *New World A'Coming*, pp. 91–2.
23. New York *Amsterdam News*, 22 June 1932 and 22 June 1935; New York *Herald Tribune*, 16 January 1935; *Negro World*, 2 April 1935.
24. For the CLFP's campaign, see Meier and Rudwick, *Along the Color Line*, pp. 319–20; W. Muraskin, 'The Harlem Boycott of 1934: Black Nationalism and the Rise of Labor-Union Consciousness', *Labor History* 13 (Summer 1972) pp. 362–9.
25. Ibid., p. 364.
26. Ibid., pp. 365–7; New York *Age*, 1 September 1934; New York *Amsterdam News*, 4, 8 and 25 August 1934.
27. *Along the Color Line*, ed. Meier and Rudwick, pp. 319–20; Muraskin, 'The Harlem Boycott', pp. 368–9.
28. *Negro World*, 15 July 1933; New York *Post*, 18 February 1967; Ottley, *New World A'Coming*, pp. 119–20.
29. M. E. Pollard, 'Harlem As Is; vol. 2: Negro Business and Economic Community' (unpublished Master's thesis, College of the City of New York, 1937) pp. 143–4; typescript in Schomburg Center.
30. *Negro World*, 15 July 1933.
31. Muraskin, 'The Harlem Boycott', p. 368.
32. There was disagreement within the Harlem Section of the Communist Party. Cyril Briggs and Richard B. Moore, veterans of the New Negro movement, were removed from leadership positions because of 'nationalistic' tendencies, partly for favouring the boycott movement. The communists organised two boycotts of their own, which enlisted the support of the white employees of the boycotted businesses. The Fifth Avenue Coach Company was unsuccessfully boycotted from February to July 1934. In August 1934, there was a successful boycott of the Empire Cafeteria which put four black counter staff into employment without displacing any white employees. See Naison, *Communists*, pp. 95–124.
33. For ethnic business ownership, see McKay, *Harlem*, p. 29; for Reid and the pushcarters, see ibid., pp. 92–3; Baltimore *Afro-American*, 15 February and 25 July 1936.
34. Reports of the Sufi's statements at two trials, in October 1934 and January 1935 appear in: New York *Age*, 19 January 1935; New York *Amsterdam News*, 13 and 20 October 1934, 19 January and 2 February 1935; New York *Herald Tribune*, 16 January 1935; New York *Times*, 16 January 1935; New York *World Telegram*, 9 October 1934. A defence of the Sufi is given in McKay, *Harlem*, pp. 198–203. New York *Amsterdam News*, 13 April 1935 reports a handbill on which the Sufi advertised himself as 'the most talked about black man in the country, Abdul Hamid, called the Black Hitler'.
35. CLFP spokesmen did not deny that the selected employees were light-complexioned, rather they accused the Picket Committee of colour bias in favour of dark-skinned girls; New York *Age*, 25 August and 22 September 1934.
36. New York *Amsterdam News*, 13 November 1937.

37. Ibid.; and an election leaflet in WPA in New York City, *Negroes of New York*, microfilm reel 5 in Schomburg Center.
38. Under threat of deportation in 1935, the Sufi claimed that his real name was Eugene Brown and he was born in Massachusetts in 1903; New York *Amsterdam News*, 22 June 1935; McKay, *Harlem*, pp. 192, 206.
39. M. E. Pollard, 'Harlem As Is, vol. 1: Sociological Notes on Harlem Social Life' (Unpublished Bachelor's thesis, College of the City of New York, 1936) p. 26; typescript in Schomburg Center. See also New York *Age*, 30 March 1935. Most comments by black spokesmen on the riots mentioned the fact that white business in Harlem did not employ black sales clerks as a contributory factor in causing the rioting; see, for instance, 'Editorial', *Opportunity* 13 (April 1935) p. 102.
40. New York *Times*, 6 July 1935.
41. Among those who complained to the police and Mayor LaGuardia about the Sufi were the larger merchants in the Uptown Chamber of Commerce; the smaller merchants in the Harlem Merchants Association; the leadership of the CLFP; the editor of one of Harlem's black-owned newspapers, the New York *Age*; and the Communist Party. See New York *Amsterdam News*, 29 September and 29 December 1934, and 19 January 1935; *Liberator*, 6 October 1934; New York *Times*, 26 September 1934 and 20 January 1935; New York *Sun*, 21 and 22 March 1935; New York *World Telegram*, 20 March 1935.
42. New York *Amsterdam News*, 22 June 1935; New York *Times*, 16 and 20 January 1935.
43. The Communist Party, with its greater resources, took most advantage of the hearings, but other speakers and ordinary black citizens made voluble contributions. An account of the Mayor's Commission public hearings from the communist point of view is given in Naison, *Communists*, pp. 145–8.
44. W. R. Scott, 'Black Nationalism and the Italo-Ethiopian Conflict 1934–1936', *Journal of Negro History*, LXIII (April 1978) pp. 118–19.
45. Joel A. Rogers was the pre-eminent black popular historian. Ottley described him as the street speakers' Karl Marx; Ottley, *New World A'Coming*, pp. 101–3. See, for instance, J. A. Rogers, *The Real Facts About Ethiopia* (New York: Rogers, 1936) *passim*.
46. Naison, *Communists*, pp. 138–9, 155–8, 174–6, 195–6; 'Black Nationalism', pp. 124–9.
47. Baltimore *Afro-American*, 25 July 1936; 'To the People of Harlem – Don't Buy From Italians', APL pamphlet, in WPA in New York City, *Negroes of New York*, microfilm reel 5 in Schomburg Center; Naison, *Communists*, pp. 155, 176; Scott, 'Black Nationalism', p. 123.
48. For 'gum beatin'' in New York see New York *Amsterdam News*, 20 July 1935; for reports of disturbances see ibid., 5 October 1935, 23 and 30 May and 6 June 1936; *Crusader News Agency*, 11, 18 and 29 May 1936; *Daily Worker*, 10 October 1935; New York *Times*, 4 and 5 October 1935; Scott, 'Black Nationalism', p. 130.
49. Denunciations of the street speakers and the boycott appear in the New York *Age*, 27 July 1935, 30 May and 8 August 1936; and the New York *Amsterdam News*, 23 and 30 May 1936.

50. New York *Age*, 25 July 1936; New York *Amsterdam News*, 18 July and 1 August 1936; *Crusader News Agency*, 20 July 1936; *New York Times*, 14 and 18 July 1936; 'The Case of the People of Harlem Against Bella Restaurant' in Pollard, 'Harlem As Is', vol. 2, appendix 5d, pp. 441–3.

51. New York *Amsterdam News*, 6 and 27 June 1936; *Crusader News Agency*, 20 July 1936.

52. The Communist Party, in response to the riot and the Mayor's Commission, had formed an, apparently brief, alliance with the NAACP and the Urban League, called the United Civil Rights Committee of Harlem. It was intended mainly to monitor police activity in the black community. This delegation seems to have been a development of that alliance; New York *Amsterdam News*, 25 July 1936; *Crusader News Agency*, 27 July 1936.

53. Pollard, 'Harlem As Is', vol. 1, p. 317 and vol. 2, pp. 143–4, 147–8.

54. New York *Amsterdam News*, 28 March 1936.

55. Ibid., 21 November 1936; New York *Post*, 17 November 1936; Muraskin, 'The Harlem Boycott', pp. 370–1.

56. Foner, *American Socialism*, pp. 338–9; P. S. Foner, *The Negro Labor Committee, What it is and Why* (New York: Harlem Labor Center, 1935) *passim*.

57. New York *Amsterdam News*, 21 November 1936, 21 August 1937, 7 May, 4 June, 23 July, 3 and 17 September 1938; New York *Post*, 17 November 1936, 13 May and 30 August 1938; *Unions or Rackets? Negro Workers Beware!* (New York: Harlem Labor Center, 1937?) *passim*; C. McKay, 'Labor Steps Out in Harlem', *Nation* 145 (16 October 1937) pp. 399–402; Naison, *Communists*, pp. 262–3.

58. Election leaflet in WPA in New York CIty, *Negroes of New York*, microfilm reel 5 in Schomburg Center.

59. New York *Amsterdam News*, 13, 20 and 27 November, 11 December 1937.

60. New York *Age*, 8 and 16 April 1938; New York *Amsterdam News*, 26 February, 2 and 30 April 1938; *Crusader News Agency*, 31 January, 7 and 21 February and 18 April 1938.

61. New York *Amsterdam News*, 13 August 1938.

62. New York *Age*, 15 November 1938; New York *Amsterdam News*, 22 and 29 October, 5, 12, 19 and 26 November and 31 December 1938.

63. *Along the Color Line*, ed. Meier and Rudwick, pp. 328–9; A. Meier and E. Rudwick, 'Communist Unions and the Black Community: The Case of the Transport Workers Union 1934–1944', *Labor History* 23 (Spring 1982) pp. 171–82; Naison, *Communists*, pp. 267–9, 271–2, 304, 306–8.

64. New York *Age*, 16 and 23 December 1939; New York *Amsterdam News*, 16 and 30 December 1939; *Crusader News Agency*, 5 June 1939; *Voice of Ethiopia*, 10 June 1939; Muraskin, 'The Harlem Boycott', pp. 372–3.

65. *Voice of Ethiopia*, 13 and 27 January, 3 and 24 February 1940.

66. New York *Amsterdam News*, 23 May 1940; *Fifth Anniversary of the Negro Labor Committee* (New York: Harlem Labor Center, 1941).

67. New York *Amsterdam News*, 6 August 1938.

68. Pollard, 'Harlem As Is', vol. 2, pp. 145–6.

69. See, for instance, Ottley on 'Hustlers' in New York *Amsterdam News*, 11 January 1936; and Pollard, 'Harlem As Is', vol. 2, p. 146.
70. New York *Amsterdam News*, 7 September 1932; Naison *Communists*, pp. 39–40, 62–3.
71. On Daniels, see: Samuel Daniels, 'Death or Salvation! The Part the Black Man Must Play in the Present World Conflict', *Negro Youth* 1 (June–July 1941) pp. 1–2; New York *Age*, 27 August 1933 and 23 January 1937; New York *Amsterdam News*, 24 January and 24 March 1934, 16 February, 13 and 20 July, 31 August and 2 November 1935. On Reid, see *Jewish Review*, 22 May 1941; Ottley, *New World A'Coming*, pp. 119–20. There seem to be no charges of anti-Semitism against Reid until after 1940; but he is probably the model for the viciously anti-Semitic street demagogue, Reeves, in Offord's *The White Face*.
72. New York *Amsterdam News*, 15 July 1939.
73. Ibid., 29 July 1939.
74. There were three periods of contention and dissension: the early Jobs Campaign; the Italo-Ethiopian campaign; and, finally the 'Popular Front' phase. See Naison, *Communists*, pp. 95–111, 174, 270–1.
75. This was the International African Friends of Abyssinia, chaired by George Padmore, which later developed into the Pan African Federation (1944). The New York Ethiopian campaign was in contact with the International African Friends, through Dr Willis N. Huggins, who visited London on behalf of the PCDE in 1935. He set up a Friends of Ethiopia in America on his return, but nothing further developed; G. Padmore, *Pan Africanism or Communism? The Coming Struggle for Africa* (London: Dennis Dobson, 1956) pp. 144–51.
76. United Aid for Ethiopia became United Aid for People of African Descent in 1936. From 1936 to its demise in 1939, it organised a number of meetings on West Indian affairs in cooperation with Caribbean organisations. In 1940, two of its most important members, Dr P. M. H. Savory and Cyril Philip, served on the West Indian National Emergency Council in New York. New York *Amsterdam News*, 24 and 31 July 1937, 21 and 28 May, 25 June and 10 December 1938, 20 and 27 July 1940.
77. Naison, *Communists*, p. 263. In 1939, Reid recognised the limitations of the HLU: 'Nit wits who think that I have set up a rival union to the AFL or CIO are foolish. I'm only concerned with Negroes being integrated into the economic life of America'; New York *Age*, 16 December 1939.
78. Baltimore *Afro-American*, 25 July 1936.
79. Reid had been a manufacturer of black dolls; Kemp had been the owner of a children's clothing factory; New York *Amsterdam News*, 13 November 1937; Ottley, *New World A'Coming*, p. 119.
80. Baltimore *Afro-American*, 25 July 1936.
81. Ibid.; Pollard, 'Harlem As Is', vol. 2, pp. 143–4.
82. McKay, 'Labor Steps Out', p. 400.
83. 'Editorial', *Negro Quarterly* 1 (Winter–Spring 1943) p. 296; G. Charney, *A Long Journey* (New York: Quadrangle, 1968) pp. 101–2.
84. The Sufi, Reid and Kemp, all condemned by the black press when in

full career, received accolades on their death or retirement from the street; New York *Age*, 30 December 1939; New York *Amsterdam News*, 11 December 1937 and 6 August 1938.

85. Ottley, *New World A'Coming*, p. vi.
86. Powell, *Marching Blacks*, *passim*, while often factually inaccurate, is faithful to the spirit of the times and Powell's own place in them.
87. 'Editorial', *Negro Quarterly*, p. 296.
88. Malcolm X, *The Autobiography of Malcolm X* (Harmondsworth, Middx: Penguin, 1968) pp. 317–22 describes his evangelism in New York as Minister of Temple Seven of the Nation of Islam.
89. Pollard, 'Harlem As Is', vol. 2, p. 114.

# 9
# The Image of Black Harlem in Literature

## JAMES L. de JONGH

The question of what writers make of Harlem is a fascinating one, for in literature as in other fields, black Harlem has become a familiar landscape of the modern imagination. Harlem was a landscape where in the lifetime of the literary generations of the Black Awakening, black New Yorkers had performed an epic deed and wrested a desired territory from the foe in the face of extraordinary obstacles in the years following the end of the First World War, creating a black city which promised to be the cultural capital of the race in this country. Ever since, the idea of Harlem has inspired large numbers of writers, black and non-black alike, in a remarkably high number of works. After each of the race riots of 1919, 1943 and 1964 in American cities with large black populations, a new international generation of Africana writers – authors of African descent and heritage writing in modern European languages (usually English, French, Spanish or Portuguese) – has emerged throughout the black world employing the Harlem motif as the emblem of an ethos of racial renewal. Many authors who are not black have also celebrated the city-within-a-city north of Central Park, for the idea of Harlem has come to be part of the figurative geography of modern writers of all the races.

Harlem's figurative character was defined initially in a period when racial selfhood was being articulated by the literary movements of the Black Awakening, and when Harlem was perceived generally as a liberated landscape free of the repressions and oppressions of Babbittry and Jim Crow. After the First World War, an international literary generation of young black writers took Harlem as a portent of the primacy of their own experiences and perceptions over the authority of European culture. Africana authors representing this purview included Claude McKay, Langston Hughes and the New Negro writers of the United States;

131

Nicolás Guillén and the Negrist poets of Cuba, the Dominican Republic and Puerto Rico; Jacques Roumain and the Indigenist writers of Haiti; and Léopold Senghor and the Negritude poets of French West Africa and the Caribbean. For these literary movements of the Black Awakening, Harlem's rise was identified with a resurgent racial consciousness and a comprehensive philosophy of racial selfhood which defied the hegemony of so-called 'universal' standards whose ethnocentric norms denied the worth of the Negro's African patrimony. Harlem was recognised as a mythological landscape in which their African inheritance was being reclaimed in the diaspora.

This initial formulation of black Harlem as a dreamscape of reasserted African values in exile resonated ironically with Harlem's alternative formulation by a daring but disillusioned international assortment of young writers of the same generation who were not black, including William Rose Benét, Maxwell Bodenheim, Federico García Lorca, Yvan Goll, Yonezo Hiroyama, Fannie Hurst, Alfred Kreymborg, Salvatore Quasimodo and Carl Van Vechten. Facing a crisis of confidence in their own western patrimony, they identified Harlem as a conveniently urban heart-of-darkness celebrated for the exuberance of its primal joy, a readily understandable setting of profound otherness close at hand; their idea of Harlem often seemed insulated by the power of preconception from the paradox of how so alien a place could also offer such facile meanings.

Two works of fiction, Carl Van Vechten's *Nigger Heaven* (New York: Alfred A. Knopf, 1926) and Claude McKay's *Home to Harlem* (New York: Harper & Bros, 1928), stand as paradigms of contrasting literary conceptions of Harlem in the 1920s between which a spectrum of figurative usages developed and evolved. In the opening chapter of *Home to Harlem*, black Harlem is evoked lyrically and figuratively rather than depicted by fictional technique:

> 'Harlem for mine!' cried Jake. 'I was crazy thinkin' I was happy over heah. I wasn't myself. I was a man charged up with dope everyday! That what it was. Oh, boy, Harlem for mine!
>
> Take me home to Harlem, Mister Ship! Take me home to the brown gals waiting for the brown boys that done show their mettle over there. Take me home, Mister Ship. Put your beak right into that water and jest move along.' (pp. 8–9)

Jake is rhapsodising on the theme of Harlem; the elements of his evocation are literary figures – personification, apostrophe, synecdoche, metonymy, etc. – rather than literal details of the landscape. And later, after one night of love in Harlem, we are given to understand that Jake has found the Harlem he came seeking. His cry of 'Harlem for mine!' (p. 8) with its subjunctive and conditional modalities becomes a triumphant 'Harlem is mine!' (p. 17), when Harlem responds by allowing him the freedom to be himself within the nurturing frame of a Negro community. McKay's lyrical evocation of Jake's personal Harlem contrasts with the larger portion of *Nigger Heaven*. Most of Van Vechten's novel is guided by a didactic imperative skilfully integrated with the fictional necessities of the story. The narrator, in his own phrase, is 'a careful observer' (p. 151) who depicts Harlem dispassionately and varies the setting systematically to convey a comprehensive and informed view of Negro life in America *circa* 1925. Mary Love's estrangement from so many elements of life in black Manhattan permits the 'careful observer' to catalogue and contemplate many facets of the Harlem landscape without violating either the love story or his narrative point of view. With Mary, the reader tours a variety of Harlem environments: the Gatsby-like indulgence of the Long Island set, the St Nicholas Avenue pretensions of the Albrights, the Striver's Row luxury of Adora Boniface, and the refined comforts of the Sumners. All combine with glimpses of Craig's Restaurant, the 135th Street Public Library, and the United Charities Ball to depict a variegated Harlem landscape. Similarly, an exploration of Byron's need to earn a living and his ambition to be a writer permits a tour of working-class Harlem on the job along with an informed consideration of the status of black literature. In addition, the narrator explores the topology as well as the top-ography of Harlem. Mary Love's visit to Adora Boniface's townhouse becomes the occasion for nostalgic reminiscences of the Tenderloin area of black Broadway at the turn of the century which anticipated and set the style of Harlem cabaret life, and the family histories of the Sumners and the Loves hint at the roots of the talented tenth's prosperity and urbanity. This careful observer is so thorough that a careful reader should be able to dismiss a minor character's stereotyped view that Harlem is typified by the Black Venus cabaret:

> Well, it's wonderful up here, Baldwin exclaimed. I had no idea it would be like this. It's as wild as a jungle. . . .

> God, but this place is great! I could live up here. Is all Harlem like this?   (pp. 209–15 *passim*)

Byron Kasson, to whom the question is directed, has been characterised, however, as an urban tragic mulatto: a person more white than black, sensitive to the finer ways of life in the white world, but condemned to languish within the confines of the black because of his share of Negro blood. He is tortured by the proximity of the place from which he is excluded, and projects a defensive psychology and abject aesthetic on the Harlem landscape which he has labelled 'Nigger Heaven'. Now he is depicted as confused enough to accept a judgement based on just one jaunt to a Harlem cabaret:

> The question awakened a swarm of perverse, dancing images in Byron's brain. They crowded about each other, all the incongruities, the savage inconsistencies, the peculiar discrepancies, of this cruel segregated life.
>
> Yes, he replied, I suppose it is.   (p. 215)

Once Byron begins his affair with Lasca Sartoris, the narrator discards the pose of a careful observer to immerse himself in the sensational side of Harlem. As Byron's middle-class persona is stripped away, the cabaret landscape of Harlem becomes an expression of a mental state which the narrator implies is racially characteristic of the primitive Negro psyche. When the urbane youth succumbs to the primitive forces within, the careful observer's precise pictorial descriptions give way to evocations of Harlem from Byron's feverish point of view. The pace of the language accelerates until conventional syntax is lost in a concatenation of isolated words and phrases. Van Vechten's careful observer has become a voyeur resonating with Byron's obsessions. The Harlem setting and Byron's deranged state of mind merge and become one:

> It all became a jumble in Byron's mind, a jumble of meaningless phrases accompanied by the hard, insistent, regular beating of the drum, the groaning of the saxophone, the shrill squeeling of the clarinet, the laughter of the customers and occasionally the echo of the refrain.

If you hadn't gone away!

A meaningless jumble. Like life. Like Negro life. Kicked from above. Pulled down from below. No cheer but dance, drink and happy dust . . . and golden browns. Wine, women, and song, and happy dust. Gin, shebas, Blues, and snow. However, you looked at it. . . . Whatever you called it.   (p. 278)

In *Nigger Heaven*, Van Vechten reduced his own carefully observed and varied depiction of black Harlem to the narrow scope of a stereotype by insisting in the final chapters on Harlem's atavistic and bizarre primitivism. In *Home to Harlem*, on the other hand, McKay's sense of place, captured by describing figurative and imaginative perceptions rather than by depicting physical details and observations, evoked a sense of Harlem's authentic inner life. Ironically, McKay achieved this using the same narrow slice of Harlem cabaret life which Van Vechten advanced as the epitome of the 'meaningless jumble' (p. 278) of Negro life. Significantly, both McKay in *Home to Harlem* and Van Vechten in *Nigger Heaven* predicted the tendency of writers of the different races to characterise Harlem as a figurative and symbolic landscape, a realm of myth and imagination as well as actual place.

Harlem's promise as a black culture capital in the 1920s was overwhelmed by the ghetto's actuality under the stress of economic depression and global war. By 1940 black Harlem was sufficiently wretched to undermine the idea of a liberated racial landscape it had come to symbolise in the 1920s. The naturalistic fictional techniques of newer novelists, such as Ann Petry of *The Street*, Ralph Ellison of *Invisible Man* and James Baldwin of *Go Tell it on the Mountain* could explore Harlem's demoralising decline after the Harlem riots of 1935 and 1943, but the emerging Harlem ghetto presented other black writers with a formidable problematic. Africana poets in particular were overwhelmed and for a time avoided Harlem altogether. Only Langston Hughes among the New Negro writers was able to write creative literature about Harlem much past its voguish heyday in the 1920s. What most distinguished Hughes's career-long commitment to the motif was his early identification of Harlem with the modalities of Afro-American folk culture, initially with the aesthetics of jazz and blues. The Harlem poems of *The Weary Blues* (1926) were as marked by irony, paradox, contradiction and ambiguity as the Harlem works of his Afro-American contemporaries, but Hughes associated the dualities of black Harlem with the quintessential pattern of twoness (i.e. call and response, problem and resolution, being and becoming) which are the structure and spirit of the blues. Langston Hughes wrote about Harlem and the urban folk experience it represented in the forms and the idiom the folk had chosen to bring with them to the city. His usage of the folk forms of blues and jazz corresponded to the challenge of Afro-American selfhood in the crucible of the urban environment where blacks in the 1920s and 1930s were transforming themselves from a rural people. Today one may have to remind oneself that Langston Hughes's identification of Harlem with jazz and blues, which now seems so natural, perhaps even a bit trite to some, could have been severely criticised and rejected in its own time. In fact, it took a streak of daring and independence as well as genius for Hughes to invoke the cultural traditions of the Harlem folk and vest his literary vision of Harlem with the authority of Afro-American musical and philosophical frames of reference in the 1920s. Few of the major Afro-American writers of Hughes's generation followed his lead in this respect, and Hughes's Harlem of jazz and blues was reflected first outside the United States by writers of the parallel generations of the Black Awakening, for example the Negrist poetry of the Afro-Hispanic Antilles, in a famous verse of Nicolás Guillén's 'Pequeña oda a un boxeador cubano':

> ahora que Europa se desnuda
> para tostar su carne al sol
> y busca en Harlem y en la Habana
> *Jazz* y son . . .

> now that Europe strips naked
> to brown its hide in the sun
> and seeks in Harlem and Havana
> Jazz and *son*[1]

The Indigenist poetry of Haiti in Jean Brièrre's 'Me Revoici, Harlem' (Here I am again Harlem) addressed all Afro-Americans through the symbolic figure of Harlem:

> Au rythme de tes blues dansent mes vieux chagrins
> Et je dit ton angoisse en la langue de France.[2]

To your blues rhythm, my old sorrows dance,
And I tell your anguish in the language of France.

Portuguese Negritude's foremost exponent Francisco José Tenreiro dedicated his poem 'Fragmento de Blues' to Langston Hughes; in it he associates Harlem with a blues piano, recalling Hughes's first volume of poetry:

> Vem até mim
> ao cair da tristeza no meu coração
> a tua voz de nigrinha doce
> quebrando-se ao som grave dum piano
> tocando em Harlem:[3]

> When sadness falls into my heart
> your voice of sweet blackness comes to me
> breaking in the grave sound of a piano
> playing in Harlem:

Unlike the Harlems of his literary contemporaries – Countee Cullen's sacramental ghetto in 'Harlem Wine', Claude McKay's ineffable lost identity in 'Harlem Dancer', Helene Johnson's touching spectres of Africa on the streets of Harlem in 'Sonnet to a Negro in Harlem', Sterling Brown's demystifying burlesque of the fakery of the Harlem vogue in 'Mecca' and even Rudolph Fisher's city of inviting surfaces and insidious undercurrents in 'City of Refuge' – Hughes's motif of Harlem as the landscape of blues and jazz could respond to disheartening alterations in Harlem's circumstances as well as to her initial promise; leadership in reconciling the initial optimism and racial confidence with the deterioration and oppression of the emerging ghetto fell largely to Langston Hughes. In *Shakespeare in Harlem* (1942), Hughes could still identify the Harlem environs as landscapes of jazz and blues, although the favour and texture were very different, and escape – the solution in so many country blues luring blacks from the rural South to the city – seemed the only option in the blues landscape of the city of refuge itself. As Simple puts it, 'The blues can be real sad, else real mad, else real glad, and funny too. I ought to know. Me, I growed up with the blues.[4] In fact, the same folk culture which had provided Hughes with his jazz and blues aesthetic now offered him the blues idiom of Jesse B. Simple to conjure with the oblique and ironic possibilities of Harlem in the 1940s. When someone asked Simple 'What on earth makes you think you are going to heaven?' he said, 'Because I have already been in Harlem.'[5] Simple also said, 'But as long as what *is* is – and Georgia is Georgia – I will take Harlem for mine. At least, if trouble comes, I will have *my own window* to shoot out of.'[6]

It is Hughes's *Montage of a Dream Deferred* (1951), however, which restored a credible sense of possibility and offered a new key to the Harlem motif. In *Montage* Hughes synthesised the facts of racial oppression in America with the faith of black Americans through the contemporary jazz modes of boogie-woogie and bebop, and the cinematic concept of montage, in the unifying and comprehensive symbolic locus of Harlem. By identifying Harlem as the montage of a dream deferred. Langston Hughes not only reclaimed the *topos* of Harlem for the spiritual geography of the black world, as he had defined its terms a generation earlier, but also reasserted the challenge of Harlem by rhyming 'What happens to a dream deferred' with the tag, 'Good morning, daddy, Ain't you heard', thereby pointing the way for the coming literary generation. With Langston Hughes's renewed vision of Harlem as the present denial of a historic faith in the reformulated concept of the dream deferred, black Harlem was restored to its place in the literary geography of the black world. Enabled by Hughes's reinterpretation of Harlem a new generation of Afro-American poets turned again to the evolving theme of Harlem. As the drama of racial struggle in the United States focused on the non-violent push for civil rights in the South, the spirit of Harlem was renewed for LeRoi Jones / Amiri Baraka and younger Afro-American poets associated with the Umbra Workshop in New York City and *Dasein: A Quarterly Journal of the Arts* at Howard University; these included Ray Johnston, Oliver Pitcher, Walt Delagall, William Browne and Calvin Hernton, who wrote:

> Wake up o jack-legged poet!
> Wake up o dark boy from 'way down South!
> Wake up out of Central Park and walk
>         through Harlem Street.
> Walk down Seventh Avenue, Eight,
> Madison, Lenox and St Nicholas,
> walk all around –
>         It's morning in Harlem.

Wake up jack-legged poet!
Wake up dark boy from 'way down South!
Wake up out of Central Park –
wash your face in the fountain water,
take a long stretch,
light up your cigarette butt, and walk defiantly
    through the streets of Harlem town.[7]

And outside the United States, other black poets, particularly
Afro-Portuguese writer–revolutionaries of Angola, Mozambique
and the island colonies, heard the voice of Harlem in the global
call for an Africana consciousness and employed black Harlem as
an emblem of solidarity in a common struggle. Viriato da Cruz,
Noemia de Sousa, José Craveirinha, Agostinho Neto and Francisco
José Tenreiro took Harlem as an emblem of civil injustice corre-
sponding to their own colonial situations as they struggled for
political autonomy.

At the same time, a disaffected new literary generation of
white writers seeking liberation from the rigidity of bourgeois
complacency and conformity flipped the meaning of the neighbourhood north of Central Park from an earlier significance of primitive
joy to one of preternatural suffering. Ironically, this suffering made
Harlem an effective spiritual buffer where white bohemians of the
Beat Generation could find cultural and psychological relief, just
as blacks had sought social and physical refuge there a generation
earlier. As Jean-Paul Sartre and Norman Mailer enunciated more
hip renditions of the myth of black primitivism in 'Orphée noir'
and 'The White Negro', the Harlem motif was reinterpreted by
bohemian writers who perceived mocking contrasts and ironic
coincidences between their personal circumstances and the plight
of blacks in Harlem under the colour line. Seymour Krim, for
example, writing about the Harlem he calls 'dark dream mistress
of my adolescence and educator of my so-called manhood!' in 'Ask
for a White Cadillac', declared:

I sincerely doubt that even God could marry the discrepancies:
namely the boots and joys of Harlem life for soul-as-well-as-
penis-starved human beings like myself, who could get the
needed equivalent nowhere else in the greatest city on the globe,
along with its ugliness, .45 calibre toughness, and kick-him-
when-he's-just-getting-up attitude (not when he's down – that's

too easy). . . . And yet if you look at Harlem without morality
at all, from a strictly physical and blindly sensuous point of
view, it is the richest kind of life one can ever see in American
action as far as fundamental staples of love, hate, joy, sorrow,
street-poetry, dance and death go.[8]

In 1948, an apartment in East Harlem was Allen Ginsberg's
retreat after his explusion from Columbia University, where in
Aram Saroyan's delightful phrase, 'Harlem and Lionel Trilling
intersect in an extraordinary urban mambo',[9] and in his poetry
Ginsberg almost always associated Harlem with the formative taste
of visionary awareness and/or madness he experienced there.
John Tyrell has described Ginsberg's visionary experiences in East
Harlem:

> One day [Ginsberg] was relaxing in bed, reading Blake while
> masturbating, and as he reached climax, he experienced a
> sweepingly blissful revelation. He saw 'Ah! Sun-Flower,' the
> poem over which he had been musing, as a manifestation of the
> universe freed from body. . . . Simultaneously, he heard a deep,
> grave voice sounding like 'tender rock' reciting 'Ah! Sun-Flower,'
> and a few minutes later, 'The Sick Rose.' Catalyzed to the vitality
> of the universe, he would now see his own poetic attempts as
> part of a tradition of magic prophecy.[10]

The Blake visions were evidently a threshold experience in the
evolution of Ginsberg's literary identity, and 'Vision: 1948', an
early poem about the Harlem visions, includes the assertion of an
ironic coincidence between the poet and Harlem:

> Outside, great Harlems of the will
>     Move under Black sleep:
> Yet in spiritual scream,
>     The saxophone the same
> As me in madness call thee from the deep.[11]

The saxophone of Harlem, like the madness of the poet, calls to
the same 'Dread spirit in me that I ever try/with written words to
move', anticipating the 'eli eli lamma lamma sabacthani/saxophone
cry that shivered the cities' in 'Howl' which conflates the 'spiritual
scream,/The saxophone the same/As me in madness' with the

despairing call of the crucified Christ. More than simply the place where Ginsberg's vision occurred, Harlem was the spiritual cosmos of the famous lines:

> I saw the best minds of my generation destroyed by madness,
>     staring hysterical naked,
> dragging themselves through the negro streets at dawn looking
>     for an angry fix . . .[12]

The 'negro streets' are by implication Harlem, and the 'angel-headed hipsters burning for ancient heavenly connection' are touched by Pentecostal fire, like the Apostles in the upper chamber:

> on the sixth floor of Harlem crowned with flames
> under the tubercular sky surrounded by orange crates of
>     theology.[13]

In 'Sunflower Sutra', Harlem is summoned up from memory when Jack Kerouac points out a sunflower to Ginsberg:

> Look at the Sunflower, he said, there was a dead gray shadow
>     against the sky, big as a man, sitting dry on top of a pile of
>     ancient sawdust –
> – I rushed up enchanted – it was my first sunflower, memories
>     of Blake – my visions – Harlem.[14]

In 'My Sad Self', as he gazes at his world from the top of the RCA Building in New York City, Ginsberg's 'History summed up' in the places he sees and remembers includes another reference, 'my absences / and ecstasies in Harlem'.[15] In 'The Lion for Real', Harlem is recalled in the phrase 'real lion starved / in his stink in Harlem', in which the lion symbolises the 'roar of the universe' and the 'starved and ancient presence' of the Lord which the poet seeks again after 'a decade knowing only your hunger'.[16] And so on in nearly two dozen poems written over three decades. It is ironic that in the very period when Harlem had ceased to be considered a city of refuge from American racism for blacks, the emerging New York ghetto could be taken by Beat poets as a haven from the oppressive cultural and psychological values of bourgeois American life at mid-century.

The Harlem riots of 18–21 July 1964 initiated a turbulent new phase to the Negro Revolution of the 1950s and 1960s in the United States, and to the motif of black Harlem. The enactment of the Civil Rights Act of 1964 on 2 July of that year had marked the culmination of a decade of achievement for the non-violent crusade against the structure of custom and law which had constituted Southern apartheid. Yet on 18 July 1964, a mere fortnight after the signing of the Civil Rights Act, Harlem exploded as it had twenty years earlier, and this time the violent uprising lasted for four days, setting the pattern for a historic series of similar outbreaks over the course of the next five summers. Still the symbolic centre of the black world, Harlem was the first ghetto to have rioted in the 1960s, and the impact was stunning and immediate. Similar outbreaks followed on 20 July in Brooklyn's Bedford-Stuyvesant, on 24 July in Rochester's Negro North Side, on 2 August in Jersey City, New Jersey, on 11 August in Patterson and Elizabeth, New Jersey, on 16 August in the Chicago suburb of Dixmoor, Illinois and on 28 August in North Philadelphia. Harlem had spoken and Harlem's violent statement was affirmed resoundingly in the ghettos across America. After the riots of 1964, the motif of black Harlem in literature was associated with the riot itself; it seemed difficult for writers, regardless of race, to perceive Harlem except in some dimension of the insurrection, and because Harlem also brought its unique resonance to bear on the issue of the burning ghettos, writers turned to Harlem most often as a primary symbol of the contemporary black condition. Riots, generally ignored as a subject for poetry after the violence of 1919 and 1943, were interpreted as events of quasi-mythic dimensions after 1964. The riots had markedly different means for black and non-black writers, however.

Non-black writers generally used black Harlem after the riots for its oblique perspective on the grasping, racist, self-destructive tendencies of a misguided social order. Barbara Bellow Watson's 'Echoes in a Burnt Building', for example, imagines Harlem after the riots as a burned-out wonderland in which Alice awakens to find herself become black. Alice sits astonished between 'fire-demented walls' in a world where 'rats long as ribbons roll about/ crackling across their battle and its rout', and as she waits 'amazed, awake among the ash/sitting asplit/untaught', a parody of Elizabethan song evokes details of the post-riot Harlem setting with echoes of Shakespeare, Spenser and T. S. Eliot:

Babies born in the pit, sing me one song:
Sweet Thames, sweet Harlem, roll my sins along,
comfort me with hailstones, hang my head,
swing me alive among the dancing dead.
Alice born black, unwashed among the ash,
whiter than that sweet snow
that sleeping hope the sad ones push
which thou ownedst long ago.

Whiter than water are thy mistress lips,
pale hoarding for a merchandiser's quips.
Behind their boards far mandarins shall fake
syrups of sight to medicine thee awake.

Money my fame, Harlem my happy name:
trade is the trick and truth is just the same;[17]

The impact of Watson's high literary resonances is an unsettlingly ironic reflection of western culture in the riot-torn landscape of Harlem where black Alice 'sits hypnotic stiff among the charred / garbage and bricks, the doors and windows barred, / the flag of heaven furled'. For black writers on the other hand, the reaching out of a third Africana generation for a new racial sensibility seasoned the cultural and political dynamics of the previous two after the Harlem uprising. While the newly independent nations of Africa and the Caribbean struggled with the creation of their post-colonial identities, the Black Arts Movement in Harlem sought an aesthetic for the inner city as an element of nation-building within the riot-torn landscapes of the ghettos. In this third phase after 1964, the Africana usage of Harlem resembled its initial formulation as a celebration of black selfhood, but with a bitter difference. Black writers, apprehending the Harlem riot and the subsequent uprising across America as events of mythic significance symbolising the resurgence of Africanadom, synthesised the reawakened spirit of racial possibility in the 1920s with the disenchanted actuality of the dream deferred of the 1950s in an unprecedented flowing of black literature which envisioned Harlem as the metaphor for resurgent black being in the inner city. Harlem became again a primary motif of black racial consciousness for another young generation of Afro-Americans, including Charles Cobb, Conyus, Victor Hernandez Cruz, Henry Dumas, David

Henderson, Gayle Jones, Etheridge Knight, N. J. Loftis, Audre Lorde, Haki R. Madhubuti (Don Lee), Larry Neal, Ntozake Shange, Charles Wright and many others. The Black Arts idea of Harlem as an interior landscape as well as a physical setting merged with the contemporary euphemism for racial slum to identify Harlem as the 'inner city' of the black spirit in the soul land of America. Black writers generally began to sense the fundamental unity of the Africana experience. Post-riot Harlem was seen from outside the United States as a shared motif of the common tragedies and potentialities of black life by Lebert Bethune, René Depestre, Lamine Diakhaté, Jean Louis Dongmo, Valère Epée, Keorapetse Kgositsile, Nicolas Pasteur Lappe, Lennox Raphael and Juan Romero, for blacks outside the United States accepted the motif of eruptive Harlem, nation-building within the riot-torn ghetto, as a microcosm symbolising a resurgent spirit throughout the diaspora.

After 1964, three international generations of black authors were writing together of Harlem, an unprecedented glory in Africana literatures after the holocausts of slavery and colonial exploitation. In fact, the celebration of a multigenerational sense of Harlem is a characteristic feature of several of the most inventive works of this period: Melvin B. Tolson's *Harlem Gallery, Part I: The Curator*; Ismael Reed's *Mumbo Jumbo*; and Audre Lorde's *ZAMI: The Spelling of My Name*. Melvin B. Tolson's comic ode is set in a Harlem that is simultaneously of the 1920s, the 1950s and the 1960s. Ismael Reed's hoodoo detective story cum history of the world is set in an identifiable Harlem of the 1920s that, nevertheless, transcends chronology. In Audre Lorde's mythobiography, as she terms it, the various perceptual Harlems she recalls from various stages of her personal development as a woman and a writer, resonate with each other and with the respective experiences of Harlem of her immigrant mother and father.

The literary *topos* of black Harlem is a twentieth-century original, a modern motif created by Afro-American writers inspired by the initial fervour of racial awakening of the Manhattan neighbourhood north of Central Park, and reinterpreted over the decades by three generations of writers of different races. Neither borrowed from western literary sources nor inherited from African or Africana traditions and verbal modes, the figure of Harlem rechannelled and redirected the legacy of both cultures nevertheless. The force of these confluences differed in characteristic ways, however, because the figurative usages of black Harlem evolved in a parallel but bifurcated progression from the dual visions of Harlem of black and non-black authors in the 1920s. With some exceptions, notably Federico García Lorca, writers who were not black focused on Harlem as a fundamentally alien landscape but one readily employ-able as a metaphor for issues of the moment in western culture (i.e. primitivism in the 1920s, anti-bourgeois alienation in the 1950s, revolutionary idealism in the 1960s). Because their Harlem was conceived initially as a landscape of fundamental human otherness, albeit one in the heart of the great modern metropolis, they simply interwove the motif of black Harlem into the cultural and mythological fabric of the west as an occasional *topos* for its picturesque and exotic texture when it served the ethos of the times.

The initial elaboration of the Harlem motif by Africana writers, on the other hand, was influenced by the need to make a new mythology of racial being which defied not only the historic, sociological and cultural status of the Negro race but also his place in the mythology of the west. Their usage of Harlem with a concern for a self-created ontology of blackness incorporated manifold significances of Afro-American life in the twentieth century and was understood in other Africana literatures as expressive of a parallel ethos. Their evolution of the Harlem motif followed the traditional figurative usage of the legendary and historical places of the diaspora, for those places, real or imaginary (such as the briarpatch in Afro-American folktales, Egypt and the Promised Land in the diction of the spirituals, Guinea in the cosmology of Haitian voodoo, and Babylon and Ethiopia in the imagery of Rastafari), in which black peoples have vested their spirit and history in the diaspora are the cultural precedents for the literary usage of the figure of black Harlem by black writers. Afro-America vested its psyche in the idea of Harlem as in few other symbolic places, and this extraordinary aesthetic and spiritual investment was accepted and given symbolic currency by black writers around the world in a spirit of racial renewal.

The question of how writers view Harlem uncovers a rich lode of coherence and continuity transcending national and linguistic boundaries in the modern literatures of the black world, and opens a significant approach for the growing scholarly consciousness of an existing Africana literary tradition composed in the European languages of the diaspora but deriving its identity and authority from the continuity of its distinctive forms, practices and achievements. The question also points to an intriguing instance of the complex interplay between the Africana literatures and the literatures of the west. Writers who employ the figure of black Harlem reflect a modernist synthesis of intermingled currents, for the evolution of the literary figure of black Harlem traces a significant path of convergence between traditional Afro-American and western usages of symbolic landscapes. Thus, an inflection of western literature's motif of the symbolic city and the traditional Africana usage of historic and legendary places have been alloyed in the innovative literary figure of black Harlem, the evolution of which has been deliberate, self-conscious and incremental from one international generation of writers to the next.

## NOTES

1. *Man-Making Words*, ed. and trans. R. Marquez and D. A. McMurray (Amherst, Mass.: University of Massachusetts Press, 1970) pp. 54–5.
2. *Anthologie de la nouvelle poésie nègre et malgache de langue française*, ed. L. Senghor (Paris: Presses Universitaires de Frances, 1969) p. 123.
3. *Obra poética de Francisco José Tenreiro* (Lisbon: Editora Pax, 1967) p. 91.
4. Jesse B. Simple, *Simple's Uncle Sam* (New York: Hill & Wang, 1965) p. 17.
5. Ibid., p. 20.
6. Jesse B. Simple, *The Best of Simple* (New York: Hill & Wang, 1961) p. 23.
7. *Sixes and Sevens: An Anthology of New Poetry*, ed. P. Breman (London: Paul Breman, 1962) p. 21.
8. Seymour Krim, *Views of a Nearsighted Cannoneer* (New York: E. P. Dutton, 1968) pp. 100–2.
9. Aram Saroyan, *Genesis Angels* (New York: William Morrow, 1979) p. 8.
10. John Tyrell, *Naked Angels: The Lives and Literature of the Beat Generation* (New York: McGraw-Hill, 1973) p. 89.
11. Allen Ginsberg, *Gates of Wrath* (Bolinas: Grey Fox Presses, 1972) p. 7.
12. Allen Ginsberg, *Howl and Other Poems* (San Francisco: City Lights Books, 1965) p. 9.
13. Ibid., p. 13.
14. Ibid., p. 28.
15. Allen Ginsberg, *Reality Sandwiches: 1953–60* (San Francisco: City Lights Books, 1963) p. 72.
16. Ibid., pp. 54–5.
17. All references for Barbara Bellow Watson, 'Echoes in a Burnt Building' are to *Kenyon Review* (Autumn 1965) pp. 762–3.

# 10

# The Black Capital of the World

## CHRISTOPHER MULVEY

This chapter takes as its theme a relationship of Harlem to the general culture of Americans. In particular, it focuses upon that moment of entry into the city which is celebrated in the autobiography and art of major black artists who made the journey from the provinces of America to the 'black capital of the world'. It concentrates on an experience especially of the young black seeing very often for the first time the full potentialities of self and people.

The epic event of twentieth-century black America is the Great Migration which remade the American South as much as it remade the American North. Its shaping of the lives of black urban populations was recognised in the attention given it by the Report of the National Advisory Commission on Civil Disorders (the Kerner Report of 1968). Three major routes out of the South had been established in the decade between 1910 and 1920 when blacks began moving along the Atlantic seaboard towards Boston, up the Mississippi towards Chicago and Detroit, and out to the west towards California. This pattern accounted for the present population distribution of black Americans, making them in the twentieth century an urban people. In the nineteenth century they had been essentially a rural people and 90 per cent had then lived in the South.[1] The 'magnitude of this migration' meant that between 1910 and 1960 nearly four and a half million blacks left the South.[2] In half a century this was an internal migration of a fair portion of a people. By 1940 the black population of New York City had grown to 458,000; it was to grow to 1,000,000 by 1960.[3] The Kerner Report further estimated that 50 per cent of the non-white migrants to the New York Metropolitan Area were from five Southern states, North Carolina, South Carolina, Virginia, Georgia and Alabama.[4]

These were the figures. James Baldwin's account of the Great Migration gave the figures flesh and blood – quite a lot of blood.

'The reason my father left the land', he wrote in 'The Language of the Streets', 'and came to the city was because he was driven by the wave of terror which overtook the South after the First World War when soldiers were being lynched in uniform, slaughtered like flies. So daddy came to New York – others went to Chicago, others went to Detroit – and we know what happened when we got there.'[5] That summed up one family's memory of the Great Migration along the Atlantic seaboard route out of the South. In the economist's terms, Baldwin's father was as much influenced by the pull factor of the New York City economy as he was by the push factor of Southern violence, and, it should be added (though Baldwin did not add it), by the push factor of the Southern economy which could not support its population. 'So daddy came to New York': there James Baldwin was born. Baldwin did not write of the South with any affection because for Baldwin the South was a white place. The affection for the South expressed by so many blacks in the North found no echo in him. There was no love of its landscapes and no aching after a lost black world of grandfathers and great aunts, of extended families and communities of affection.

'So daddy came to New York' and when he arrived in New York, it was to Harlem that he went. 'In the very process of being transplanted the Negro is being transformed', Alain Locke wrote in 1925 in *The New Negro*.[6] And Locke rejected the demographic and statistical explanation of the 'New Negro' which was to become the kernel of the *Kerner Report*.

> The tide of Negro migration, northward and city-ward, is not to be fully explained as a blind flood started by the demands of war industry coupled with the shutting off of foreign migration, or by the pressure of poor crops coupled with increased social terrorism in certain sections of the South and Southwest.[7]

Alain Locke was already in 1925 distancing the migration from the South from the terms in which James Baldwin's daddy (his stepfather, that was) formulated it for his son: 'soldiers [black soldiers] were being lynched in uniform, slaughtered like flies'.[8] Alain Locke described the flight to the city in terms very like those which the mainstream American culture used to explain that even greater migration which, as Locke said, had by 1925 been 'shut off': the migration, or immigration, of the tens of millions from

Europe to America in the period of the late nineteenth and early twentieth centuries.

This movement of peoples had been mythologised in terms of the text of the American Dream so that it might be read as Emma Lazarus read it in her monumental inscription 'The New Colossus':

> Give me your tired, your poor,
> Your huddled masses yearning to breathe free,
> The wretched refuse of your teeming shore,
> Send these, the homeless, tempest-tossed, to me:
> I lift my lamp beside the golden door.

White immigrants passed in front of the Statute of Liberty on their way to New York; black migrants mainly passed behind it. But blacks too arrived by boat and James Weldon Johnson arrived that way on his journeys from Jacksonville, Florida. He did not need to land at Ellis Island since he was already an American. In his novel, *Autobiography of an Ex-Colored Man*, he gave an account of New York City from the bay different from that in the classic text of arrival:

> New York City is the most totally fascinating thing in America. She sits like a great witch at the gate of the country, showing her alluring white face and hiding her crooked hands and feet under the folds of her wide garments – constantly enticing thousands from far within, and tempting those who come from across the seas to go no further. And all these become victims of her caprice. Some she at once crushes beneath her cruel feet; others she condemns to a fate like that of galley slaves; a few she favours and fondles, riding them high on the bubbles of fortune; then with a sudden breath she blows the bubbles out and laughs mockingly as she watches them fall.[9]

The guardian image of New York in Johnson's novel was not Lazarus's new Colossus with beautiful hands boldly displaying the book and torch of liberty for the newly arrived. She was instead a witch, a cripple, a slave driver, a sadist. Johnson linked black migrant with white immigrant here; he believed that the immediate deal offered to both by New York City in 1901 was the same. Johnson's inversion of the American myth of arrival was not to become the common view for blacks arriving in New York City any more than it was for whites.

'The American Negro has the great advantage', said James Baldwin in 1962, 'of having never believed that collection of myths to which white Americans cling: that their ancestors were all freedom-loving heroes, that they were born in the greatest country the world has ever seen, or that Americans are invincible in battle and wise in peace.'[10] But the American Negro, the American black, did not escape quite as completely as Baldwin believed the pervasive influence of the dominant culture. If blacks did not share with whites the myth 'that their ancestors were all freedom-loving heroes', Alain Locke none the less preferred in 1925 to explain the great migration in terms of a mythology which had been used to interpret movement towards New York for at least a hundred years.

> The wash and rush of this human tide on the beach line of the northern city centers is to be explained primarily in terms of a new vision of opportunity, of social and economic freedom, of a spirit to seize, even in the face of an extortionate and heavy toll, a chance for the improvement of conditions. With each successive wave of it, the movement of the Negro becomes more and more a mass movement toward the larger and the more democratic chance.[11]

The Negroes had not moved towards America as towards freedom, they had come in chains, but they were moving north, they were moving towards New York as other American people had moved across the Atlantic towards a vision of opportunity, of freedom, of democratic chance.

There was a tension here between the mythologically enhancing reading of the city of New York as a place which spoke of opportunity, freedom, democracy and the demographically reductive reading of the city as a place which spoke of statistics, politics, economics. People did not want their own experience to be aggregated in mass patterns which reduced their actual or apparent self-determination. Some preferred the aggrandisement of individual endeavour which myth permitted but math denied. To this end, Locke availed himself of the images of the New Man and the New Dawn, co-opting De Crevecoeur's New American man so that he became Alain Locke's New Negro who would possess the future itself, so long colonised by the white, so that it became black:

> We have tomorrow
> Bright before us
> Like a flame.

Locke, quoting Langston Hughes, expressed the conviction of the Young Negro that this was 'the promise and the warrant of a new leadership'.[12] This promise and this conviction were also confirmed by the seizure here of the imagery and the voice of European Romantic and Revolutionary texts to make them black texts. There was a price to be paid, however, because what was seized was already poisoned.

The prize, as opposed to the price, of this seizure was the splendid intoxication, the oceanic stimulus, the visionary excitement with which *The New Negro* was filled. The myth pattern of New Man and New Dawn needed completion by the image of the New Land, the City on the Hill, to which the renewed people would flock. Again Alain Locke was ready to complete the formulation. 'Here in Manhattan is not merely the largest Negro community in the world, but the first concentration in history of so many diverse elements of Negro life.'[13] Locke celebrated the diversity of New Negroes, coming as they did from North and South, from city, town and village, from Africa, the Caribbean and America. In doing so, Locke echoed the celebration of the diverse origins of the eighteenth-century New American Man. The celebration of the fusing of these diverse elements in 'the laboratory of a great race-welding',[14] as he put it, updated with a modernist image and co-opted for a black readership one of the most powerful myths of nineteenth-century white America, that it was the mixing place of races.

Israel Zangwill had developed the image for New York in his play *The Melting Pot*, in 1914 just when the First World War was shutting off white immigration to America and when the demands of the war industry were accelerating black migration to the North. In little more than a decade Alain Locke had adapted and adopted the image of the melting pot to make it refer to his new people, new land and new nation. The whites, when they came to New York and their New World, had to remake themselves by abandoning whatever nationalism they brought with them and by

adopting the nationalism of the United States of America. This for
the most part they effectively did. It was a massive demonstration
of the culture-bound status of the nation-state – something that
remained for many, both in Europe and in the United States, one
of the facts of nature. The case was less straightforward for the
Southern migrants. Alain Locke indicated that the black coming
from the South had to do something more than take up the
nationality offered to the white.

For Alain Locke, black Americans had still in 1925, like the
peoples of Ireland and Czechoslovakia, to make a new national
consciousness. The settlements that had followed on the ending
of the First World War had seen the creation of a number of new
nationals, and the nineteenth-century myth of nationalism required
that this political act be matched by the spiritual act which consisted
of the willing into being of a new national consciousness; indeed,
if this could not be achieved, there was little hope that the new
nation would be able to survive. 'The chief bond' between a people
had to be that of a 'common consciousness' not, as Locke said was
the case with all those made in the image of the Old Negro, a
'common condition'. In Dublin, the world had seen the creation
of just such a new consciousness in what Locke called the 'New
Ireland'. The arrival of this 'new people' had been heralded by the
manifestation of artistic energy very much like that which was to
be called the Harlem Renaissance. The task of the artist hero was
nothing less than 'to forge in the smithy of [his] soul the uncreated
conscience of [his] race'.[15] So said Stephen Dedalus, the craftsman,
the artificer, when he abandoned the Old Dublin for the world
capital of Paris in the last pages of *A Portrait of the Artist as a Young
Man*. Stephen Dedalus repudiated the political for the imaginative
and the mythical; he refused to take any part in the nationalist
endeavour; his name was a guarantee of that.

The Joycean clash between myth and ideology, consciouness
and politics, was exactly that to be found in Alain Locke's *New
Negro* and it was plainly stated at the end of Locke's celebration of
Harlem as the laboratory of a great race-welding. 'Without pretense
to their political significance, Harlem has the same role to play for
the New Negro as Dublin has had for the New Ireland or Prague
for the New Czechoslovakia.' The rejection of a claim to political
significance for Harlem was one with Locke's mythologising of the
Great Migration as something with origins beyond those of politics
and economics. But this left Harlem none the less with a role to

play in the forging of the consciousness of the New Negro in the smithies of the souls of all those poets, artists and musicians who made Locke's Renaissance, who became his literati, who set the pattern for writing about Harlem through the 1930s and through the 1940s.

This art mythologised the migrant's arrival in Harlem as the moment when the New Negro was born out of the Old; it was the moment that stirred the emergence of the new consciousness. Economics determined that it should be New York City which provided the locus for texts which celebrated this apotheosis of the migrant as well as the immigrant, the one to become the New Negro, the other to become the New American Man. But in this black version of the myth it was the South which equalled the Old World and Harlem which equalled the New. It was a classic motif of the American literary tradition (though its starting-point was pre-American). Locke was not inventing his pattern; he was reflecting it. Exactly what Harlem meant for the migrant hero was represented by Rudolph Fisher in a short story, 'The City of Refuge', first published in the *Atlantic Monthly* of February 1925. This was included later in the same year in Alain Locke's *The New Negro* as part of a selection of short stories introduced by Locke under the general title: 'Negro Youth Speaks'.

The hero of 'The City of Refuge', King Solomon Gillis, took the train from North Carolina to New York's Penn Terminal and the subway from Penn Terminal to Harlem to the 135th Street stop:

Heat, oppression, suffocation – eternity – 'Hundred 'n turdy-fif' next!' More turnstiles. Jonah emerging from the whale.[16]

The moment of rebirth, renewal and resurrection was clearly pointed. From the hellish heat of the subway, the hero, a king, was delivered from his suffocating imprisonment. 'Jonah emerging from the whale.' He came into the New World as a man awakening in the New Dawn: 'Clean air, blue sky, bright sunlight.' A major theme of this rhetorical structure was that of the world populated by the hero's own kind, 'Negroes at every turn . . . Negroes predominantly, overwhelmingly everywhere.' It was important in fact that there was 'here and there a white face' because that emphasised for King Solomon Gillis and the reader that the Negro predominated. The predomination of the Negro made for the New World.

Gillis had known that this was the Harlem reality before he had
left North Carolina because he had read 'occasional "colored"
newspapers from New York: newspapers that mentioned Negroes
without comment, but always spoke of a white person as "So-and-
so, white". That was the point. In Harlem, black was white.'[17] By
the act of travelling from Waxhaw, North Carolina to Harlem, New
York, King Solomon Gillis had accomplished the revolutionary act
of transforming the world, turning authority on its head, making
black white. Seeing with distinctly mythical vision, as who would
not who had just been delivered from a whale, but seeing without
distinctly political vision, King Solomon Gillis saw a world in which
the black man had power:

> For there stood a handsome, brass-buttoned giant directing the
> heaviest traffic Gillis had ever seen; halting unnumbered tons of
> automobiles and trucks and wagons and pushcarts and streetcars;
> holding them at bay with one hand while he swept similar tons
> peremptorily on with the other; ruling the wide crossing with
> supreme self-assurance; and he, too, was a Negro![18]

The moment of gaping amazement was not only one of renewal
and rebirth; Rudolph Fisher saw his hero as ambiguously placed
at the entrance of a new life. Gillis was not only to be initiated into
the mysteries of black consciousness; he was also to become the
victim of black betrayal. But his first reflections, at the point 'where
you find all the jay birds when they first hit Harlem – at the subway
entrance', as one of the less-recently arrived inhabitants put it, was
that he had experienced resurrection. '"Done died an' woke up in
Heaven", thought King Solomon, watching, fascinated.'[19] Harlem
as heaven was a repeated motif of this literature and it brought
with it the corollary of Harlem as hell. The apocalyptic and demonic
imagery alternated. Harlem was opposed to the Old World of the
White South against which it could be seen to be a heaven; Harlem
was opposed to the Old World of the Black South against which
Harlem could be seen to be a hell. Harlem was by this comparison
a horrifying version of New World of the North. This hellishness
of Harlem was reinforced by the very fact that the heroic New
Negro would be betrayed by his own kind; King Solomon Gillis
was being sized up and set up even as he stood at the entrance to
Harlem by Mouse Uggams from his home town.

The notion of the home town exactly drew together the oppositions, since Harlem could be seen simultaneously as the big city which represented everything the small town or village did not (here black literature echoed the rural bias of the mainstream American culture and literature) and as the true home of the black, the place where he was most at home, the place where he came into his own. Home to Harlem could then be the dominant motif, and getting there might be all the hero needed to achieve. 'King Solomon Gillis had longed to come to Harlem. The Uggams were always talking about it; one of their boys had gone to France in the draft and returning, had never got any nearer home than Harlem.' Claude McKay's hero returning to the US from France after the First World War came *Home to Harlem.* When he did so he was able to live through once again the enrapturing moment of the entrance, now re-entrance, and initiation, now re-initiation.

> He left his suitcase behind the counter of a saloon on Lenox Avenue. He went for a promenade on Seventh Avenue between One Hundred and Thirty-Fifth and One Hundred and Fortieth Streets. He thrilled to Harlem. His blood was hot. His eyes were alert as he sniffed the street like a hound. Seventh Avenue was nice, a little too nice.[20]

The menace was real enough but so was the excitement. The hero, Jake, was on the prowl for Locke's freedom, opportunity and democratic chance. He met it in 'a little brown girl'; she not only charged him fifty dollars at the outset but returned it at the close. The male orientation of this ritual of entry and initiation was particularly emphasised in Claude McKay's version of the pattern for a woman, called a little girl, actualised Harlem, 'Chocolate Harlem! Sweet Harlem!'[21]

But New York City was for the rural innocent a foreign land, and the black hero shared in this configuration with all the heroes who landed on America's shores to make their name and win their fame. Arrival overland obscured this dimension of the pattern and for this reason, Langston Hughes's account of his arrival in Harlem following a boat journey from Mexico both drew the analogy between the patterns of migrant and immigrant arrival very clearly and indicated how other black writers focused their emotional attention on Harlem not on New York City. Gillis in 'City of Refuge' and Jake in *Home to Harlem* passed straight through white New York; it was part of the journey, not part of the arrival.

Langston Hughes arrived on the evening of Sunday 4 September 1921.[22] His particular journey, following the grief and anxieties of a reluctant period in Mexico at his father's bidding, made him as excited as any traveller by the sea approach to New York

> But, boy! At last! New York was pretty, rising out of the bay in the sunset – the thrill of those towers of Manhattan with their million golden eyes, growing slowly taller and taller above the green water, until they looked as if they could almost touch the sky! Then Brooklyn Bridge, gigantic in the dusk! Then the necklaces of lights, glowing everywhere around us, as we docked on the Brooklyn side. All this made me feel it was better to come to New York than to any other city in the world.[23]

The young black poet experienced none of the misgivings of James Weldon Johnson's 'ex-colored man'. Langston Hughes had to take a room in a hotel off Times Square that first night. It was not until the Monday morning that he displaced the great immigrant scene of New York Bay from the ship's rail with the great migrant scene of Harlem from the subway entrance at 135th Street. The initiating event of 1921 was repeated as a centrepiece of Hughes's autobiography of 1940, *The Big Sea*:

> Like the bullfights, I can never put on paper the thrill of that underground ride to Harlem. I had never been in a subway before and it fascinated me – the noise, the speed, the green lights ahead. At every station I kept watching for the sign: 135TH STREET. When I saw it, I held my breath. I came out onto the platform with two heavy bags and looked around. It was still early morning and people were going to work. Hundreds of colored people! I wanted to shake hands with them, speak to them. I hadn't seen any colored people for so long – that is, any Negro colored people.
>
> I went up the steps and out into the bright September sunlight. Harlem! I stood there, dropped my bags, took a deep breath and felt happy again. I registered at the Y.[24]

The climactic moment of Harlem itself, combining a promise for a black future with a splendid appearance in a black present, must have come shortly after Langston Hughes's arrival there in 1921:

'In the make-up of New York', wrote James Weldon Johnson in 1925,

> 'Harlem is not merely a Negro colony or community, it is a city within a city, the greatest Negro city in the world. It is not a slum or a fringe, it is located in the heart of Manhattan and occupies one of the most beautiful and healthful sections of the city. It is not a 'quarter' of dilapidated tenements, but is made up of new-law apartments and handsome dwellings, with well-paved and well-lighted streets.'[25]

Johnson dated the beginning of black Harlem to 1900 so that its growth coincided with his own life in New York and he made arrival in Harlem not a once-only experience but a continuous, endlessly repeated happening: 'A stranger', he wrote,

> 'who rides up magnificent Seventh Avenue on a bus or in an automobile must be struck with surprise at the transformation which takes place after he crosses One Hundred and Twenty-fifth Street. Beginning there, the population suddenly darkens and he rides through twenty-five solid blocks where the passers-by, the shoppers, those sitting in restaurants, coming out of theaters, standing in doorways and looking out of windows are practically all Negroes; and then he emerges where the population as suddenly becomes white again. There is nothing just like it in any other city in the country, for there is no preparation for it; no change in the character of the houses and streets; no change, indeed, in the appearance of the people, except their color.'[26]

The *locus classicus* of the Harlem entrance and initiation was Ralph Ellison's representation of the trope in *Invisible Man*. Ellison created the great migrant text which contained in its title the full political negation of the mythological positive which would make the New Negro the New American Man. Ellison effectively denied the promise of Alain Locke and the Negro literati. Ellison's hero was eventually to go unseen altogether in a world which was blind to colour. But before the political reality overwhelmed the mythical vision, Ellison let the pattern have full play.

All the elements were present, the terrifying subway ride, the delivery into Harlem, the world of black people, black women

serving behind counters, black policemen directing white traffic,
the directions to the Men's House where the hero would first
room:

> This really was Harlem, and now all the stories which I had
> heard of the city-within-in-a-city leaped alive in my mind. The
> vet had been right: For me this was not a city of realities, but of
> dreams; perhaps because I had always thought of my life as
> being confined to the South. . . . I moved wide-eyed, trying to
> take in the bombardment of impressions.[27]

The Invisible Man stood as wide-eyed as King Solomon Gillis. The
Invisible Man's emergence from the subway matched that of
Langston Hughes's emergence from the subway at 135th Street in
1921 but Ellison's writing was a more knowing writing. The
Invisible Man heard 'a small voice' telling him of 'a new world of
possibility' but he left the scene of his enlightenment in fear. 'I
was careful not to look back lest I see a riot flare.'

The new world of Harlem represented for the hero of the black
text exactly what the New World always represented in the
American text, a land of plenty. The hero was a Dick Whittington
making his way from childhood poverty to adult wealth in the
capital city where he would find the streets paved with gold. In
white stories, the poor boy had every chance of becoming Lord
Mayor; in black stories, the chances were not so good. Like the
Invisible Man, every black hero carried with him a letter of
introduction which would close the doors of the land of opportunity. 'I had seen the letter,' the Invisible Man said, 'and it had
practically ordered me killed. By slow degrees.'[28] The white hero
might carry a deathletter in his pocket but the white hero could
hand it on to someone else, and for this reason he was a hero.
The black hero could not, and for this reason he was a hero. The
deathletter was of course concealed only from the naive hero newly
emerging from the subway, the underground, the underworld. He
carried his *todesbrief* not only in a closely enveloped message secure
in his briefcase but in the openly displayed message written on
his skin.

The hero was to be kept running and the hero on route to
Harlem was typically a hero in flight to Harlem, as the title of
Rudolph Fisher's story, 'The City of Refuge', made plain. 'Back in
North Carolina Gillis had shot a white man and, with the aid of

prayer and an automobile, probably escaped a lynching . . .; and so he had come to Harlem. . . . The land of plenty was more than that now: it was also the city of refuge.'[29] Harlem became then an alternative to the prison and death represented by the old country of the South. Defying the white man, killing the white man, was the heroic crime and even the well-meaning Invisible Man came close to giving his white man a nearly fatal heart attack.

Defying the white man made the black man a hero and in writing a preface to *Native Son* in New York in 1940, Richard Wright identified a variety of ways in which the black man might defy the white. To the defying blacks, Wright gave the name of his hero, Bigger Thomas. 'The Bigger Thomases were the only Negroes I know of who consistently violated the Jim Crow laws of the South and got away with it, at least for a sweet brief spell. Eventually, the whites who restricted their lives made them pay a terrible price. They were shot, hanged, maimed, lynched, and generally hounded until they were either dead or their spirits broken.'[30] Wright said he saw no other kinds of blacks ever defy the Jim Crow laws of Dixie, especially not those blacks called 'leaders', but Wright heard one man after another wish for another way, another country, an escape. Religion, blues, jazz, swing, alcohol, education helped some. For Wright himself, escape came with migration North to Chicago and there he learned two ways in which Bigger represented something larger than waywardness: 'First, being free of the daily pressure of the Dixie environment, I was able to come into possession of my own feelings. Second, my contact with the labor movement and its ideology made me see Bigger clearly and feel what he meant.'[31] For Wright, the transformation that migration worked upon the migrant was from slave to proletarian. For Wright, that meant something which the 'nationalist' and racial thrust of this textual pattern in other black writers could not mean: 'I made the discovery', said Wright, 'that Bigger Thomas was not black all the time; he was white, too, and there were literally millions of him, everywhere.'[32]

Wright delineated precisely the distinction to be made between the mythical and the ideological meanings of the black city to the black hero. If it were read in the mythic mode then the hero swelled with every kind of glorious but delusory fulfilment. It was a land of plenty, a land of freedom, a city of refuge, a black kingdom. If it were read ideologically, then the hero did not allow his mind to be dazzled by the image of a black policemen or a black shop-girl and recognised that he still carried his deathletter about with him wherever he went. But Wright did not belittle the escape, as he called it, from 'the daily pressure of the Dixie environment',[33] which was represented by the complete segregation of a black city such as the South Side or Harlem. Dixie was a prison and the black artist, like the black hero in flight to the South Side or to Harlem, had to escape that prison before he could sing. The link of artist, exile and imagination established by Alain Locke and identified by him with James Joyce and the New Dublin was endorsed by later black texts in a powerful fashion. Wright moved north to Chicago and from Chicago to New York and, as it were, in the same spiritual direction from New York to Paris. James Baldwin moved in the same trajectory except that, starting in New York, his first move was to Paris.

While Wright did not subscribe in his autobiography, *Black Boy*, to any ordinary version of the American Dream – 'I had sense enough', he wrote, 'not to hope to get rich' – he was subscribing to Alain Locke's notion that the black was choosing to go north. Opportunity, freedom and democratic chance seemed even more a thing chosen in the case of the black artist. 'Yet I felt that I had to go somewhere and do something to redeem my being alive.'[34] The authenticity of the individual's experience of his own reality should not be denied, but the reality of the black's going north was just as well expressed in a scene which James Weldon Johnson recalled from Jacksonville, Florida, during the First World War. After the government and the big industrial concerns had started to send 'hundreds, perhaps thousands, of labor agents into the South who recruited Negroes by wholesale', he wrote,

I sat one day and watched the stream of migrants passing to take the train. For hours they passed steadily, carrying flimsy suit cases new and shiny, rusty old ones, bursting at the seams, boxes and bundles and impedimenta of all sorts, including banjos, guitars, birds in cages and what not. Similar scenes were being enacted in cities and towns all over the region. The first wave of the great exodus of Negroes from the South was on. Great numbers of these migrants headed for New York or eventually got there, and naturally the majority went up into Harlem.[35]

Naturally they went to Harlem, he said. If it were not in fact a fact of nature but very much one of economics and demography, it might as well have been a fact of nature for the millions caught up in the exodus. They took banjos with them and guitars and singing birds and they took musicians with them and poets and novelists. Wright was born in the state of Mississippi and when it came his turn to go north in the 1930s, he just as 'naturally' went to Chicago. And in the shape of his own personality he took the South with him as it had been ingrained by the violent love of his mother, his grandmother and his aunt. He lived with it in the North as much as the hero of his novel lived with his mother and sister in Chicago. The protective and imprisoning love of the black Southern family was identified by Ralph Ellison as a mechanism which repressed in the black individual the urge towards individualism. It was a mechamism as much at odds with one thrust of mainstream American culture as it was in line with another.

> The pre-individualistic black community discourages individuality out of self-defense [wrote Ellison]. Having learned through experience that the whole group is punished for the actions of the single member, it has worked out efficient techniques of behavior control. For in many Southern communities every one knows everyone else and is vulnerable to his opinions. In some communities everyone is 'related' regardless of blood-ties. The regard shown by the group for its members, its general communal character and its cohesion are often mentioned. For by comparison with the coldly impersonal relationships of the urban industrial community, its relationships are personal and warm.[36]

The great Northern ghettoes could represent a real liberation from the direct interference of the family just as it could represent a real liberation from 'the daily pressure of the Dixie environment'. It was as a release from imprisonment that entry into Harlem could figure for its residents. 'I was part of that generation', wrote Baldwin in *Notes of a Native Son*, 'which had never seen the landscape of what Negroes sometimes call the Old Country.'[37] But in his story 'Sonny's Blues', an account of a convict's return from an upstate prison, Baldwin reworked in 1957 the classic tropes of Harlem entry, the return to the black city, the black homecoming. The returned man met by his brother at Penn Station asked that their taxi take a route along Central Park West on the way to Harlem.

Yet [said the narrator brother], as the cab moved uptown through streets which seemed, with a rush, to darken with dark people, and as I covertly studied Sonny's face, it came to me that what we both were seeking through our separate cab windows was that part of ourselves which had been left behind. It's always in the hour of trouble and confrontation that the missing member aches.

We hit 110th Street and started rolling up Lenox Avenue. And I'd known this avenue all my life, but it seemed to me again, as it had seemed on the day I'd first heard about Sonny's trouble, filled with a hidden menace which was its very breath of life.[38]

Baldwin did not in 1957 retain very much of Alain Locke's image of Harlem. It too had become a trap and it too could represent the Old Country. The fine avenues and brownstone houses had become ugly with drugs, death, decay and development. The boundary line between black Harlem and white Manhattan had moved further south since Johnson gave it as 125th Street in 1925. But the trope of entry and initiation was still not without some energy as the streets 'seemed, with a rush, to darken with dark people'. Harlem, by comparison with the white Manhattan – 'stony, lifeless' – was breathing life, even if it was a life of menace. Sonny was to find work in Harlem and was to discover himself, or be discovered by his brother, to be an artist of deep, traditional power who had learned to sing the blues in a way which represented all those who have gone before him. 'He had made it his: that long line, of which we knew only Mama and Daddy. And he was giving it back, as everything must be given back, so that passing through death, it can live forever.'[39] Ineluctably the text comforted itself with intimations of immortality for which there could no more be justification than there could be verification. The sacramental food of myth is addictive.

As the myth of entry and initiation became or gave way to the myth of re-entry and renewal, it drew with it evocations of the myth of return. Claude McKay's *Home to Harlem* of 1929 explicitly evoked that pattern but it was a pattern implicit in a number of the statements and restatements of the myth of entry. Harlem's image as the new Black World was shadowed by its being made the image of the black's true Old World, not the South, that was, but Africa. The ambiguities felt about the 'old country' which was once the Slave States were not to be felt about the continent from which the ancestors were abducted. When Sonny sang the blues in Harlem, the line in which he was singing and of which the narrator knew only the last link, 'that long line, of which we knew only Mama and Daddy', reached back through time, to the black's lost past. James Baldwin's hard prose was never far from this sentimentalisation. Characteristically, he left it to the last pages or lines of his tellings.

As the spell of Harlem failed, fewer and fewer writers were able or willing to invoke the trope of arrival in Harlem as a triumph of black youth, as a moment of any kind of mythical, mystical significance for the black race. In his *Autobiography*, Malcolm X wrote: 'New York was heaven to me. And Harlem was Seventh Heaven! . . . This was in 1942. I had just turned seventeen.'[40] But by 1962, Malcolm X spoke of Harlem as spent: 'Even for Negroes Harlem nightlife is about finished. Most Negroes who have money to spend are spending it downtown somewhere in the hypocritical "integration".'[41] So that for Maya Angelou, in *The Heart of a Woman*, arrival in Harlem in 1957 was a significant but not a unique experience. Like Malcolm X, she had to move to Africa itself before her text initiated the ritual of entrance. It was there, first but incompletely, in the City of Cairo, whose 'avenues', she said, 'burst wide open with such a force of color, people, actions and smells I was stripped of cool composure'.[42] But real entrance and full initiation to the black city come only with arrival at the city of Accra, south of the Sahara, in black Africa. She entered by the airport not by the subway:

The airport at Accra sounded like an adult playground and looked like a festival. Single travelers, wearing Western suits or dresses which would be deemed fashionable in New York, were surrounded by hordes of well-wishers, swathed in floral prints or rich plaid silk of Kente cloth. Languages turned the air into clouds of lusty sound. The sight of so many black people stirred my deepest emotions. I had been away from the colors too long. Guy and I grinned at each other and turned to see a sight which wiped our faces clean. Three black men walked past us wearing airline uniforms, visored caps, white pants and jackets whose shoulders bristled with epaulettes. Black pilots? Black captains?

It was 1962. In our country, the cradle of democracy, whose anthem boasted 'the land of the free, the home of the brave,' the only black men in our airport fueled planes, cleaned cabins, loaded food, or were skycaps, racing the pavement for tips.[43]

James Weldon Johnson, Alain Locke, Langston Hughes, King Solomon Gillis, the Invisible Man, Malcolm X, even Baldwin's narrator had shared these feelings. The black traffic policeman of 1925 became the black airline pilot of 1963 when early twentieth-century Harlem became mid twentieth-century Africa, for arrival in Harlem was a type of the arrival of life itself. A pattern of black writing was working itself out and it was a pattern re-enacted not only by writers but by musicians, painters, actors and every kind of black striver who was drawn to prove him- or herself in the black capital of the world. Not only are these self-reflexive patterns of black fiction and black biography to be laid against one another, these patterns may in turn be laid against those replicated by parallel movements in American culture and politics. Beyond mythic harmonies lie ideological struggles and beyond both lie demographic determinations.

## NOTES

1. Kenneth Fox, *Metropolitan America* (London: Macmillan, 1985) p. 118.
2. Kerner Report, *Report of the National Advisory Commission on Civil Disorders* (New York: E. P. Dutton, 1968) p. 240.
3. Fox, *Metropolitan America*, p. 118.
4. Kerner Report, p. 240.
5. James Baldwin, 'The Language of the Streets', in *Literature and the Urban American Experience*, ed. M. C. Jaye and A. C. Watt (Manchester: Manchester University Press, 1982) p. 135.
6. Alain Locke, 'The New Negro', in *The New Negro*, ed. A. Locke (New York: Atheneum, 1975) p. 6.
7. Locke, 'New Negro', p. 6.
8. Baldwin, 'Language', p. 135.
9. James Weldon Johnson, *The Autobiography of an Ex-Colored Man*, in *Black Joy*, ed. J. David (Chicago: Cowles, 1971) pp. 77–8.
10. James Baldwin, *The Fire Next Time* (New York: Dell, 1969) p. 136.
11. Locke, 'New Negro' p. 6.
12. Ibid., p. 7.
13. Ibid., p. 7.
14. Ibid., p. 8.
15. James Joyce, *A Portrait of the Artist as a Young Man* (Harmondsworth, Middx: Penguin, 1974) p. 253.

16. Rudolph Fisher, 'The City of Refuge', in *The New Negro*, ed. A. Locke (New York: Atheneum, 1975) p. 57.
17. Fisher, 'City of Refuge', p. 58.
18. Ibid., pp. 58–9.
19. Ibid., p. 59.
20. Claude McKay, *Home to Harlem*, in *Black Writers of America*, ed. R. Barksdale and K. Kinnamon (New York: Macmillan, 1972) p. 498.
21. Ibid., p. 499.
22. Arnold Rampersad, *The Life of Langston Hughes*, vol. 1 (New York: Oxford University Press) p. 50.
23. Langston Hughes, *The Big Sea* (New York: Hill & Wang, 1977) p. 80.
24. Ibid., p. 81.
25. James Weldon Johnson, 'Harlem: the Culture Capital', in A. Locke (ed.), *The New Negro* (New York: Atheneum, 1975) p. 301.
26. Ibid., pp. 301–2.
27. Ralph Ellison, *Invisible Man* (Harmondsworth, Middx: Penguin, 1982) p. 132.
28. Ibid., p. 159.
29. Fisher, 'City of Refuge', p. 59.
30. Richard Wright, *Native Son* (London: Jonathan Cape, 1970) p. v.
31. Ibid., p. viii.
32. Ibid., p. viii.
33. Ibid., p. viii.
34. Richard Wright, *Black Boy* (London: Longman, 1977) p. 148.
35. Johnson, 'Harlem', p. 305.
36. Ralph Ellison, 'Richard Wright's Blues', in *Black Writers of America*, ed. R. Barksdale and K. Kinnamon (New York: Macmillan, 1972) p. 691.
37. James Baldwin, 'Sonny's Blues', in *Dark Symphony: Negro Literature in America*, ed. James A. Emanuel and Theodore L. Gross (New York: The Free Press, 1968) p. 301.
38. Ibid., p. 326.
39. Ibid., p. 347.
40. Malcolm X, *The Autobiography of Malcolm X* (New York: Grove, 1966) pp. 162–4.
41. Malcolm X, *Autobiography*, p. 204.
42. Maya Angelou, *The Heart of a Woman* (London: Virago, 1986) p. 212.
43. Angelou, *Heart of a Woman*, p. 258.

# 11

# New York as a Third World City

## ARTHUR E. PARIS

It remains axiomatic that New York City is both the premier American metropolis and a world-class city as well. Indeed, its advanced position has led American scholars to see it as unique, rather than typical, especially in regard to its problems. This tendency has been heightened by the changes and transformations that this metropolis is undergoing, and has undergone since the Second World War. These changes are fundamental and structural and are altering the fabric of urban and metropolitan life there (and I would suggest in other American and even some European cities) as well. Further, and more importantly for this discussion, some of these changes parallel developments in a number of Third World cities.

Western social scientists are unaccustomed to thinking of their own advanced industrial societies in terms applied to developing countries. Comparative analysis most often treats the developing countries in categories derived from western examples. In this instance it seems useful to reverse that procedure and look at American urban life, at least in the case of New York City, from within concepts applied to Third World cities. Those ideas and the analysis within which they are situated offer (more) useful analytical schemas than the conventional analysis for some currently observed phenomena.

I would like to outline some of the transformations which New York City is undergoing and which are giving it characteristics more akin to Kingston, San Domingo, *et al.*, and then note some implications of these developments for social policy and planning. Before doing that, let me set the context of discussions by giving some historical background.

## STRUCTURAL BACKGROUND

Since the end of the post-Korean war recovery (roughly), New York City's economy has been in a state of stagnation, if not long-term decline. The process has been uneven. Some sectors and geographic areas have enjoyed steady, even explosive, growth, while others have experienced stagnation and decay. This is partly a result of the peculiarities of US land-development policy and state and municipal practice. Growth and development are most dynamic on the geographic frontiers of US cities. This is where land, and therefore housing, is cheapest to acquire and build; this is where the biggest increases in population growth are recorded; and this where (at least initially), taxes and the other out-of-pocket civic costs of metropolitan life are lowest. Hence jobs and people flock to these areas, from the more developed areas of the metropolis. The state and municipalities facilitate this exodus of their affluent middle-class populations by building highways and rail links back into the central city for the new suburbanites and by subsidising their mortgages. This makes it yet more attractive to leave the 'crowded', 'crime-ridden', increasingly non-white central city, for the (white) pastoral suburbs – which the new residents none the less leave during the day to work in the city.

The catch is that the frontier is always moving and, since about 1920 in the East, has surpassed the political bounds of the municipality. Thus people are no longer moving about *within* the city, but have escaped its political and tax obligations, while still availing themselves of its services, culture and jobs. Thus the cost of continued suburban growth for cities has undergone a qualitative upward shift. No longer are municipalities providing new infrastructure for citizens settling new territory within their bounds, but services to affluent non-residents, who are able to evade the costs of those services, thereby saddling the city citizenry with the added costs for services, from which they derive little benefit.

Since the end of the nineteenth century this pattern of economic cum geographic growth has changed American cities, first into metropolises, and now megalopolises, for example 'BosWash' – the eastern strip of metropolitan development running from Boston to Washington. The Regional Plan Association for New York has moved from dealing with the metropolitan region as a twenty-two-county area in 1950 to a thirty-one-county region in 1985. Currently, it includes not only the five counties of New York City proper, but some in the adjoining states of Connecticut and New Jersey, and counties from formerly 'upstate' New York as well.

The counties and towns immediately outside and adjacent to New York City (Teaneck and the Oranges in New Jersey; Mt Vernon and New Rochelle, Armonk, Yonkers and Port Washington in Westchester; and Hempstead, Freeport and Rockeville Centre on Long Island) experienced substantial growth in population, commercial and even industrial activity, at least through the 1950s. As the developmental frontier has swept past them, they too have begun to slide into stagnation and decay like the central cities before them. Again within the region, however, some economic sectors have gained ground (health, finance, and real estate, etc.) while others have continued their steady decline (apparel, manufacturing, etc.).

Overall, while New York City and the surrounding metropolitan area remains the cultural and economic capital of the US, its economy and population have stagnated and it has lost some of its eminence relative to other American cities. This overall weakening has been noted only in recent hindsight. Such awareness was forced upon public officials and their advisers by the fiscal crisis of the mid-1970s. At that time New York City effectively defaulted on its debt obligations, and the city government and more specifically its budget and taxing power were rendered hostage to the banks to ensure that its debt-holders held first claim upon the city treasury.[1] Prior to the mid-1970s public officials were too busy 'managing growth' to pay much attention to the signs of long-term decay.[2]

The fiscal crisis swept away the more comfortable preoccupations with growth, and in its wake political and social science analysis has been much more sombre. Scholarly opinion has continued to see New York City as unique, and has resisted viewing the city as merely the leading example of large-scale changes which are affecting more and more American (and even European) cities as well.

As noted above, the fiscal crisis of the mid-1970s swept away the grander delusions of continued growth. It revealed more clearly the underlying weakness of the city's industrial structure. What had previously seemed a not-too-serious cut became a haemorrhage. Between 1974 and 1979, job losses averaged 68,000 a year; 43,000 of these were in manufacturing, and of these, 12,000 a year were in garment and apparel production.[3]

The 267,000 drop in factory employment from 1970 to 1980 accounted for nearly three-fifths of the city's 447,000 net job loss for the decade . . . This decline [in manufacturing] followed a 181,000 drop between 1960 and 1970, and a 1950–60 loss of 92,000. In percentage terms, the 35% rate of decline for the 1970s was nearly double the 19% rate for the prior decade and about quadruple the 1950–60 rate of 9%.[4]

Over the course of the last decade one-third of the industrial jobs disappeared from the city's economy. Not all of these simply evaporated. Some went to the adjacent suburban regions, others to the newer booming sunbelt areas and still others went overseas. The net effect, however, was that a quarter of a million (mainly working-class) New Yorkers suffered economic dislocation or disruption at best, or structural unemployment (in the neutered language of the policy analysts) at worst. Between 1968 and 1976, the low point during the fiscal crisis, the number of unemployed jumped from 104,000 to 343,000, and the unemployment rate went from 3.1 to 11.2 per cent. At 8.3 per cent in 1985 it was still more than double the 1968 low.[5]

A greater sign of the scale of the economic decline was its impact on the city's minority population. The unemployment rate for blacks went from 8.5 per cent in 1974 to 13.6 per cent in 1984. For younger blacks these unemployment rates were a marker of the social disaster they had experienced in the past fifteen years.[6] In 1971 black youth unemployment (persons 16–21 years old) was 27.4 per cent; 'in 1982 (latest available data) fewer than one in ten black teenagers held jobs'.[7]

## DEMOGRAPHIC BACKGROUND

In the boom induced by the Second World War, New York, like other northern and western cities, attracted large numbers of Afro-Americans from the South, who came seeking civil liberties denied them in their home areas, but more importantly jobs in the industrial war economy. This migration was not new, since it had been occurring in waves since early in the century. But the influx of Afro-Americans, during and after the war, coincided with the urban exodus of suburb-bound whites. This dual migration began to change the demographic profile of the electorate, and, of equal significance, the in-migration of unskilled black workers occurred at the moment that the city's industrial economy started to falter.

The in-migration of Afro-Americans has been followed in rapid succession by the immigration of large numbers of, first, Caribbean, and, more recently, other Third World peoples (e.g. Koreans, East Indians, etc.) This continued immigration of peoples of colour has led to the transformation of the labour force along racial lines. The dual inflow and exodus of blacks and whites and the stagnation of the city's industrial economy noted above, produced initially a situation where black workers not only entered the industrial economy at the start of its decline but were also trapped in this decaying sector, because of racism and discrimination and the erosion of better-paying jobs as the job and career ladder – the normal channel of upward mobility – decayed. Thus black workers were trapped in central city ghettoes at the bottom of the industrial order, while whites either lost better-paying jobs or those jobs followed their holders out of the central city.

The continued immigration of Third World peoples has further altered this situation. Not only is the economic order stratified along racial lines, but it is becoming segmented along ethnic lines as well, with one or another new immigrant group concentrated in a particular occupational area or economic niche: there are concentrations of Chinese in the garment industry, Greeks in the restaurant trade, Latin (women) in light manufacturing, etc.

Looking at the continuing migration stream and the steady industrial decline, one must ask: Why do these people continue to come? What opportunities can they find in these decaying industrial cities? And what is the connection between these developments and the parallels to Third World cities I invoked at the beginning of this chapter?

The answers to these questions have to do with (1) factors in the domestic situations out of which the immigrants come; (2) the specifics of the places they find or make for themselves here; (3) the ways in which the ecology of First World cities is being reshaped amidst the decline of their industrial bases in the late twentieth century.

## THE THIRD WORLD(ISATION) OF NEW YORK

First, immigrants, especially more recent ones, to north-eastern metropolises, such as New York City, are by and large not coming from field and farm, but are people with prior urban life and work experience. They are products of step and stem migration moving not from field to factory, but from lesser-developed towns and cities to bigger, more developed (American) ones in search of more opportunity. As the century has progressed, the shape of those opportunities has altered. There are fewer and fewer unskilled and semi-skilled factory jobs available, but there remain numbers of equally low-skill, low-wage service jobs (hotel and office cleaners, caretakers, hospital workers, etc.) into which such groups have moved, as indigenous workers moved on. Younger, native-born workers have refused to enter such jobs as either too low-paying, or beneath them (too hard, dirty, menial, etc.). The newer immigrants are free of the cultural baggage preventing the indigenous workers from taking such employment. Further, they often possess cultural characteristics, enabling them to make a living from work paying wages which American workers insist are too low to survive on.

Second, in industries under increasing pressure from overseas competition, such as the garment industry and consumer electronics, the employment of immigrant Third World labour in a local segmented labour market conveys important comparative advantage to the producer. Because the labour market is segmented, the producer can maintain a lower labour price, even in the presence of unionisation, than would be possible in a more open market setting.[8] In this way the American producer appropriates much of the labour cost advantage enjoyed by foreign producers. In this case domestic producers bring the Third World labour force directly into the metropolitan American economy, rather than 'putting out' the components of production to Asia, Mexico, Haiti, etc. The profits ensuing from the lowered wage bill, enable such producers to compete more effectively with foreign employers of that same labour in its native setting. Such a scenario has been repeated in a number of competitive sector manufacturing settings.

It is sometimes argued that it is in precisely this fashion that immigrants take jobs away from native-born American workers. I am not engaging in that argument here. Rather the thrust of my argument is that the availability of such immigrant labour allows

small and medium-sized domestic producers to continue competitive production against overseas suppliers whose costs are often
dramatically lower.[9] In a world defined by global markets and
lacking tariff protections for national entrepreneurs, producers can
no longer offer the increased wages necessary to attract or retain
the indigenous worker. Without other options on the labour front,
these businesses would lose out to international competition.

Further, while much, if not most, of this foreign labour goes into
conventional jobs, the fact remains that much of the above-ground,
mainstream economy of the city is shrinking, and there are not
enough jobs to go around. Yet numbers of people continue to
come here, to New York and other metropoles. What are these
people doing? What is the economic attraction?

Third, while the mainstream economy may be stagnating, there
has been explosive growth in the economy's informal and underground components. Innumerable niches have been opened and
filled by enterprising foreign workers. For example, as traditional,
petty ethnic retailers and independent service businesses (dry
cleaners, shoemakers, candy store operators, etc.) have declined,
their roles have been reinvigorated by Oriental and Latin entrepreneurs, Greek pizza and lunch counter operators, etc. Korean
merchants have refilled the retail fruit and produce niche, in danger
of passing away because of the ageing of the ethnic Italian
entrepreneurs who dominated it heretofore. The Koreans, because
of their use of the kin group as the productive unit, and consequently their much lower labour costs, have been able to compete
effectively against the supermarkets in both quality and price.

In the public sector, a similar process can be observed. Just as in
the commercial sector, where the decline of one group of workers
and services has opened the way for a newer group, so also in
public services; public need and the pruning of civic action have
combined to create new niches for job creation. There has been
significant growth of 'gypsy cabs', and even jitney cab and van
services, as complements to public mass transit. The need for and
provision for such services has grown as the city has cut its transit
service, especially in the outer boroughs and in off-peak hours.
Again, it has been non-whites (blacks and circum-Caribbean immigrants) in the jitney trade who have seized this opportunity as
public service has declined. The number of legitimate taxi drivers
has grown for the same reasons.

A similar set of processes is transforming the underground

economy and the illegal activities and businesses which are part of it. There has been significant growth in the scale of some of this business, and the opening up of new market niches and even ethnic succession in many criminal occupations, as the Italian 'mob' ages and is not revitalised by new Sicilian recruits.

The drug trade is a prime example of these developments. Since the 1950s, distribution and sales of drugs, hard, soft and otherwise, has steadily increased, despite adoption of the most draconian measures to stem the tide of drug trafficking and abuse. Not only has there been substantial growth in the sale of illicit drugs since the end of the Second World War, but multiple drug markets have opened up as well. The spread of marijuana and acid use in the 1960s and early 1970s opened up new market niches for exploitation and new occupations in these markets for recent immigrants. Thus, one not only finds Columbians, Jamaicans and others from the circum-Caribbean discovering occupational opportunities in cannabis-related market niches, but also ethnic succession in the opiate-related segment(s) as first blacks and Cubans, and more recently Columbians and Chinese have gained 'market share', partly at the expense of the Italians.[10]

While the drug trade is perhaps the most spectacular example, similar developments typify growth patterns in other 'mob-related' businesses. In racketeering, newer immigrants, for example the Chinese, have expanded the geographical scope of their activities from bases within their own group enclaves, and are poised to go beyond the confines of ethnicity.[11]

All these examples combine to show in the informal sector a pattern of growth, that is, an expansion in the size of existing markets (produce, transportation, drugs) and the opening up of new niches within such markets for newer immigrants. Further, one observes stratified ethnic succession at both the lower occupational levels and through the middle of the distribution channels. Looking at the casual labour market and the underground economy as a whole, one sees similar patterns manifested. Thus while the economy of New York City and other older industrial cities is being transformed according to the imperatives of the post-industrial era, with attendant job and income loss and other suffering for the existing citizenry dependent on the older modes of production, newer and different opportunities are emerging in the wake of this transformation, which some of the more recent immigrants have proved agile at exploiting. This is so especially in the service and informal areas enumerated.

It is the growth of the casual and information sectors attendant on the transformation of the domestic metropolitan economy which strikes a familiar chord for observers of Third World cities. The new presence of large numbers of street vendors, food-sellers and other petty traders makes one wonder if one is in Kingston or New York.[12] The growing numbers of street people and the homeless, no longer just Bowery derelicts but increasingly able-bodied young men, and even whole families, suggests an American Calcutta.[13] The proliferation of jitneys, minibuses and other private substitutes for public transit Caribbean-style makes the question of more than speculative or academic interest. Finally, the filling of such new occupational slots by recent immigrants already familiar with such careers and niches from their home territories, the growth of segmented labour markets in construction, manufacturing, services, etc., with the unofficial segments filled with alien workers, and entrepreneurs operating according to rules and practices imported from 'home' markets fortify an impression that metropolises such as New York are not so much 'post-industrial', but segmented into modern sectors and others operating along more old fashioned, competitive, paternalistic and ethnically oriented lines.[14]

Indeed, it often seems that the modern sectors feed on the old-fashioned ones. In the garment industry the growth of subcontracting is resurrecting sweatshops, outworking and other abuses of the archaic modes of production of a century ago, and also enabling larger, 'modern' operators to share (along with the ethnic entrepreneurs) in the profits from the superexploitation of the growing numbers of workers in Chinatown sweatshops; in the restaurant and retail produce trade 'yuppie diners' have seen their lunch and dinner expenditures fall because of the lowered prices charged by proliferating ethnic restaurants and the spread of Korean fruit and produce vendors.

If taken on a broad scale, these developments presage a different kind of American city and metropolitan future than usually assumed, one in which the glowing star of the high-tech future is fed from some very old-fashioned sources. Indeed, the current and continuing dynamism of metropoles such as New York may have more to do with the re-emergence of these older, more traditional forms of production relations than with the glitter of post-industrial development. These developments raise policy questions, as well, about the character of the American urban polity as we approach the next century. Will we now have to deal with a metropolitan population split not only by race, but segmented by ethnicity as well? These developments and the issues they raise will require the close attention of scholars in the years to come.

NOTES

1. J. Newfield and P. DuBrul, *The Abuse of Power* (New York: Viking, 1977).
2. New York City Planning Commission, *Plan for New York City 1969* (Cambridge, Mass.: MIT Press, 1969).
3. *Post-Industrial America: Metropolitan Decline and Inter-Regional Job Shifts 1975*, ed. G. Sternlieb and J. W. Hughes (New Brunswick, NJ: Center for Urban Policy Research, Rutgers University, 1975) p. 118; Sternlieb and Hughes also note that 'The absolute number of jobs in New York City remained virtually unchanged between 1953 and 1973', ibid., p. 113.
4. S. M. Ehrenhalt, 'Some Perspectives on the New York City Economy in a Time of Change', in *New York City's Changing Economic Base*, ed. B. J. Klebaner (New York: Pica Press, 1981) p. 17.
5. J. Bigel, 'New York City's Fiscal Situation: Recurring Crisis of Long-Term Stability?', *City Almanac*, vol. 17, no. 2 (August 1983) p. 2; J. Mollenkopf, Political Science Department, Graduate Center, City University of New York (CUNY), personal communication.
6. *Geographic Profile of Employment and Unemployment 1974*, Report no. 452, US Bureau of the Census, p. 16, table 4; *Geographic Profile of Employment and Unemployment 1984*, Bulletin no. 2234, US Bureau of the Census, p. 93, table 23.
7. M. Ehrenhalt, 'New York City's Labor Force – Change and Challenge', *City Almanac*, vol. 17, no. 4 (December 1983) p. 10; *The Social and Economic Status of the Black Population in the United States* (1971) Current Population Reports Series p. 23, no. 42, p. 145, table 113.
8. This is a key factor behind the growth of Chinese subcontractors in the New York garment industry. These ethnic entrepreneurs employ their own countrymen and women at lower cost(s) than they could workers from other groups; as such, they enjoy a cost advantage over other (non-Chinese) suppliers, which they have efficiently translated into enterprise growth. Cf. Abeles, Schartz, Haeckel and Silverblatt, Inc. (Roger Waldinger), *The Chinatown Garment Industry Study* (New York: Local 23–5, International Ladies Garment Workers Union, 1983).
9. A local retailer told me that the cheapest domestically produced tee shirt he can get costs $2.40. He can get Pakistani shirts for $0.30–0.35. (This was in 1986; the differential has narrowed somewhat since then: e.g. in 1987, a US-made shirt could be had for $0.75.)
10. F. A. J. Ianni, *Black Mafia* (New York: Simon & Shuster, 1974); New

York City Police Department, 'Rasta Crime: A Confidential Report', *Caribbean Review*, vol. 14, no. 1 (Winter 1985) p. 12.

11. 'A Gang Preys on Chinese Restaurants on L.I.', *New York Times*, 5 January 1986, p. 26.

12. 'Street Peddlers from Senegal Flock to New York', *New York Times*, 10 November 1985, sect. 1, p. 52.

13. P. Kerr, 'Homelessness isn't Skipping a Generation on City Streets', *New York Times*, 3 November 1985, p. E7; J. Purnick, 'Sleepless Nights for Homeless in Welfare Office', *New York Times*, 16 December 1985, p. B1.

14. R. Buck, 'New Sweatshops: A Penny for Your Collar', *New York Magazine*, 29 January 1979, p. 40; M. Santos, *Shared Space: The Two Circuits of the Urban Economy in Underdeveloped Countries* (New York: Methuen, 1979).

# 12

# The Changing Face and Role of America's Primate City

## JOHN F. DAVIS

So now we come to New York City, the incomparable, the brilliant star, city of cities, the forty-ninth state, a law unto itself, the Cyclopean paradox, the inferno with no out-of-bounds, the supreme expression of both the miseries and the splendours of contemporary civilisation, the Macedonia of the USA.[1]

Thus Gunther opens his chapter on New York in *Inside America;* he then goes on to remark that it has been called nothing but a 'cluster of small islets in the North Atlantic'. If so unpromising, why then is it so important?

The reasons for the importance of New York are the subject of this chapter, but first it is necessary to answer two questions: what is a primate city, and what is New York? A primate city can be best described as one which is above all others, one which stands at the top of the league tables of such criteria as population, employment and wealth. A primate city is also the city which is of fundamental importance to its country.

The question 'What is New York?' is perhaps more difficult to answer. This is partly because, over time, New York has grown from being a small settlement on Manhattan Island to a city extending out on to the mainland, and if one goes beyond the actual New York City as defined by the census then one includes a much wider area. This wider metropolitan area was designated a 'Standard Metropolitan Statistical Area' by the Bureau of Census, but very recently this term has been altered to 'Consolidated Metropolitan Statistical Area'. Thus New York to some people is really Manhattan, to many it is the city of five boroughs – Bronx, Brooklyn, Manhattan, Queens and Richmond – while for many

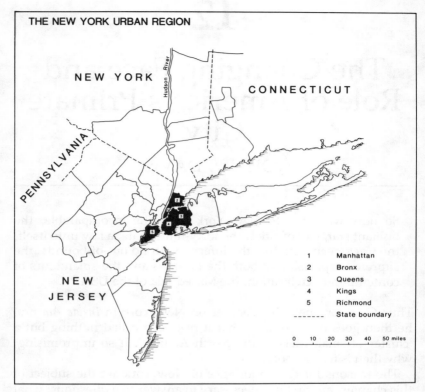

*Map 2    The New York Urban Region*

purposes it consists of a wider area, extending beyond New York
state boundaries into New Jersey and Connecticut. In 1980, in
population terms, this meant a range from 1.4 million living in
Manhattan, and 7 million in New York City to 17.5 million living
in the Consolidated Metropolitan Statistical Area. Inevitably, at
various times within the chapter reference will be to each of
the three versions, partly because New York has grown from
Manhattan to New York City and partly because, from some points
of view, it is impossible to discuss the importance of New York
City without reference to the 'whole'.

Boundaries are necessary, but at the same time we must not
be restricted by the purely administrative political convenience
provided by boundaries; our theme is partly conceptual in that the
role of New York is more than just position in a league table. In

other words, a city spreads beyond its official boundaries. To understand the present role we must briefly discuss the city's setting and historical growth.

## HISTORICAL AND GEOGRAPHICAL FACTORS

Manhattan Island stands at the mouth of the southward-flowing Hudson River where it enters the Atlantic Ocean. The original European visitors to the place were attracted by the good, protected anchorage, the scope for inland trade via the rivers, and the availability of fresh water, all of which combined to make Manhattan Island attractive for settlement. In 1609 Henry Hudson, abroad the *Half Moon*, wrote in the ship's log that New York Harbour was 'a very good place to fall in with'. Two years later Adrian Block came to Manhattan Island to trade furs with the Indians and in 1615 the New Netherland Company was granted a charter by the States General of Holland to trade for three years. It was this company which built a storehouse and fort at the south end of Manhattan Island. In 1624 a group of Protestant families arrived, but most moved on to Fort Orange (Albany). More settlers arrived in 1626 with Peter Munuit, the first Director General, who was succeeded first by Twiller and then by the able Peter Stuyvesant. It was in 1653 that a city wall was started (Wall Street) and other defences were also erected, for example at Battery Point. Shortly afterwards there came conflict with Britain and, in 1664, New Amsterdam was renamed New York. The settlement prospered and by the mid-eighteenth century was regarded as a focal point of resistance to royal authority and became a major focus of opposition to the British government's attempts at taxation.

New York was immensely aided in its growth in importance by its situation astride both north–south and east–west routes. Standing on the east coast with a very good, large harbour it was well located for the growth in trade between Europe and America which grew from a mere trickle in the seventeenth century to a major flow in the nineteenth century: a traffic both in goods and people. Nearby there was both woodland and farmland, and in addition New York was situated on the coastal water route from the northern colonies of New England to the southern colonies. The settlement grew rapidly from being a mere fur-trading point to becoming a port of the 'middle' or 'bread' colonies. Consequently, it developed a trade pattern both with Europe and other colonies and had local fish, furs, food, forestry products and trade. It was also able to develop inland trade with the interior via the south-flowing Hudson. None the less in colonial times there were also other east coast ports some of which had a richer immediate hinterland, for example, Baltimore and Philadelphia.

In one sense New York's importance was checked for a while when in 1797 the state capital was moved to Albany. New York's reign as national capital was ended but a few months before, when this was moved first to Philadelphia and then finally to Washington in 1800.

The first national population census was taken in 1790, and from it New York emerged as the most populous city, a position it has held ever since (Table 12.1). How did the city not only reach but maintain this rank? As has already been observed, New York was one of a number of east coast ports of the colonial period but was really only on a par with such towns as Boston, Charleston and Philadelphia. In 1800 Philadelphia lost the national capital when this was movd to Washington; one of New York's greatest potential competitors was thus made less of a threat in that Philadelphia now did not have the additional accolade of a national capital to go with its rich hinterland.

In the post-revolutionary period people increasingly were moving into and settling the Ohio valley and further west. Consequently there was a determined search for routes from the coast to the interior. Such searches were fostered and then financed by city and business interests in the various ports. Of all the proposed schemes the one that was the most practicable technically, most economic to build and the first to come into operation was the Erie Canal, which opened in 1825. The Erie Canal not only linked Lake Erie with the Hudson River and so through to the Atlantic but it enabled New York City to become the undisputed port for handling traffic with the West. It gave the city unrivalled and unprecedented access to the interior and this water route enabled New York to develop and maintain its economic and in some respects political leadership. The opening of the canal led to dramatic falls in freight rates, to significant changes in farming and other aspects of the economy. These are largely outside the scope of this chapter; however, the existence of a good route to the interior, initially by water but later by rail as well, emphasised New York's position as a wholesale centre. In the mid-nineteenth century about one-third

TABLE 12.1    *Population of New York and its nearest rivals, 1640–1980*

| Date | Population of New York | Nearest rival | Population of nearest rival | Third |
|------|------------------------|---------------|------------------------------|-------|
| 1640 | 400 | Boston | 1,200 | ? |
| 1660 | 2,400 | Boston | 3,000 | Newport |
| 1690 | 3,900 | Boston | 7,000 | Philadelphia |
| 1730 | 8,622* | Boston | 13,000 | Philadelphia |
| 1760 | 18,000 | Philadelphia | 23,000 | Boston |
| 1775 | 25,000 | Philadelphia | 40,000 | Boston |
| 1790 | 49,400 | Philadelphia | 28,000 | Boston |
| 1800 | 79,000 | Philadelphia | 41,000 | Boston |
| 1810 | 120,000 | Philadelphia | 54,000 | Boston |
| 1820 | 152,000 | Philadelphia | 64,000 | Baltimore |
| 1830 | 242,000 | Baltimore | 81,000 | Philadelphia |
| 1840 | 391,000 | Baltimore | 102,000 | Philadelphia |
| 1850 | 696,000 | Baltimore | 169,000 | Philadelphia |
| 1860 | 1,175,000 | Philadelphia | 566,000 | Baltimore |
| 1870 | 1,478,000 | Philadelphia | 647,000 | Chicago |
| 1880 | 1,912,000 | Philadelphia | 847,000 | Chicago |
| 1890 | 2,507,000 | Chicago | 1,000,000 | Philadelphia |
| 1900 | 3,427,000 | Chicago | 1,699,000 | Philadelphia |
| 1910 | 4,767,000 | Chicago | 2,185,000 | Philadelphia |
| 1920 | 5,620,000 | Chicago | 2,702,000 | Philadelphia |
| 1930 | 6,930,000 | Chicago | 3,376,000 | Philadelphia |
| 1940 | 7,455,000 | Chicago | 3,397,000 | Philadelphia |
| 1950 | 7,892,000 | Chicago | 3,612,000 | Philadelphia |
| 1960 | 7,782,000 | Chicago | 3,550,000 | Los Angeles |
| 1970 | 7,895,000 | Chicago | 3,369,000 | Los Angeles |
| 1980 | 7,072,000 | Chicago | 3,005,000 | Los Angeles |

NOTE    Years 1790–1980 are based on National Census. Data only for cities.
* Census on New York.

of all imports were textiles and New York had a near-monopoly of this trade, becoming the centre of both clothing manufacture and fashion. It also became the wholesale centre for a range of other commodities, including chemicals, furniture, jewellery and machinery.

Other east coast ports also gradually established links to the interior, though only one other was by water and all were later. With the coming of the railway a number of new routes were opened to the interior, but New York, having been the first in the field together with good rail access along the same route as the Erie Canal, was never seriously threatened in its premier position. Indeed, the development of rail links further enhanced the city's position. Thus, while in 1800 New York handled about 9 per cent of the country's foreign trade, by 1830 this had risen to 37 per cent and in 1870 to 57 per cent.

Economics and political factors influenced the fortunes of all east coast ports and some of those of significance in colonial times soon passed into relative decline as the nineteenth century progressed, for example Charleston. Technological change also played a role. As the nineteenth century progressed ships increased in size, in draught and length voyages became both faster and more regular and the volume of traffic increased enormously. New York was fortunate in that what were good site factors in the seventeenth century were still so in the twentieth century. The approaches to Manhattan Island from Long Island Sound were suitable for the increased size of ship and there was deep water close to land. Admittedly, docks and wharves had to be redesigned and rebuilt but New York did not suffer decline through inadequate water access. It was also an ice-free port, as are all other Atlantic coast US ports. However with the opening of the railway to Montreal in 1853, New York became a port of entry not only for the USA but also for goods and people heading to Quebec and Ontario in winter.

The original site of the city was Manhattan Island and this had many advantages for water transport; an island location was a serious snag, however, when it came to either the landward expansion of the town or to the development of links with the interior other than by water. Almost by necessity New York showed great initiative in the development of ferry services to link its various parts. Bridges and tunnels also became necessities; the High Bridge over the Harlem River was opened in 1846, the Brooklyn Bridge in 1889, the first rail tunnel came in the late nineteenth century and the first road tunnel (the Holland Tunnel) in 1927. Since the Harlem and East Rivers were easier to bridge than the Hudson, the Jersey shore developed more slowly. Today there are five tunnels and over a score of bridges, of which the most recent – the Verrazano Narrows Bridge – was opened in 1964.

This reference to bridges and tunnels serves to indicate the growing importance of movement into and out of the city core. It is around this core, especially the waterfront, that much of the city's economic *raison d'être* focused and indeed, to a large extent, still focuses. Transport and wholesaling were magnets for the development of manufacturing in the city – initially clothing but later a whole range of commodities. Along with trade and transport developed a whole range of other servies – banking, brokerage, finance and insurance to name but a few – and all combined to emphasise the primacy of New York.

## POPULATION GROWTH

As a port with connections to Europe, and especially Britain, it was inevitable that not only manufactured goods and raw materials should be handled but that New York would also grow as a passenger port. During the nineteenth century New York quickly became the foremost port of entry for immigrants. Originally a number of ports had shared this function and indeed throughout the nineteenth century other ports, especially Boston and Philadelphia, continued to disembark passengers; New York was supreme, however, and with its developing rail links to the interior and the fact that many railways had headquarters in the city it was all the more important for new immigrants. The city's booming economy also made it a magnet not only for those with skills but for the unskilled, who could be absorbed by the expanding demand for such labour in New York.

Perhaps another attraction of New York as the premier port of entry was that from a very early date its population was cosmopolitan with very varied European origins. Thus information flows would tend to be via New York and new immigrants would be drawn to a city where they stood a very good chance of finding people of their own language and culture already in residence. This was especially important after the 1840s when increasingly the immigrants were non-English-speaking. The 'Gateway to the New World' became a fitting description of New York, a position it still retains. It could be said that the Statue of Liberty is the epitome of this. Being the premier port of entry gave the city its diversity and richness of language and culture. It is probably the most polyglot of all US cities and around two hundred newspapers are published here. Here, too, distinctive ethnic enclaves have been established, some for over two centuries, such as Dutch, German, Irish, White Russian, Jewish, Puerto Rican and Italian. Perhaps the best known of all ethnic areas is Harlem – but there are really a number of distinct Harlems: black, Puerto Rican and Haitian. It should also be mentioned in passing that Harlem does not consist only of slums, but contains rich areas and middle-income areas too.

Any perusal of nineteenth-century newspapers indicates the frequency of shipping movements to and from New York in comparison with other US ports. This great period of activity as well as the main period of immigration really came to an end with the First World War and the introduction in 1921 of the first of the major immigrant quota acts. This date too can be said to mark a natural break in the city's development.

## THE TWENTIETH CENTURY

The twentieth century, and especially the post-1920s, has seen very significant technological developments and economic changes which together have done much to alter the face of urban America. Unlike some formerly important cities, New York has been able to ride the upheavals of change and still remain on top. The spreading use and almost universal ownership of the motor car here, as elsewhere, dramatically changed the pattern of urban life. Suburbs mushroomed, freeway-building pushing them further and further outwards, and there were the associated increasing problems of central city congestion and pressure on public transport services. Partly due to the highly compact nature of employment location on Manhattan Island, an existing infrastructure and a combination of judgement and luck, New York retains one of the most comprehensive systems of public transport in the USA, and in this respect its nearest rival is probably Chicago. Commuter railways, subway services and bus lines all help to make the New Yorker the lowest user of private transport for commuting of any major US city. Admittedly much of the system is aged and enormous sums have been and remain to be spent to bring the services up to the standards of comfort and reliability desired, but, on the other hand, New York never allowed its system to disappear, as did some other large cities.

Air travel has had very dramatic effects on New York. True, the seaport still handles large numbers of passengers but today most embark for only a few days at a time – or perhaps weeks – as they are cruise ship passengers. No longer is it possible to look down upon the Hudson from the Rockefeller Building and count the long line of transatlantic liners moored.

Today it is difficult to cross the Atlantic in the winter half of the year by passenger liner service. Now the old liner terminals between 48th and 52nd Street have been rebuilt as a three-level modern terminal with heating and air conditioning which is able to handle a fleet of luxury liners and cruise ships, has rooftop parking for 1,000 cars and handles over 300,000 passengers annually.

Notwithstanding these changes, the Port of New York Authority still handles the bulk of US passenger arrivals from overseas (in 1979 14.0 million of them) but that is only because by an administrative quirk the Authority administers the three airports Kennedy, La Guardia and Newark. In 1979 these three handled nearly 41 million domestic and 14 million international passengers and carried 0.67 million tons of foreign air freight (i.e. about 43 per cent of the nation's total foreign air freight). By 1982 these figures had risen to nearly 57 million passengers and 1.5 million tons of air freight. From being the major ocean liner hub of the USA, New York has now become the major air hub if the three airports are grouped together; if one considers each individual airport, however, then Atlanta comes first for passengers, while Chicago handles more air freight in total. Nevertheless as a *city* hub New York is still primate.

While discussing transport one has to acknowledge that in the field of rail transport New York has had to take a back seat in comparison with Chicago, which has long been the nation's rail centre. Chicago's more central position in the country makes it eminently more capable of fulfilling that role than any seaport. Even so, New York is a key element in the densely served (by American standards) Metroliner system (passenger rail) linking Boston and New York with Philadelphia, Baltimore and Washington.

Though for passenger travel the aeroplane has replaced the ship it must not be supposed that port activities are unimportant. New York is still the chief port of the country on the basis of tonnage handled. The port has over 700 miles of shoreline and more than a thousand waterfront facilities ranging from liner piers to drydocks and is used regularly by over a hundred steamship lines. The main channel is dredged to 45 feet and the tidal range is only 4 feet. In 1982 the port of New York recorded over 3,200 commercial ship arrivals and handed over 12 million tons of cargo as well as more than 2 million containers. The Port of New York Authority was one of the pioneers of container traffic and is linked to the Pacific coast by 'land bridge' – a system whereby containers from Pacific-rim countries can be shipped to the US west coast, transferred to rail, and taken to New York where they are loaded on to ships for the Atlantic crossing – a quicker route than an all-sea one. In 1982 New York handled over 20 per cent of the nation's total container traffic – more than twice that of its nearest rival. The geographical area served by the jurisdiction of the Port of New York Authority extends over a radius of some twenty-five miles. It not only handles port-related matters but also administers the airport and some of the commuter services and recently has become involved more directly in trying to attract new industrial development to the city.

The long-time existence of a port has been a major factor in encouraging industrial development and today manufacturing is still a significant source of both direct and indirect employment. Within the metropolitan area are approximately a million manufac-turing jobs in some 35,000 establishments. The range is wide indeed: the metropolitan area contains representatives of about 85 per cent of the designations in the Standard Industrial Classifica-tion. However its dominance in specific industries has declined; other centres, such as those on the west coast, have eroded its supremacy in fashion clothing, for example.

The general trend in employment in the USA is towards the tertiary and quaternary sectors (services) and here the importance of New York is unsurpassed. For well over a hundred and fifty years it has been regarded as the financial and commercial capital of the country, a situation partly exemplified by the fact that of the 254 foreign banks in the USA in 1978, 242 of them had headquarters or branches in New York, and of the world's 80 largest non-American banks, 75 had offices there. Not only banking and finance but a wide variety of other services related to insurance, brokerage and wholesaling are found here. In a sense the World Trade Centre, with its offices for over 900 shippers, importers, exporters, banks, brokers and government agencies within it, is an epitome of the larger city. The dominance is not as great as it was; a combination of the Depression years, the Wall Street crash, changes in the taxation system and the increased importance of government control and influence has meant that much of the control of credit has moved directly or indirectly from Wall Street to Washington. Many corporations too have been tempted to leave New York City for other, more convenient or more economic, locations.

It was during the 1970s that the city of New York suffered a loss of some of its corporate big names. In the late 1960s and early 1970s government-related employment was the major growth industry, and in a sense both city and state tried to build their economies on the public payroll. The result was a significant rise in taxes, and they continued to rise as the city became increasingly involved in various welfare programmes. This in turn threatened the tax base itself; business voted with its feet and, as was stated in *Fortune* magazine on 14 May 1984, New York State lost over 367,000 jobs in 1970–6 as well as 33 of the listed Fortune 500 companies; in all, some 700 firms left the state and 1200 closed down. Much of this change occurred in the New York metropolitan area. True, some of these closures or moves would have come in any case but many were related to the increasing cost of operation in New York. However, to overcome these problems as far as possible, the state cut some three billion dollars off its tax budget, promised not to charge unitary taxes on the world earnings of companies and their subsidiaries (as twelve states did) and made other modifications. This has helped stem the flow. Some of the loss of firms, especially major companies from New York, has been only partial in that they have moved beyond the official bounds of New York City but still remain within the New York area. These moves have often been made to obtain lower rents, lower land and congestion costs and sometimes to achieve greater proximity to air transport links. On the other hand, some companies have left the region completely and moved west or south.

The chairman of Pfizer Inc. (Pharmaceutics) stated, 'It always costs more to operate in New York City than in say Alabama but New York has a critical mass of services, background and education. It's worth paying a price to get that.' Many agree but compromise by moving 'non-essential to New York operations staff' elsewhere. Pfizer made economies, as have many other companies, by closing or reducing overseas marketing offices and bringing them back to New York – relying on air transport, telex and telephone to keep in quick and easy contact with the 'field' areas. An example of the communications age is Teleport – the first-in-the-world satellite communications centre and office park located on Staten Island and, interestingly, a joint venture of the Port Authority, New York

City Public Development Corporation, Merrill Lynch and Western Union.[2]

A widely used barometer has been the Fortune 500 – the index of the top 500 industrial corporations in the USA – and by comparing their addresses over time we can get an idea of how many remain in New York. This gives a crude indicator of primacy (see Table 12.2).

TABLE 12.2    *Fortune 500 Industrial Corporations in the USA*

|            | 1956 | 1960 | 1976 | 1983 |
|------------|------|------|------|------|
| New York   | 140  | 156  | 84   | 74   |
| Chicago    | 47   | 52   | 27   | 40   |
| Pittsburgh | 22   | 24   | 14   | 14   |

SOURCE    Based on annual surveys of the Fortune 500 Industrial Corporations.

Again, if one looks at a similar list of the top fifty utilities, transportation, savings, insurance, retailing and diversified financial corporations, then of these six groups (i.e. 300), New York was headquarters of seventy-two in 1972 and Chicago second with twenty-seven; in 1983 New York had fifty-one and its nearest rival less than twenty. However, if one looks at the six separately then Houston comes out top for utilities and Chicago for transport companies. Therefore, in summary one can say that while New York has shown a decline in both industrial corporations and also services, it still retains the lion's share.

Part of the change in the degree of dominance is a reflection not of the fiscal issues facing New York but of the general population and economic shifts that are taking place in the country. The old adage of 'go west, young man' cannot only be altered to include both sexes and all ages but should also now add 'and go south'. The resurgence of economic growth in the South over the past forty years and the continued lure of the West has meant that, for a variety of reasons associated with the development of resources, amenity attractions and space for development, there has been a decline in the dominance of the manufacturing belt in general; along with this, the towering dominance of New York City itself has diminished. The attractions of the sunbelt have had repercussions on the economic health and prosperity of the rustbelt, frostbelt or snowbelt, or whatever other title one wishes to place on the area. Surprisingly, perhaps, but really a reflection of the power of New York and its great supremacy in many facets of life, these trends have not resulted in New York losing its place at the top of the league table except in a very few very specialised instances.

Today's typical American city is most easily described as an outward-spreading sprawl of suburbs and subcentres with often a declining or almost hollow core. Not so New York. Though New York has its share of suburban spread yet it still retains a large and vibrant core. This is partially epitomised in the enormous concentration of skyscrapers in Manhattan. The Manhattan skyline has been called many things – 'gypsum crystals', 'a ship of living stone', 'dividends in the sky', 'an irregular tableland intersected by canyons'; however, H. G. Wells made an apt description in one sense: 'piled up packing cases outside a warehouse'.[3] Today the two areas of high-rise concentration – Wall Street and Midtown – contain the greatest concentration of skyscrapers in North America. For much of the last century and a half, New York has boasted the highest building in North America – initially with Trinity Church (284 feet) in 1846, the Singer Building in 1905 and the Empire State Building in 1930. However today the 1971 World Trade Center at 1350 feet is topped by the Chicago Sears Tower at 1454 feet. (Though there is talk of building a 1555-foot building in New York.) One can also look to other indicators of primacy. It is still the major headquarters for corporate law firms and other related special services. In a different sphere it retains the lead with regard to daily newspapers and literary, political and financial magazines. The *New York Times* remains the most influential of US newspapers and the city is also the headquarters location of all three major television networks as well as a host of radio stations. While other cities also have theatres, symphony orchestras, museums and art galleries, New York has the greatest variety and greatest concentration in most fields of the arts. In the field of education, with its sixty four-year colleges and thirty two-year ones as well as more than fifty community and eighty vocational colleges, it is the major centre of education in the country if one uses numbers as a yardstick. This one would expect as being a direct reflection of size; however, the number is larger than size alone would indicate. The same also applies to health care, with over 200 general care hospitals containing more than 60,000 beds.

In April 1983, *The Economist* made a very astute comment about the city: 'New York's lack of rivals at home tempts other Americans to treat it as a foreign land. Geography is on their side. The only bits of the city on the mainland are the Bronx and Marble Hill. Other Americans tend to think New York untypical (rightly). But then consider (wrongly) that it cannot really be America.'[4] In a country where cities are characterised by outward spread, Manhattan, with some 63,000 residents per square mile, is the densest concentration by far of any US city and is about five times denser than its nearest rival, San Francisco. This density increases each weekday with over 2 million commuting into Manhattan daily.

From the above discussion there can be no doubt that New York remains the country's primate city and also retains much of its role as a leader; what it has lost in the political and some of the consumer-related fields has been more than compensated for by its continual dominance in all things relating to finance, insurance, trade and similar areas. The metropolitan region as a whole is home for over 17.5 million people living in 6 million households, and its total effective purchasing power is some 20 per cent ahead of its nearest rival. While its port may see fewer tansatlantic liners today, in 1982 the three airports accommodated nearly 800,000 aeroplane movements and 57 million passengers. It is not without serious problems; near-bankruptcy in the 1970s was only painfully averted and there continues to be the problem of a declining property tax base in some areas alongside mounting costs. Surrounding Manhattan itself are parts of the other boroughs where urban redevelopment, economic revival and financial injections are still urgently needed. In this sense it shares with other major US cities the problems of the central cities, the main difference being that in the case of New York the core – Manhattan – is largely vibrant while it is the surrounding areas that are in difficulty: beyond them come the more affluent suburban sectors and associated urban centres.

New York has been called a city of extremes and a city of superlatives. It is not only an American city and partly a European city, but now also a world city. Old-time jazz musicians used to say that although there were many apples on the tree, when you picked New York then you picked the Big Apple. The main theme of this chapter has been to suggest that it is still the core of the nation.

NOTES

1. J. Gunther, *Inside America* (London: Hamish Hamilton, 1949) p. 459.
2. *Fortune: International Edition*, 14 May 1984.
3. All quotations are from an essay on New York City by Vincent McHugh published in *The WPA Guide to New York City* (New York: Pantheon Books, 1982).
4. *The Economist*, 2 April 1983, p. 51.

# Index